THE THIRD EYE and Other Works

THE THIRD EYE and Other Works

Mahatma Phule's Writings on Education

Rohini Mokashi-Punekar

Foreword by

Bhalchandra Nemade

Orient BlackSwan

THE THIRD EYE AND OTHER WORKS: MAHATMA PHULE'S WRITINGS ON EDUCATION

ORIENT BLACKSWAN PRIVATE LIMITED

Registered Office
3-6-752 Himayatnagar, Hyderabad 500 029, Telangana, India
e-mail: centraloffice@orientblackswan.com

Other Offices
Bengaluru, Chennai, Guwahati, Hyderabad, Kolkata,
Mumbai, New Delhi, Noida, Patna

First published by Orient Blackswan Private Limited 2023

ISBN 978-93-5442-380-2

041930

Typeset in
Adobe Garamond Pro 11/13
by Le Studio Graphique, Gurgaon 122 007

Printed in India at
Kensington Printing & Packaging, Noida 201 301

Published by
Orient Blackswan Private Limited
3-6-752 Himayatnagar, Hyderabad 500 029, Telangana, India
e-mail: info@orientblackswan.com

Dedicated
to
Eleanor Zelliot
(1926–2016)
crusader and generous friend,

and
students on the wrong side of divides,
modern and endemic

Contents

Foreword by Bhalchandra Nemade ... *ix*
Preface ... *xix*
Acknowledgements ... *xxiii*

Phule in His Times: A Brief Note on His Life and Works ... 1

The Significance of *Tritiya Ratna*: Phule's Play of Ideas ... 14

The Third Eye ... 76

Political Uses of Poetry: 'Vidyakhatyateel Brahman Pantoji' ... 112

'Brahmin Teachers in the Education Department' ... 119

Situating Phule within the History of Education in India ... 124

'Preface' to *Gulamgiri* ... 179

Memorial Addressed to the Education Commission: A Statement for the Information of the Education Commission ... 191

Works Cited and Referred ... 204
Index ... 212

Foreword

It can be rightly said that colonialism has distorted the native conceptual system, as a result of which it is often problematic to assess the work of a writer born and dead in the colonial period. On the one hand, the ante-colonial 'Land of Gold' that was destabilised by the extractive capitalism of alien rulers, and on the other hand, the post-colonial hybridised reality that one has to live in do not allow even the most objective criteria to assess a revolutionary work such as Mahatma Jotiba Phule's *Tritiya Ratna*. Written in 1855 and published for the first time in 1979—124 years after it was written and thirty-two years after Independence—it is a classic example of how Hindu society treats its rebels like Phule. He was a pioneer in women's education, opened the first school for the lower castes and untouchables, initiated several movements against horrendous social evils such as widow-burning (sati), child marriage, inequality of castes and gender, and Brahminical hegemony.

It is indeed commendable that Dr Rohini Mokashi-Punekar has translated the play so faithfully and with such meticulous care. The translation is the result of a long period of research and reflects the genuine interest she shows in the literature of commitment and in social protest, and her multilingual skills have been fully tested in such difficult tasks as finding equivalents in English of the various nineteenth-century sociolects used profusely by the characters that represent different castes and religious groups. Dr Mokashi-Punekar has thoughtfully included in the collection two other representative educational writings of Phule: the first, a *powada* (ballad) on the Brahmin teacher and the second, the text of Phule's celebrated document 'Memorial Addressed to the Education Commission'

(1882), thus making its scope broad enough to represent Phule's textual engagement with the question of education for all, including lower classes as well as untouchables and women of all strata. She has also included Phule's 'Preface' to *Gulamgiri* for reasons of continuity between this work and the educational petition submitted to the Hunter Commission. These texts connote the anti-hegemonical struggle against the Brahminical hold over society by means of religious practices.

The introduction to the play will be, I am sure, a valuable aid to students of Indian drama as well as of colonial India of the nineteenth century. As stated by Dr Mokashi-Punekar in her introduction, 'The Significance of *Tritiya Ratna*', Phule's play, if staged, would have been a misfit in the contemporary Marathi theatre of pseudo-romantic musical comedies of middle-class entertainment. If we believe in the observation that every type of culture has its corresponding type of protest, here is a play of ideas initiated much before it appeared in Europe with Ibsen and Shaw. We witness a kind of protest in the play which is indicative of the morbid pathological syndrome of the age-old structure of Hindu society, dominated by the priestly caste even during the British regime. The manuscript of *Tritiya Ratna* was submitted by an angry young man of twenty-odd years to a grant-in-aid committee manned by Brahmin pundits and influential British officials; yet it was rejected. Obviously the Victorian British rulers, who advertised themselves as custodians of justice and equality, could not support or uphold the explosive contents of Brahminical exploitation and other religious evils such as superstition, blackmail and discrimination. Surprisingly there is the character of a Christian missionary in the play who openly canvasses for Christianity, just stopping short of an attempt to proselytise. Another major character, Vidushak, praises the Englishmen because they 'always fraternise with the Malis and Kunbis and treat them as their equals' (p. 104, this volume). Even in his later writings Phule continued to praise the English rulers' sense of justice and their kindness towards the downtrodden people of India. Vidushak in *Tritiya Ratna* says, 'Ishvar himself has sent the English to our country to end the Brahmin's proscription of education for the Shudras and Atishudras and to empower them' (p. 107, this volume).

Can religion bind people together or does it divide vertically and/or horizontally? This is a fraught question in the pre-modern period in the context of the multi-religious pluralistic structure of age-old Hinduism. Phule was categorically antagonistic to polytheist Hinduism, and in all his books and pamphlets, which he printed, published, sold and distributed on his own in very hostile conditions, he satirised the Brahminical notions of the utility of a common cultural heritage floated by 'Aryan Brahmin invaders' who subjugated the indigenous people and treated them as slaves. 'Of what use is it to be born a Brahmin and not scheme and trick!' says the Brahmin Joshi to his wife (p. 92, this volume).

Since dominant ideas invariably come from the dominant class, any resistance to these ideas naturally targets the Brahmins who mercilessly exploited every activity of the marginalised classes. The Jain, Buddhist, Nath, Sikh, Bhakti and Veerashaiva—all rebellious religions—show the same pattern of anti-Brahminical sensibilities in the long history of India. Phule also attempted to establish his own religion called the 'Truth-Seekers' Society' which, after a brief span of dramatic spread all over western India during the colonial period, did not survive for reasons we cannot discuss here; but *Tritiya Ratna*, the play Phule wrote as a young man, expresses several revolutionary ideas of the author through the mouth of Vidushak—condemning idolatry and polytheism, belief in one Creator and the equality of all His creations.

Regarding women's freedom and rights, Phule was categorically radical. Now all cultures are more or less misogynist. Phule's ideology was openly against Hinduism, especially the post-Buddhist Brahminical hierarchical structures of all types—the absurd theories of *avataras* or incarnations, the ridiculous myths taken for history, the varna system and casteist Dharmashastras, and so on. The infamous Manu writes in his *Manusmriti*: 'What educated Brahmins say should be the undoubted law' (Ch. 12.105). The implicit hierarchy in Hinduism is what Phule wanted to annihilate, and it is this credo that inspired the many later non-Brahmin movements in India, including the most powerful subaltern revolts by Dr Babasaheb Ambedkar and the Dalit movements.

Tritiya Ratna is the first play of ideas that presents a cross-section of nineteenth-century rural Indian society in a carefully constructed plot with the utmost economy of characters: the exploitative Brahmin Hindu (Joshi), the exploited working-class Kunbi farmer and the even more oppressed housewife, the Christian missionary and the Muslim—both antagonists of polytheist Hinduism—and the omnipresent Vidushak, the author's mouthpiece who interprets the thematic content that Phule wanted the Hindu audience to share with him.

It is for the first time that a play portrays so many subaltern classes voicing, through their representatives, their standard views against the establishment. Even in the rich tradition of Sanskrit drama, nobody except Shudraka, author of the renowned play *Mricchakatika*, had the courage to present the lower-class reality that one finds in *Tritiya Ratna*. Tamasha, or the popular Marathi folk drama, which has roots in Prakrit drama, seems to be Phule's source in his portrayal of Vidushak as a *songadya*, a comic intermediary between the author and the audience. It also alludes to the *sutradhar* in Sanskrit drama.

Phule seems to have avoided the basic issue of the dual exploitation of the farmer in colonial India—political by the British, and religious by the Brahmins—which is significant in the context of his indebtedness to the Scottish Mission Church and other Christian influences such as American Reformist thought.

Unlike the author, Phule's protagonists, the farmer and his innocent wife Jogai, do not seem to know that they were working tirelessly for the farmyard of England, in order to make the Industrial Revolution a great success. Added to this oppression was the spiritual degradation caused by another kind of exploitation by the Brahmins, who were also equally exploited politically by the East India Company, but insulated from menial work and farming conditions by the varna system. Their basic needs such as food, clothing and money had to be met by the lower castes who were permanently harnessed to superstition and dogma. Phule had in mind a total revolution within Hinduism that would crush the Brahminical monopoly and intolerance, and initiate reforms such as caste and gender equality. Since learning scriptures and Sanskrit texts was in general a forbidden space for the lower castes, untouchables and women as well as tribals, no heresy was ever possible. Added to this was the legendary tolerance of Hindus, fed for centuries on superstition and the karma theory. Again the British had their own axe to grind here, especially in not displeasing the Brahmins, who were regarded as the pillars of British Raj in their widespread nascent administration in the subcontinent—Bengali and Marathi Brahmins especially. We must remember here the heated debates among Brahmins as to whether social reforms should precede political freedom.

In these circumstances, 'social-reforms-first' activists like Phule were very clear in their priority. As Vidushak says in the last scene of *Tritiya Ratna*, '[I]f…the English too ill-treat their subjects, then… the newly educated Shudras and Atishudras will establish their own state and, like the Americans, will govern it themselves' (p. 107, this volume).

It may be noted here that Phule dedicated one of his major books *Gulamgiri* (1873), the title of which was translated into English by the author as *Slavery*, to the leaders of the abolitionist movement in the United States who led the movement for the emancipation of the black population. Phule chose to write his preface to *Gulamgiri* in English. The preface makes a number of insightful observations on education and is therefore also included here.

The sub-text of Phule's *Tritiya Ratna* would give us an ideology surprisingly advanced for colonial society. Vidushak's mono-dialogues reveal complete sympathy—not just pity—for women as the last frontier of compassion in Hindu culture. A pregnant housewife looking after the household, guileless, hapless and willing to make any sacrifice for the child she is carrying, is transformed into a free person, ready to join Savitribai Phule's newly started school for women.

Education in Phule's agenda holds priority over everything else because it democratises knowledge and the power associated with knowledge. Only education can emancipate women and the lower castes in India. It also leads to self-knowledge and awareness of all kinds, such as the farmer telling his wife, 'We will eat together today', and an awakened consciousness which enables him to see through 'the Bhatbrahmans' deceitful exploitation' that has been duping the ignorant lower castes for generations with all their 'lies about God and religion' (p. 109, this volume).

The missionary's Socratic dialogue with the farmer on the futility of idol worship, his justifying the destruction of Somnath and other Hindu idols by Muslim invaders, praising a newly started missionary journal in Marathi and schools under British administration as well as commending Semitic monotheism—all these ideas reveal Phule's ideology of a new religion.

However, these Christian-Muslim-Semitic ideals of monotheism had a negative effect on the self-perception of later thinkers on Hinduism. The British Parliament in fact restrained missionary activities after the war of independence in 1857, just two years after *Tritiya Ratna* was written. This war was ignited by a strong religious issue—that the British Christians were greasing the cartridges used by Indian soldiers with the fat of pigs and cows, and thus both Muslim and Hindu soldiers in the British army united in a now-or-never war against their Christian masters.

Still, *Tritiya Ratna* was a good beginning.

In his powada 'Vidyakhatyateel Brahman Pantoji' (1869?), composed in a traditional rhyme popular with the common people, Phule refers to the fairly well-established indigenous system of basic education—the private schools run all over the country by Brahmins or *pantoji* (see Dharampal, *The Beautiful Tree*[1]).

It had existed for centuries before 'English' education was initiated by the Education Departments in the 1840s. The pantoji, who was handily recruited by the government, was accustomed to teaching in the vernacular language basic literacy tools such as reading and writing skills, elementary mathematics and cost accounting. Now the switch-over to 'English' education, which was not even 'European' as educationists would opine, could easily be described as fanatical, unjustifiable and irrational. The Victorian loyalists Lord Thomas Macaulay in 1835 and Sir Charles Wood in 1854 thoughtlessly imposed a foreign language on the poor children of the whole continent, only to develop rote habits and cramming through the vernacularist pantoji's mouth. Moreover, the utopian 'downward filtration theory' envisaged by the Imperial Government was bound to fail in such a hierarchical society as Hindus had no sense of responsibility towards the underprivileged. Phule seems to overlook the basic problem of the medium of instruction.

Dr Mokashi-Punekar has attempted the difficult task of translating a satirical poem written in the traditional form and metre of a powada. So far there have been very few translations of Phule's poetic experiments in English, and her translation is one of the first attempts. As a poetic form which enjoyed popularity and currency in Marathi culture and literature, Phule must have intended the poem to be performed. In the introductory note to the powada, translated as 'Brahmin Teachers in the Education Department', Dr Mokashi-Punekar provides a comprehensive background and discusses the cultural significance of the powada in the Marathi-speaking region as a genre that traditionally celebrated the military exploits of the Maratha and Peshwa rulers. *Shahirs*,[2] traditional folk artistes and poet-musicians of Maharashtra, were very versatile and brought in references to contemporary cultural and political specificities in their performances to hold the interest of their audiences. Phule built upon this innate potential of the powada to comment on contemporary issues, and used the form to satirise the pantoji. Just as he revolutionised the dramatic form in *Tritiya Ratna* to produce a play of ideas, in 'Vidyakhatyateel Brahman Pantoji' he reinvented the form of the powada to show the existing social reality in villages, where rampant poverty was matched by the people's ignorance. Rural India and all its inequities are presented in both these texts.

Phule's 'Memorial Addressed to the Education Commission' (1882) is unique in many respects, particularly in its excellent critical interpretation of the colonial government's English education system. A superb specimen of Phule's robust style of arguing with statistics and reason, and based on the strength of his personal experience of efficiently administering the several major institutions he had founded for the lower castes and women, the Memorial exposed the deplorable state of education at all levels. He repeatedly adverted to the system that helped only the upper castes, who contributed little to the state exchequer and absolutely ignored the ryots, who paid the greater part of the revenue to the British Imperial government by the toil and sweat of their brow. Elaborating on details of how children of the lower castes were ill-treated by the Brahmin teachers, the document, with admonitory references to the white administrators, disclosed how, owing to dreadful poverty, children of tender years were forced to quit school as soon as they found manual occupation.

Dr Mokashi-Punekar locates these texts by Phule within a broad and comprehensive overview on developments in the field of education during the nineteenth century. This is an excellent and meticulously researched discussion which is bound to be of immense interest to scholars. It begins with the Charter Act of 1813 and ends with the Indian Education Commission of 1882. The overview situates Phule's interventions within a detailed summary of the contemporary trends and directions of the historiography of educational development in India. It examines the role of reformist and evangelical discourse in the making of the policies of the East India Company in the metropole. It notes the importance of tracing developments in the colony in the context of the changing discourse in the metropole, also examining the significant role of Indian elites in the shaping of colonial policy. Based on illuminating studies by scholars in the field, it shows the struggles of the lower castes and untouchables in asserting their right to education.

Dr Mokashi-Punekar has made a judicious selection of Phule's writings on the subject of education. These writings are of great importance since they enable us to establish the visceral connection between the issues and problems of our times with those of the nineteenth century. We see that two of these texts belong to the literary genres of drama and poetry, which she has felicitously translated into English. The other two are prose pieces written by Phule in English. In all these writings, Phule offers radical insights into Brahminical society and the historical control of the upper classes over the generation and transmission of knowledge. Since these texts were written over a period of time it is possible to see the development of Phule's ideas on education in the trajectory of their chronology. It is also possible to see these texts as Phule's responses to the implementation of different colonial policies on education.

A humanitarian in essence, Mahatma Jotirao Phule expresses genuine concern for the education of the children of the poor, including Muslims, and pleads for grants to private schools run by Brahmins too. He aimed to unite all the marginalised sections of society, including all categories of women, and Muslims. His concept of the Shudratishudra was an inclusive idea, which anticipated the conception of the Bahujan Samaj. A few years after Phule's demise, Maratha reformer and committed Brahmo Samajist Maharshi Vithal Ramji Shinde conceived of the Bahujan Samaj as a solidarity of the oppressed sections resisting the dominance of the privileged classes in his work *Bharatiya Asprushyatecha Prashna*. Through organisations such as Nirashrit Sahayyak Mandal (Depressed Classes Mission), Vithal Ramji Shinde worked to educate the lower castes and untouchables. He carried forward the legacy of Phule in the conception of the Bahujan Samaj and in focussing on educating the oppressed sections of society.

Phule also inspired untouchable leaders before Ambedkar such as Gopal Baba Valangkar and Shivram Janba Kamble who had been members of the Satyashodhak Samaj. These leaders formed the link in the ongoing struggle for the empowerment of the lower castes and women. In the twentieth century, when Dr Babasaheb Ambedkar arrived on the scene to directly represent the untouchables, he acknowledged Phule's radical contributions to caste and gender reform by naming him as one of his three gurus.

Bhalchandra Nemade
20 October 2020, Mumbai

Notes

1. Dharampal, *The Beautiful Tree: Indigenous Indian Education in the Eighteenth Century* (1983). In *Essential Writings of Dharampal*, edited by Gita Dharampal (New Delhi: Publications Division, Ministry of Information and Broadcasting, Government of India, 2015; second edition 2022).

2. The Dalit Shahirs of Maharashtra have been effective and powerful disseminators of the anti-caste movement who have taken Dr Ambedkar's teachings to the people. See https://feminisminindia.com/2021/03/05/dalit-shahir-maharashtra-anti-caste-art-form/; and https://www.firstpost.com/living/dalit-shahirs-of-maharashtra-from-bhimrao-kardak-to-sambhaji-bhagat-tracing-a-legacy-of-anti-caste-music-and-poetry-8273941.html (accessed 14 January 2023).

Preface

Context

There is little doubt that the education system that exists in India, a creaky, top-heavy relic that has lumbered on from colonial times, is stratified and biased towards the privileged sections of our riven and hierarchical society, and towards textual rote learning. In recent years the curriculum obtaining in schools and undergraduate programmes has been the subject of contestations. The development of curricula and text books at the school level is decided by government bodies at the state and/or central level. This construction of knowledge and the enforcement of pedagogy are filtered through ideological biases. Digital modes of instruction, introduced in a concerted manner in the wake of the Covid pandemic, despite the real advantages of the medium in terms of its capacity for storage and dissemination of educational material, have only deepened these inherent biases in the system.

The New Education Policy (NEP) introduced since 2020, despite its nobly worded intentions, is ominously silent on the word reservation, which has, in the decades after independence, enabled a small fragment of socially backward and deprived groups to enter elite institutions. Moreover, the privatisation of education envisaged will only serve to put education beyond the reach of socially and economically weaker sections. Such students who do enter the portals of private institutions on scholarships instituted by state regulations are bound to find themselves in a social minority. Divisions amongst the student community will encourage weaker students to drop out. The NEP makes provisions for the exit of students and indicates that these students will be accommodated with a certificate or a diploma; but this consolation will not sell in the job market. It also recommends that such students can get into vocational training, when in fact any vocational training ought to follow after a full basic education. Partial education in combination with vocational training will only continue the traditional duality between textual knowledge and skill-based knowledge.

Interlaced with these issues is the flood of information disseminated by means of social media, often of dubious origin and mischievous in its intended targeting, which overwhelms the young and old alike. In the absence of quality basic education and the lacunae of critical thinking in the curricula of both run-of-the-mill and elite institutions catering to professional courses, half-baked and scurrilous bites of information accompanied by visual content inflame feelings of righteous entitlement and suspicion. This peculiar crisis of knowledge occurring paradoxically in an age characterised by the undeterred surge of information technologies cannot fail to strike any academic invested in addressing the challenges of education.

It would be a useful exercise to take some steps back into history, if only to revisit the long, hard battles fought for equitable access to education and to locate the present crisis in the education system of the country within the larger historical context. This book attempts to focus on the attempts of subaltern groups in nineteenth-century Maharashtra under the leadership of Mahatma Jotiba Phule who spearheaded the first modern struggle for the rights of the marginalised castes, and to examine his heroic battle for the right to access learning by reading some of his writings.

Plan of the Book

Planned initially as a translation of Jotiba Phule's play *Tritiya Ratna*, with a detailed discussion introducing it to readers in English, this book has grown in scope and ambition. Considering the ferment in Indian educational institutions on the question of inclusivity and the yearning amongst the populace for quality education and commensurate openings for employment, it seemed meaningful to take the opportunity to link the aspiration for modern education in colonial India with its continued intensity in the present times. Phule wrote with passion on the subject of inclusive education; he also made substantial interventions by founding several schools for marginalised sections, women and working caste adults. Included in this book are two of his literary works on the seminal importance of education that have been translated for the first time into English. *Tritiya Ratna*, translated as *The Third Eye*, is a play and 'Vidyakhatyateel Brahman Pantoji', translated as 'Brahmin Teachers in the Education Department', is a poem in the genre of a ballad or *powada*. A prolific writer, Phule also wrote prose texts. *Gulamgiri* (1873), his best-known work, contains a preface in English where Phule dwells on the subject of state funding for the education of the lower castes. Phule quoted from parts of this preface in his address to the Indian Education Commission constituted by the colonial government under the chairmanship of Sir William Hunter in 1881. Both these texts are included in the present volume along with a detailed discussion locating Phule in the history of modern education in India. It is hoped that the inclusion of all of Phule's major texts on education in a single volume will enable a historical perspective on the subject of inclusive education and be of some help to scholars working in this field.

G. P. Deshpande's edited volume of translations of Phule's prose works, published in 2002 by LeftWord, has expanded the understanding of subaltern assertion and literature in India. However, Phule's literary experiments in the service of ideological critique have seldom found attention even in Marathi literary circles. The intention of the present volume is to make available in English translation two such experiments that focus on education for the lower castes and women: Phule's play of ideas *Tritiya Ratna* and his satirical ballad 'Vidyakhatyateel Brahman Pantoji'. It is this translator's hope that these translations and their inclusion in a dedicated volume on Phule's educational writings will deepen our understanding of the pivotal significance of education to the history of subaltern protest in India.

On Translation

Always tricky, translation poses unique problems when it has to manage a transfer of meaning from texts complexly anchored in cultural specificities into a language that is ignorant of these. The world of nineteenth-century rural, western India presented in both works is structured on linguistic and cultural exclusivities of caste and religion that are yet interdependent on one another. Language has to negotiate the boundaries of these different worlds and achieve control over the nuance of tone and experience. *Tritiya Ratna* is a play that is premised on the politics of identity and hierarchy. The translator has to be sensitive to colloquial idioms, the linguistic differences embedded in social identity and the cultural mores intrinsic to those worlds. She has to walk the thin precipice between the rarified heights of sounding too 'English' or too stolidly cleaved to the original and becoming fatally florid. In translating the ballad 'Vidyakhatyateel Brahman Pantoji', contrary to my standard practice while translating from non-modern Marathi poetry, I chose to use rhyme and metre. As a political and social satire, the dark humour of the original, I felt, would be captured best in verse that employed a loose rhythmic structure. The syntax, however, is in modern English idiom. I have also taken the liberty of dropping some phrases or a line or two of the original poem when doing so seemed to better fit the sound and effect of the translation in English.

All texts of Phule included in this volume are based on the 1991 fifth edition of *Mahatma Phule Samagra Vangmay* (The Collected Works of Mahatma Phule), edited by Y. D. Phadke, first published in 1969 by the Maharashtra State Society for Literature and Culture, Mumbai, edited by Dhananjay Keer and S. G. Malshe (and henceforth cited as CWMP 1991[1969]). All translations are mine unless otherwise stated; texts quoted from this volume are cited by page number alone.

Rohini Mokashi-Punekar
February 2023

Acknowledgements

I am deeply grateful to Bhalchandra Nemade and Christian Lee Novetzke for their insightful comments on the drafts of different chapters of this book, and to Bhalchandra Nemade for readily agreeing to write a Foreword to this volume.

Though I have not had the privilege of meeting or corresponding with Datta Bhagat, his comprehensive introduction as an editor, titled '*Jotirao Phule Likhit Trutiya Ratna: Marathi Bhaashetla Pahile Aadhunik Natak*', to Phule's first play was a crucially important study in the formation of my own analysis of *Tritiya Ratna*.

My thanks to Chakradhar Saswade, friend, frequent collaborator, and *sahridaya* whose inwardness with Marathi letters can only be described as grace.

Dilip Chavan and Parimala Rao shared books and articles with great generosity; Shanta Gokhale responded promptly and with the greatest kindness to my queries. A debt of gratitude to all three scholars.

Rumina Sethi invited me to submit the translation of 'Vidyakhatyateel Pantoji' together with an introductory note for an issue of the journal *Dialog* which she then edited. I am grateful to her, and to the present editors for the permission to reprint both in the present book.

Deepest thanks to M. Asaduddin, Mini Krishnan and Sudhanva Deshpande whose interventions and support nudged my manuscript to its present status and location.

A salute to Ravish Kumar (formerly with NDTV) whose series on the prevailing conditions in educational institutions in contemporary India ran parallel with my own initial reading of Phule. A rare journalist of courage, passion and poetic sensitivity,

Ravish was unfailingly kind in his responsiveness to any question or comment. For his work and for being him: only indebtedness.

My warm appreciation for the dedication of the editors at Orient BlackSwan: Vidya Rao, Nilanjana Majumdar and Moyna Mazumdar who have been incredibly thorough and empathetic.

Different chapters of this study were presented in talks given at Harvard, USA; Grenoble, France; Osmania University, Hyderabad; IIT Kanpur and IIT Ropar. I am grateful to the organisers: Kate Costello, G. J. V. Prasad, T. Vijay Kumar, G. Neelakantan, Mini Chandran and Swathi Krishna for inviting me to present my ongoing work, and to the many scholars in the audience who posed questions and sought clarifications that deepened my understanding of Phule's texts.

A teacher's daily engagement with courses and texts in the classroom, and informal exchanges with colleagues in hurried corridor encounters, or around the coffee stall feeds into much of the busy happiness that is academic life. It is sheer joy to live and work amidst the green hills and clear lake waters of the IIT Guwahati campus, arguably the prettiest in the country. I am grateful to the administration for the measures taken over many years which provide excellent facilities for research. My thanks too, to colleagues in the department; to the office staff which is unfailingly kind and supportive; and to the graduate researchers: Halim Hussain, Ajay Salunkhe, Himaxee Bordoloi, Snigdha Deka and Adeep Hussain who are so intelligent, affectionate and eager to help.

Finally, almost everything I do emerges from the bedrock that is Ravi; Prachi and Rohit; Mithu and Haley. They know what I owe them.

Rohini Mokashi-Punekar
February 2023

Phule in His Times

A Brief Note on His Life and Works

Mahatma Phule (1827–1890) is alive in public memory today as a radical reformer from Maharashtra who interrogated social hierarchies and who, together with his wife Savitribai, instituted schools for women and the lower castes in mid-nineteenth century Pune, attempting to make education accessible to all those sections that were traditionally deprived of learning. Phule is also remembered for his interventions in agriculture; many movements in western and central India in contemporary times are spearheaded by farmers who have affiliations to his name or to the Satyashodhak Samaj, the organisation which he founded, as do movements for sustainable agriculture and ecology as a whole. Not much attention has been paid, however, to Phule's creative use of many literary forms, traditional or otherwise, which he deployed for his polemical writings. Concurrently, while there may be some acknowledgment in contemporary discourses in the social sciences of Phule's lifelong struggle in the cause of his mission, there is little recognition for Phule's literary interventions even in Marathi literature. There is hardly any discussion on Phule's poetry, though he was a prolific poet, employing traditional poetic forms such as the ballad-like *powada*, which he used for political purposes; or the *abhanga*-like verse, which in a typical predilection for reinvention he termed '*akhanda*'. Very recently some note has been taken of Savitribai's writings, and a spate of articles analysing the modernity and the radicalness of her verse that speaks with great courage of sexual oppression and caste divisions has become available in the public domain. It may be noted that Savitribai's book of poetry *Kavya Phule* was published in 1854, far before Phule published any of his own work. Though their writing is highly individualistic, this remarkable couple voice similar ideological preoccupations, and a recuperation of their unique literary compositions will prove to be of great significance for ongoing social and literary movements in contemporary times.

We may at the outset trace a short account of Phule's life and map within it the trajectory of his writings and activism.

JOTIBA PHULE: THE EARLY YEARS

Jotiba Phule was born in the year 1827 into a lower-caste Mali family, barely a few years after the Peshwas had been overthrown by the British. The Malis are a Shudra caste that falls into the broad range of cultivating, land-owning castes called the Maratha-Kunbis who are spread across a hierarchy of ranks.[1] Living in Pune, the family took to its hereditary occupation, which was horticulture, and earlier generations of its members supplied flowers to the Peshwas who had awarded them a little land as a grant on the outskirts of the city. The family was fairly well-off and as a result of this, perhaps, Jotiba was sent first to a local Marathi school. On the advice of a family acquaintance, however, he was soon taken off the rolls and put to work in the fields. This episode in his life is reflected in the play *Tritiya Ratna* (1855) which he was to write in his twenties. A bright boy with a taste for reading, he soon caught the eye of another friend of the family (a Muslim as it happens) who advised his father to send him back to school. This time Jotiba was admitted to the Scottish Mission school run by the Free Church of Scotland, which had an enlightened admission policy, admitting children from the upper as well as the lower castes, including a few children from the Mahar and Mang castes.[2] In this heterogeneous group, Phule made several early friendships; interestingly these were deep, intimate bonds with Brahmin and non-Brahmin boys who were to stand by him throughout his life, becoming his associates in all his later radical initiatives and activism.

Phule was also exposed to the most current ideas and discourses of the times in this school. The most lasting impressions on his mind seem to have been formed under the tutelage of the missionaries. Not only did he read classical and modern Western literary texts, he was also exposed to Protestant literature and the emerging missionary scholarship on Indian texts and knowledge systems that questioned Brahminical Hinduism and caste hegemony. All studies on Phule acknowledge the formative and abiding influence of Western reformist thought—in particular, Thomas Paine's *Rights of Man*, which Phule read in 1847—on his thinking. It is natural to assume that conversion to Christianity must have been an option easily available to him, as it was to many upper-caste Indian intellectuals of his time. However, Rosalind O'Hanlon's detailed study shows some evidence of his religious position in these early years of his career (O'Hanlon 2010[1985]: 112). Though he and his friends in the Scottish mission school valued Christianity and thought it was a superior religion than their own, their reading of Paine's books, from which they are said to have learned passages by heart, appears to have exerted a more powerful influence. While most studies on Phule testify to the influence of *Rights of Man*, Paine's other significant work *The Age of Reason*—that affirms monotheism, the idea of a natural and universal religion, and discusses the falseness of Christian dogma and creed—seems to have exercised a greater impact on Phule. He and his friends apparently realised that there was no real justification for Christianity as a religion. Moreover, Phule himself does not seem to have believed in a revealed religion (ibid.). Though his ties with the missionaries continued almost throughout his career, involved as he was in making radical interventions in education, writing and agitating for a political identity and constituency for the Shudratishudra, Phule never speaks of conversion to Christianity as a possibility, either for himself in these early years or for the oppressed groups on behalf of whom he fought most of his adult life.[3] It is important to note this point in the context of *Tritiya Ratna*. Phule's understanding of the enlightened thinker seems to be encoded in the person of the Christian missionary, a significant character in the play, who persuades the deluded Kunbi to think and reason. At no point in the play does the missionary offer conversion as a solution to end caste hierarchy.

However, it is important to take into account the interventions made by an elite and influential group of Western-educated, upper-caste reformers in Bombay during the 1830s and 1840s. Perceiving the putative backwardness and social stagnation of Hindu society, these groups spoke and wrote fervently for its regeneration. Influenced by missionary propaganda as well as English reformism as endorsed by colonial officials, they formed associations and started newspapers and journals which were quite often bilingual.[4] The overall thrust of these published articles was anti-Hindu orthodoxy, and they appealed to caste Hindu society for the emancipation of the lower castes and women, and for the overall widening of the intellectual horizons of Indians. Some of these early reformers also converted to Christianity (O'Hanlon 2010[1985]: 98–99). While there is very little available in Phule's own writings about his early years, a few autobiographical notes by some of his close student colleagues throw light on his association with the secret society Paramahansa Mandali which was started in Bombay around 1848 with the explicit objective of breaking caste divisions and working for the remarriage of widows (ibid.: 96–99). Though it is not clear if Phule was a member of any one of the branches of Paramahansa Mandali that were established secretly in several major towns of Maharashtra, it is evident that many of the core beliefs and codes of this secret society matched with the rules of the Satyashodhak Samaj that Phule was to establish much later in 1873. In fact, the book about Paramahansa Mandali setting out many of its core tenets—based on a handwritten text by the founder Dadoba Pandurang and published years after it had stopped operating—formed the basic book of the Satyashodhak Samaj. Phule used this book for his lectures, and copies were made of it to be distributed as a part of the Samaj's propaganda campaign in and around Pune (ibid.: 99–100).

PHULE'S INTERVENTIONS: ACTIVISM AND WRITING

Phule was barely twenty years of age when he began a school for girls from the low and (formerly) 'Untouchable' castes in Pune, taking upon himself the task of teaching as well as running the school.

Savitribai, to whom he was married in 1840, was a close associate here and in all his later initiatives, as were some friends from his school days. Established in 1848, the school was a radical initiative and it posed difficulties at every step. Fearing upper-caste backlash, Phule's father turned him and his wife out of the house. No female teachers could be found and so Savitribai (herself trained by Bhavalakar, one of Phule's close Brahmin associates in these early years and a member of the Paramahansa Mandali) started teaching the girls. Funds were perennially short and the school ran on voluntary commitments of labour from the circle of friends and charity from European administrators. Most crucially it was difficult to convince parents from lower-caste communities to send their girls to school. Despite all these difficulties, Phule persevered, and started several more schools over the next few years. These were schools for Untouchable boys, another for girls of all castes and an evening school for working adults. This last school figures as a reference in *Tritiya Ratna*, a sign of Phule's intention perhaps to actively canvass for it from the stage. He was partially helped by a grant of Rs 75 from the Dakshina Fund (O'Hanlon 2010[1985]: 118). In 1852, on the recommendation of the Board of Education to the Bombay Government, Phule was conferred a mark of honour in a public ceremony where Major Thomas Candy, the principal of Poona College, presented him with a pair of shawls, a traditional gift of honour (ibid.: 118–119). We must remember in this context that Candy also figures as a very topical and contemporary reference in the discussion between the Kunbi and the missionary in *Tritiya Ratna*. In 1853, Phule formed the 'Society for Increasing Education amongst Mahars, Mangs and Others', which started two more schools for the Untouchables. It may have been around this time that Phule had a rift with some of his Brahmin fellow associates over two issues: the first concerned the kind of education that must be given to the lower castes, Phule being in favour of a thorough educational grounding; and the second issue was regarding the extent of blame that must be assigned to the Brahmin elite for the miserable condition of the Untouchables. Phule characteristically presented the Brahmin as the sole cause of lower-caste misery, a fact borne out by an essay read out to a visitor in one of Phule's schools by a fourteen-year-old girl student of the

Mang caste named Muktabai, who was ferocious in her indictment of elite Brahmins (O'Hanlon 2010[1985]: 120). Muktabai's *Mang Maharachya Dukhavisayi* (About the Grief of the Mangs and Mahars) is early evidence of the intellectual space for women and the lower castes which Phule's interventions in education had made possible.

As was to become a pattern with Phule, he creatively transformed these private differences of opinion, with friends or other intellectuals as it may be, into polemical and/or creative works. The outcome of this argument was *Tritiya Ratna*, indisputably the first modern political play of ideas in Marathi literature (Deshpande 2002: 17). With a small cast of typical characters: a Kunbi couple representing the toiling lower-caste peasant, a scheming Brahmin priest, a Christian missionary and the playwright narrator, Phule presents his understanding of Hinduism as a manipulative Brahminical structure that ideologically oppresses the lower castes. The ideology itself becomes a tool of material impoverishment of those most marginalised and in distress. Phule endeavours to show how these traditional prerogatives of the Brahminical caste find extension during contemporary times in a large number of modern institutions of the Raj, including educational institutions, thereby conferring on the Brahmins enormous power in the secular sphere in addition to the existing hegemony in the religious domain.

Though it was Phule's first literary composition written in or slightly before 1855, *Tritiya Ratna* was first printed and published in 1979, exactly a century and quarter after it was submitted to the Dakshina Prize Committee for its consideration. In the interim, the text existed only as a reference in the prose polemic *Gulamgiri* published in 1873 which is dialogic in form. To the question posed by his associate Dhondiba on the dynamics of the Dakshina Prize Committee, Phule refers, in *Gulamgiri*, to his first piece of writing thus:

> You know, I had written a play about how *bhatjoshis* deceive the shudras with tall tales of their self-serving religion and how on the other hand the Christian missionaries impart real knowledge of their impartial religion to lead their people on to the path of Truth. And I submitted this play to the Dakshina Prize Committee, long back in 1855. But here too the *bhatbrahmans* held on to their opinion and the European

> officers could do little to counter it. And so my play was rejected straight away. (CWMP 1991[1969]: 191–192)

The Dakshina Prize Committee was formed by the colonial government as a way of carrying forward the older Peshwa tradition where monies (i.e. *dakshina* or fees paid to Brahmins) had been disbursed to learned Brahmins as a kind of state patronage. While the custom may have started as an instrument to encourage *shastric* learning, quite clearly it was yet another privilege the Peshwas had implemented in favour of the ruling class. In a few years after the British had taken over the Maratha kingdom, the colonial government tweaked the form and intention of this fund in order to cater to modern educational purposes. During the initial years of colonial rule, Elphinstone had kept up with the practice by starting a school for Sanskrit from the funds kept aside for dakshina. On a suggestion made by the well-known reformer Gopal Hari Deshmukh 'Lokahitwadi' about the necessity of publishing new books in Marathi, the British administrators decided to institute a Dakshina Prize Committee which would award writers on the basis of the merit of their works, in the hope that this would result in the development of Marathi language and literature, making it richer. Ironically Phule himself supported the petitions made by the reformist members of the upper castes to widen the ambit of the Dakshina Fund's purview from merely Vedic learning to the production of knowledge in Marathi that would be of greater advantage to the public at large. On these pleas the colonial rulers reduced this fund considerably and channeled it towards emerging scholarship in the vernacular language, besides traditional learning in Sanskrit. From the 1820s the government attempted to 'replace the study of traditional, brahmanical texts by the pursuit of modern "useful" learning through the vernacular' (Naregal 2002[2001]: 83). However, the British were also very careful not to antagonise the Brahmins, giving them important positions in education and administration.

That Phule submitted his play to the Dakshina Prize Committee which was composed of a preponderance of Brahmins may be seen today as an explicitly political act meant to gauge the avowed liberalism of the reformist Brahmins and that of the colonial government. The outright rejection of his play may not have surprised Phule very much. Though the committee was instituted as a mechanism to encourage Marathi language and literature in a well-meaning bid to reform the Peshwa institution of dakshina, it was not able to support the first fledgling efforts of the subaltern castes to produce literary works. Not only could Phule's play not be published within the existing practices of social and dramatic norms of the time and the lack of minimum facilities to present modern drama, but *Tritiya Ratna* had little chance of being performed. It must be noted however that even after these facilities had developed sufficiently, *Tritiya Ratna* was not staged for more than a century. It is not difficult to gauge that there were social and political reasons why the play was consigned to oblivion. In fact, this was the theme *Tritiya Ratna* attempted to highlight unflinchingly: the exploitation of the lower castes by the Brahmins, deploying duplicity and cunning. Sadanand More makes an important point in this connection, underscoring British complicity in the rejection. Not only did the Brahmin members of the Dakshina Prize Committee reject Phule's script, he says there is no reason to believe that the English pursued it with any great conviction (More 2007: 165). It must be remembered that Major Candy headed the committee. In his play Phule takes Candy, along with other English administrators, to task for believing implicitly in all that the duplicitous Brahmin teachers report to them. Clearly, the British did not wish to upset the social hierarchies that prevailed in western India and were at pains to maintain the status quo.

No copies of this play were thought to have survived. Though Keer's biography of Phule (Keer 2000[1964]) mentioned this play, the first edition of the *Collected Works of Mahatma Phule* collated by Keer and Malshe was published without this text since the editors had not been able to track it down. However, in the late 1970s, through a fortuitous stroke of good fortune, three manuscript copies of this play were discovered in the private papers of Phule's first major biographer, Pandharinath Patil. The play was published for the first time after this momentous discovery in the journal *Purogami Satyashodhak* (Raikar 1979), with an introductory note by Sitaram Raikar.

From the early sixties, Phule began a number of initiatives in women's reform: campaigns for the remarriage of widows and a home for the prevention of infanticide. Both these efforts aimed at providing some support to upper-caste widows, who were often driven to commit suicide if they had no recourse to methods of abortion—usually crude and often with disastrous consequences—to terminate pregnancies conceived as a result of being coerced into sexual relations. Phule and Savitribai also adopted a boy born to a Brahmin widow, naming him Yashwant, Phule's name for Christ. While Phule shares with the other major nineteenth-century Indian reformers a preoccupation with women's reform, he is the only reformer whose perspective is so completely modern. He could see that caste and gender are oppressive and interlinked structures. It would be some decades after Phule that patriarchy was conceptualised as a term for male hegemony. However, he understood that all women, regardless of their position in social hierarchy, were marginalised within the cultural norms that prevailed. In 1885 Phule published two issues of a journal named *Satsar* (CWMP 1991[1969]: 357–396); these were largely devoted to the defence of Pandita Ramabai and her right to convert to Christianity even as he discussed the essence of true religion. At a time when even the so-called reformist Brahmins opposed her move in vitriolic terms, Phule's defence constitutes the only non-Christian defence of the learned Ramabai's revolutionary step (Deshpande 2002: 10).

The rejection of *Tritiya Ratna* (CWMP 1991[1969]: 1–33) by the Dakshina Committee had perhaps put a temporary break on Phule's engagement with literary forms as a vehicle for his ideas. From 1869 to 1873, however, there was a quantum spurt in Phule's experimentation with a variety of literary genres. These texts form the theoretical basis for his interventions: activist and polemical. The decades after the 1860s also mark, in fact, the gathering strength of conservative Brahminical opinion in the public sphere of Maharashtra. We will see a little later how this is reflected in theatre. A quick look at articles in highly popular print media reveals the vituperative nature of these debates: there is an ideological continuity in literary periodicals such as the *Nibandhmala* which was edited by Vishnushastri Chiplunkar, and newspapers such as the *Kesari* and *Maratha* edited by Tilak.

All three publications kept up 'a virulent anti lower-caste discourse' (Naregal 2002[2001]: 210), which explains in part Phule's own bitter campaign against upper-caste hegemony over knowledge and culture. In 1869 Phule composed a verse polemic in the form of the traditional powada on Brahmin teachers in government schools titled 'Vidyakhatyateel Brahman Pantoji' (Brahmin Teachers in the Education Department), depicting Brahmin hypocrisy and control of modern educational facilities (CWMP 1991[1969]: 83–90). The present book includes a translation of this powada together with a short discussion of its form and theme. This narrative poem continues the theme of his play *Tritiya Ratna*. The ballad *Chhatrapati Shivaji Raje Bhosale Yancha Powada* was also published the same year (ibid.: 34–81). The ballad is a traditional Marathi poetic form used to describe heroic acts, and by selecting this verse genre Phule ensconced himself within the popular oral tradition even as he attempted to underscore the figure of Shivaji as a non-Brahmin hero, the protector of the large subaltern group of castes, Shudratishudra, to which he belonged. The construction of a collective identity for all the lower castes is continued in another collection of ballads, *Brahmananche Kasab* published in the same year (ibid.: 91–118). This work, subtitled *Priestcraft Exposed* in English, offers Phule's version of a revisionist history to contest Brahminical mythology. A brave attempt to subvert Brahminical texts as the source of all knowledge, Phule deploys the then current hypothesis of the Aryan invasion as a structural strategy to interpret Brahmins as oppressive, unrighteous invaders subduing the original native inhabitants of the land, who he said were really one people: the Shudratishudras. Phule continued this theme in his best-known work, the prose polemic *Gulamgiri*, published in 1873 (ibid.: 119–201). Constructed as a dialogue between himself and a close associate, this text uses biting satire to lampoon Brahminical texts and gods: mainly the mythic stories of the ten avatars of Vishnu; it reinterprets mythology to create a counter-history for the Shudratishudra (Mokashi-Punekar 2017: 164–168).

Phule's writings constituted an ideological plank which was the foundation for his activism. In 1873 Phule established the Satyashodhak Samaj, The Society of Truth Seekers, positing truth-seeking as the essence of the organisation's activities. This association soon had branches all over Maharashtra, in towns and villages, mobilising the lower castes and offering a counterpoint to elite hegemony. The Samaj continued to challenge upper-caste political dominance till the first decades of the twentieth century and had a large role to play in the successful non-Brahmin movement of Maharashtra.[5] It began its own bilingual weekly newspaper *Din Bandhu* in 1877 which furthered its spread beyond the urban centres of Pune and Bombay to smaller towns and villages. It had the support of Telugu Mali contractors, apart from the native lower castes of Maharashtra. By the 1880s, Phule and his Mali associates Lokhande and Bhalekar had begun addressing large meetings in the rural hinterland; Satyashodhak ritual practices where the services of the Brahmin priests were dispensed with became increasingly popular in the way marriages were conducted, and in some centres the Samaj led protests by cultivators against landlords and moneylenders (Omvedt 2011[1976]).

Perhaps the first modern Indian reformer to pay attention to agriculture, Phule made a searching examination of the social and economic persecution of the Indian peasant in *Shetkaryacha Asud*, published in 1883 (CWMP 1991[1969]: 255–343). Phule lays bare the miserable conditions of the peasants, the reasons for the low productivity of agriculture in Maharashtra and the implicit connection between the social and economic aspects of agriculture. From the ballad *Brahmananche Kasab* to the two prose works *Gulamgiri* and *Shetkaryacha Asud*, Phule conceived of a two-tiered hierarchical social structure wherein the Brahmins constituted the class that oppressed all other castes; according to Phule's revisionist history, the indigent and original Kshatriyas had during the ages been designated as Shudratishudra by the Brahmins.

However, Phule's systematic and comprehensive critique of the existing society under Brahmanism (one must remember that he never once used the word Hinduism) was balanced by his formulation of the core tenets of the true faith for humankind. In 1889, even as he was ailing, Phule worked on his last book, *Sarvajanik Satya Dharma Pustak* (The Book of the True Faith), which was published posthumously in 1891 (CWMP 1991[1969]: 443–560). Instead of a deeply divisive society characterised by the hegemony and the mediation of the Brahmin in all human affairs, Phule conceived of a code of values that rule an egalitarian and bountiful world created by the *Nirmik*, the Creator who is also its benign and rather secular head (Deshpande 2002: 12). It is in this text and in the conception of the Creator that one notes the lingering influence on Phule of Paine's *Age of Reason*.

It is possible to map the trajectory of events and works in Phule's life against the developments in colonial policy on education during the nineteenth century. The changes introduced in the different Charters of the East India Company as they came up for renewal by the British Parliament under pressure from the powerful evangelical lobby and reformist opinion resulted in changes of policy in colonial India. These policies in turn were sometimes resisted or tweaked to suit the designs of elite groups in India with their own vested interests. Ordinary Indians, marginalised in the hierarchy of power, who had a stake in these changes also petitioned the government sometimes with the active support of missionary groups. Phule's schooling in the Scottish mission school, the ideas and reading to which he was exposed and the creative use he made of these to formulate his own ideological basis to resist Brahminical oppression and cultural hegemony can be examined against the larger developments of the nineteenth century. The chapter titled 'Situating Phule within the History of Education in India' attempts to do precisely this even as it hopes to provide a framework to understand Phule's two prose writings in English: the 'Preface' to *Gulamgiri* and the 'Memorial Addressed to the Education Commission'.

Notes

1. Malis and Kunbis are castes associated with occupations related to agriculture, horticulture and sometimes petty trading. They figure lower down in the broad hierarchy of castes denoted as Shudra in the Marathi-speaking region of western India.

2. Mahars and Mangs are two of several lower-caste Hindu groups formerly deemed 'Untouchable' and outside the caste system in Indian society. Their traditional occupational duties included providing menial services to the upper castes of the village. Mobilised under the leadership of Dr B. R. Ambedkar, who was himself a Mahar, these ostracised and oppressed castes call themselves Dalit today.

3. Phule used the composite term 'Shudratishudra' in which he included all non-Brahmin castes and women of all castes to indicate those oppressed by Brahminical hegemony.

4. For instance, Bal Shastri Jambhekar, Professor in Elphinstone College, founded the Native Improvement Society and ran the bilingual journal *Darpan* and the *Digdarshan*, and together with Bhau Mahajan began *Prabhakar* in which Gopal Hari Deshmukh 'Lokahitwadi' was to be one of the principal contributors. The Marathi Dnyan Prasarak Sabha was founded in 1848 by a group of reformers, which included the well-known Dadoba Pandurang. See O'Hanlon 2010[1985]: 88–102 for a detailed examination.

5. For an extensive analysis of Phule's initiatives and role in the shaping of this movement, see Omvedt 2011[1976].

The Significance of *Tritiya Ratna*

Phule's Play of Ideas

In the last couple of decades, Jotiba Phule's first work, the play *Tritiya Ratna*, has begun to be hailed by major Dalit writers as the pioneering modern play in Marathi literature. *Tritiya Ratna* is an extraordinary composition given the times in which it was written. It is radical in terms of its theme and path-breaking in the way it creates dramatic form and convention. In a sense the rediscovery and subsequent publication of *Tritiya Ratna* allowed it to be read and discussed against the context of a new efflorescence of Dalit literature which had begun to be published from the 1960s in Marathi. The play was discussed sporadically in literary forums in Maharashtra in the initial years after its discovery. But as the years passed by, more people referred to it, and now there is increasing appreciation for Phule's play, even though little was known about it during the decades after his death. In contemporary times several Marathi writers have asserted not only that Phule's first work can be seen as a forerunner to the body of writing known today as Dalit literature, but a tacit agreement prevails that *Tritiya Ratna* must also be considered the first modern play in Marathi.[1] However, though Phule's central focus is on questioning caste hierarchy and its systematic denial of education to the lower castes, his attempt is to create a broad-based solidarity of the marginalised groups in society. In this sense, then, Phule's literary writings may be seen as the expression of a subaltern voice speaking on behalf of a wide range of oppressed sections and interrogating the elite Brahminical class. These issues will be addressed in the concluding sections of this introduction.

In order to appreciate fully the significance of such statements, these assertions have to be placed against a short but detailed exploration of the birth and genesis of modern Indian drama, before arriving at an examination of modern Marathi theatre and dramatic practices. In order to appreciate the growth of modern Marathi theatre, it is necessary to trace in broad outlines both a short political account of Maratha history as well as traditional performative practices in the Marathi-speaking region. Phule's arguably precocious work must be located within this larger framework, which the next few sections of this introduction undertake to do.

MODERN INDIAN DRAMA

A scholar attempting a discussion of modern Indian drama and theatre is faced with two broad challenges. The first is the challenge of defining the scope, given the bewildering variety, complexity and the many hybrid forms of drama and theatre practices that exist in the several language cultures of the subcontinent. The second is the challenge of defining the meaning of the phrase 'modern Indian drama' and fixing its temporal markers. While a few scholars focus largely on post-independence drama in their studies on modern Indian theatre, some others make a strong and convincing argument for pushing the date back by several decades to the mid-nineteenth century, therefore breaking the easy conflation between the modern and the postcolonial.[2] These studies trace the beginnings of modern Indian theatre, which is characterised paradoxically by overlapping Orientalist, nationalist and colonialist features, right from the nineteenth century. This is not surprising given the fact that Sanskrit drama was translated first into English, followed by translations into other European languages and translated much later, in fact after nearly eighty years, into the Indian languages (Deshpande 2004[2000]: ix). A case in point is Kalidasa's *Abhijnana Shakuntala* translated by William Jones in 1789, which fired the imagination of the West, and soon plays written by Sanskrit dramatists who preceded him such as Ashwaghosha, Bhasa and others were also translated. Meanwhile Western drama had begun to be performed in theatres established specifically for this entertainment in colonial Calcutta, Bombay and a few other cities from the late eighteenth century. While these performances were restricted to the white populations in the early years, it did not take very long before elite Indians were admitted to such enjoyments. Modern Indian theatre is therefore an outcome of the combination of influences of Sanskrit and European drama on local performative practices which exhibits right from colonial times elements of traditional and Western styles of theatre. It is often a fecund blend of classical and folk, secular and ritualistic, and rural and urban dramatic forms and practices. In fact, as Anand Lal suggests, it may be much easier to determine the beginnings of modernism in Indian theatre than in Western theatre, because the shift from pre-modern forms to modern ones in India is so clearly discernible (Lal 2009: 31). Intriguingly these beginnings of modernism are also marked by an exposure to the newly available ancient Sanskrit drama in translation, together with an endorsement by European Orientalists of the superiority of this classical form over folk practices as well as its innate sophistication (Chatterjee 1993: 7; Solomon 2009). This approach also constitutes the basis of the Indian nation state imagined by the elite during the time, which is modern in form but is to be created by a return to ancient Hindu traditions. Quite clearly this form of nationalism is found embodied in emergent theatre practices. As G. P. Deshpande suggests, the modern playwright's attempt to create an 'Indianness' under the influence of colonialism is a political act and choice (Deshpande 1999a). In terms of chronology, this shift to modernism in theatre seems to coincide quite neatly with that significant turning point in Indian history—1857, the First War of Indian Independence (Lal 2009: 31). It must be emphasised, however, that the transition from pre-modern to modern forms and practices is unevenly marked across theatre regions in India: Bengali, Marathi, Hindi, Odia and Gujarati are amongst the earliest where it is reflected, and this shift is seen at work much later in theatres such as Kashmiri, Dogri and Manipuri.

A BRIEF OVERVIEW OF INDIAN DRAMA IN THE NINETEENTH CENTURY

Jotiba Phule submitted his play *Tritiya Ratna* for the consideration of the Dakshina Prize Committee in the year 1855. It is important to note that this play predates the events of 1857. Pivoted as it is on the theme of caste oppression articulated through the contemporary lives of a lower-caste couple who are presented on a stage that deploys, by and large, Western dramatic conventions, this play may well be one of the first (if not the very first) modern plays of India. Two other works are contenders for this position. The first is a play written in English by Reverend Krishna Mohan Banerjea in 1831: *The Persecuted, or Dramatic Scenes Illustrative of the Present State of Hindoo Society*, which, like Phule's *Tritiya Ratna*, was neither staged nor did it inspire any successors. However, this play is also a modern depiction of social life with an intention to critique it. Another work which, despite its religious subject matter, marks a milestone in the career of modern Indian theatre is Vishnudas Bhave's *Sita Swayamwara*. Bhave produced this play in the royal court of Sangli in 1843 and continued to present his mythological productions in different parts of Maharashtra. The huge popularity of his plays was in part because they were based on mythology and therefore considered suitable viewing for women and children. Bhave adopted for the first time the commercial strategy of a democratic sale of tickets for the staging of his play *Raja Gopichand* at Grant Road Theatre, Bombay, in 1853. He, in fact, can be considered the first Indian theatre entrepreneur, who soon paved the way to Parsi drama companies and their performances at the same venue.

While a few theatres had been set up in Calcutta by the British for their own use, the Bengali stage in its initial years was restricted to private family theatres and invited audiences. However, though limited in financial outlay and reach, Bengali theatre was informed by the spirit of reform. Some of these family theatres set up competitions for original scripts on social issues which were then staged (Lal 2009: 33). Ramnarayan Tarkaratna's plays such as *Kulin-Kulasarbaswa* (1857) and *Naba Natak* (1867) focus on the prevailing custom of polygamy; Michael Madhusudan Dutt attempted satire in

Ekei ki Bale Sabhyata (1865) and *Buro Shaliker Ghare Ron* (1867). Reform seems to be the predominant theme of drama during these decades. In the neighbouring region of Assam, Gunabhiram Barua attacked child marriage in *Ram Navami* (1857) and Hemchandra Barua presented a farce on opium addiction in *Kania Kirtan* (1861). In Hindi Bharatendu Harishchandra's *Vaidiki Himsa Himsa na Bhavati* (1873) examines violence emanating from faith. Jagamohan Lala presents a similar theme in the Oriya *Babaji* (1877), and in Gujarati Ranchhodbhai Dave examines the position of women in *Lalita Dukhdarshak* (1878). Lal lists the plays mentioned above to signal that modernism had arrived thematically in eastern India and commercially in Bombay (Lal 2009: 34). Lal's assertion is succinct and largely true: though mainstream Marathi theatre also flirted with social issues such as child marriage and the position of widows in the nineteenth century, such themes were generally presented through the prism of the orthodox, upper-caste worldview, and social drama in Marathi generally tended to be regressive (Kumbhojkar 2018). Mainstream Marathi drama till the later decades of the nineteenth century was largely given over to entertainment and pleasure. Musical plays initiated by B. P. Kirloskar's *sangeet natak* flourished and set the trend, as did the commercial Parsi theatre in the Bombay region. Only Phule's *Tritiya Ratna* presents social concerns with astonishing radicalness.

A discussion, however, on the significance of Dinabandhu Mitra's *Nil Darpan* is in order at this point to show the transition from social to political themes and its implicit connection with the Censorship Act of 1876, which extended to the whole of British India, empowering local governments to control or prohibit dramatic performances which were considered 'seditious or obscene, or otherwise prejudicial to the public interests' (Bhatia 2004: 19). This play inaugurated a nationalistic trend in Bengali drama that critiqued the British government and its discriminatory practices; this trend was to soon spread to theatre in other languages. Written by Dinabandhu Mitra, a Bengali civil servant, *Nil Darpan* was published in Dacca in 1860. The play was political in nature and exposed the exploitative conditions imposed by British planters in indigo plantations. The play (and its author) has been ascribed a radical anti-imperialist position given the pivotal role it inadvertently played in the promulgation of the Censorship Act. However, it cannot be denied that Mitra, even as he critiques British planters within the political schema of the play, hardly represents the revolutionary and organised subaltern peasant uprising, which the actual movement of 1860 had been. As Sudipto Chatterjee suggests, the plot has the distinct stamp of 'middle-class conceptions of rebellious behaviour' and the peasant characters display 'babu-like behavioural attributes…while the babu characters in the play are much more convincingly portrayed' (Chatterjee 2009: 105–106). Ranajit Guha sums it up neatly when he says that the play, 'written by a liberal in the midst of a peasant revolt, shows where the liberal stands at the time of a peasant revolt: he stands close to the power of the state seeking cover behind law and bureaucracy' (Guha 1974: 43). Mitra's address to the benevolence of Queen Victoria, the governor-general of India and the various officers in a passage in his preface to the play demonstrates both his 'reverence for the raj' as well as a fervent faith in British justice (Guha 1974: 25).

Given the tenor of the play, *Nil Darpan* in the original may not have posed quite the challenge which its translation into English by the missionary James Long managed to create. Long, who belonged to the Church Missionary Society, received a copy of the Bengali version of *Nil Darpan* a few weeks after it was first published in September 1860. At a time when the indigo controversy was on the boil, Mitra's play on the exploitative practices of the planters interested some British officials, and Long was commissioned to have the play translated into English (Bhatia 2004: 24). The circulation of the English translation under the stamp and seal of the Bengal government invited the wrath of the indigo planters, who filed a suit against Reverend Long, forcing the government to sentence him to a one-month imprisonment and a hefty fine. It may be seen that this full-blown controversy over the play did not involve Mitra at all, even if his dramatisation of peasant suffering was a significant transition in Indian theatre.

In an excellent analysis, Nandi Bhatia suggests that the politics surrounding *Nil Darpan* sheds light on the relationship between censorship, the law and nationalist drama in colonial India. The ban imposed on overt political themes led, towards the later part of the nineteenth century and well into the next century, to the recuperation of historical and mythological themes that cleverly masked nationalist agenda. However, the deployment of mythological themes as the basis for plays which could evoke nationalist sympathies 'through presentations of a Hindu nation that needed to be defended and rescued from the perils of foreign rule', may have, intentionally or otherwise, increasingly entrenched and normalised the acceptance of Hindu nationalism in public discourse (Bhatia 2004: 21).

By the 1870s, modernism in theatre was firmly in place thematically, in its professional and commercial management and in terms of the legislation enacted to proscribe certain thematic tendencies, the last of which survives well into the present century. While the trend towards mythology may seem paradoxically retrograde, one must remember that it was but the continuation of stock themes of traditional theatrical practices which were ongoing, in good health and in popular circulation. Further, the use of mythology and history in the theatrical productions of the nineteenth century had, at least for the native audiences, a symbolic and allegorical resonance of modernity coupled, as it was, with nationalist aspirations. The decades from the 1870s to 1930 perhaps mark the heyday of theatre in India: professional troupes, says Lal, had 'rapidly evolved a formula combining melodrama with musical' which was a strategy that commanded full houses and 'became the unlikely vehicle to express social or political messages' through mythological or historical allegory (Lal 2009: 34). A pan-Indian theatre had taken birth and this art form, which functioned as a unifying force across India, enjoyed a popularity that only the arrival of the first Indian talkie in 1931, *Alam Ara,* could break. Cinema struck a blow from which theatre could never recover even though commercial companies struggled on till around the 1970s. The new amateur theatre that emerged from their shadows had to mark a special niche for itself and was allied with socialist causes: concern for the oppressed had been strongly articulated in the social and political drama of the late 1850s and 1860s, as seen in the discussion on *Nil Darpan*, and it is these objectives that were to form the mainstay of the Indian People's Theatre Association founded in 1943 and Prithvi Theatres in 1944, amongst a few others in Tamil, Telugu and

Malayalam, culminating in the Marathi Dalit Theatre which was inaugurated in 1955 by M. B. Chitnis' *Yugyatra* (Lal 2009: 39–40).

It may be appropriate at this point to shift focus to the development of modern Marathi theatre in the nineteenth century and locate Phule's *Tritiya Ratna* within its context. It may be necessary, however, to also track the trajectory of this development within a broad discussion of the social and political history of the Marathi-speaking region and its traditional performative practices, which the next sections attempt to do.

MARATHI THEATRE IN THE NINETEENTH CENTURY

The pre-eminence of a specific variety of performance art and its seeming ineluctability during a particular period of history, calls for an examination of its connections to the traditional performative practices of the language culture from which it emerges as well as to the larger political and social developments that have shaped the culture's recent past. From the mid-nineteenth century to well into the first few decades of the twentieth century, Marathi drama caught the imagination of an age and its people. Keenly sensitive to the pulse of the upper-caste communities to which it largely catered, members of which also composed and produced it, not only did modern Marathi drama come into being during this period, it also transmuted throughout this long journey of almost a century, taking on variations of dramatic and musical forms that caught the political and social mood of the changing times.

This section will first attempt a quick sketch of the political history of the times followed by a short discussion of the performative practices integral to the language culture of the region. It then hopes to trace the trajectory of Marathi theatre, from the first ticketed staging of Vishnudas Bhave's mythological play in 1853 to the expansion of its genres with the 'bookish' play from the 1860s, the deepening of the popularity of Marathi theatre with the creation of the *sangeet natak* in the hands of B. P. Kirloskar and the other significant playwrights who were to employ and recreate this genre from the 1880s. It is hoped that this examination will help show up clearly the radical departures which Phule makes in terms of dramatic form and content in *Tritiya Ratna*, and indeed how his play constitutes a caustic aberration in the general trend and direction of dramatic art in nineteenth century Maharashtra.

Political History: Marathas, Peshwas and the British

For the regions constituting present-day Maharashtra, the greatest Maratha hero in recent history is Chhatrapati Shivaji, born to Shahaji Bhosle in 1630. Shivaji personally trained an efficient guerrilla army and led it on military exploits to annex new territories, in the process carving out a Maratha kingdom in the Deccan region that was dominated during the mid-seventeenth century by the Sultanate dynasties. Shivaji belonged to the Kunbi caste, but despite this social disadvantage, he was, at the age of 44, crowned ceremoniously by Brahmin priests brought specifically for the purpose from North India. A few stories of Shivaji's life, apocryphal or otherwise, have lent colour and bestowed heroism upon an entire region and language culture: these are his killing of the Mughal envoy Afzal Khan, and his escape from Mughal captivity in Agra along with his son Sambhaji. These well-loved events ascribed to him have found many narrations and representations in drama and narrative literature (Kosambi 2015: 14–15). Shivaji lived for barely six years after his coronation, meeting an untimely death. Sambhaji succeeded him and the few years of his troubled rule ended in his capture and subsequent death at the hands of Aurangzeb. Sambhaji's son Shahu was captured and imprisoned in Agra, while his younger brother Rajaram was crowned king in Kolhapur. When Shahu was freed after Aurangzeb's death in 1707, and declared Maratha king, he chose to rule from Satara and have his Brahmin prime minister, or Peshwa, appointed at the helm of administrative powers in Pune. Bajirao I was the first eminent Peshwa who inherited the office in 1720 and set up a dynastic rule of the Peshwas that lasted almost a hundred years. Maratha territories grew and flourished till Nanasaheb, Bajirao's son was defeated by Ahmad Shah in the Battle of Panipat in 1761. A few years later, Thorle Madhavrao Peshwa (Madhavrao the Elder) rebuilt Maratha power; however, he died early and none of the subsequent Peshwas were able to attain the impressive record of their ancestors' military exploits, hemmed in as they were by ambition and intrigue within the court. In 1818 when Bajirao II lost to the English East India Company, the Maratha empire had already crumbled from within: the intrigue and infighting, no less than the debauchery and decadence of its powerful rulers had made it hollow. Its confederacy headed by the Peshwa had earlier controlled a large part of India that included the Gaikwads of Baroda, the Shindes of Gwalior, Holkars of Indore and Bhosles of Nagpur. These states now became only truncated dominions nominally autonomous under the supervision of British Political Agents (Bhave 1976[1936]).

While Brahmins have traditionally enjoyed supremacy in all parts of India, this supremacy was an unchallenged hegemony in Maharashtra during the time the Peshwas were in ascendance. Ritual, political and military power was completely concentrated in the hands of the Brahmin community during Peshwa rule in Pune. Such absolute power in the hands of the upper caste spelt unprecedented oppression for large sections of the population that were under their control. For the Brahmins, however, it must have been a heady exercise of power that had to be reined in after 1818. The defeat of Bajirao II, his exile and the annexation of the Maratha dominions which were yoked together by the British to form the Bombay Presidency was a humiliation, and it is no wonder then that the Brahmin elite tended to hark back to the world of its lost glory. In the nineteenth century this past was within living memory, and with the beginnings of the national movement, it soon became 'the dominant patriotic and nationalist subtext of the cultural narrative' (Kosambi 2015: 14). The desire for self-rule, articulated famously by Bal Gangadhar Tilak in his claim 'Swaraj is my birthright' as a cogent slogan to mobilise opinion for independence, can also be read as an assertion 'reclaiming the lost Brahmin Peshwa patrimony' (Kosambi 2015: 14).

The dissolution of Peshwa political rule and the introduction of modern institutions and secular modes of administration by the colonial government transformed existing hubs of power and networks of patronage. However, as seen in earlier sections, Brahmin and other upper-caste communities continued to exert, by dint of their traditional ritual and cultural pre-eminence, an immoderate dominance even in these new and changed equations of political legitimacy. In the context of the present study, it is clear that Brahmins dominated the entire range of activities associated with theatre such as writing, acting, production as well as its consumption, constituting as they did the majority of the audience in theatres. We have seen in the preceding chapter the precise manner and mode through which Phule interrogated and challenged this Brahmin hegemony in cultural, educational and political terrains.

The foregoing section has examined hegemonic Brahmanism in Maharashtra from the times of the Peshwas and the manner in which this was extended to all activities related to Marathi drama and theatre in the nineteenth century. We must now, however, shift direction and examine traditional performance forms and practices that had continued through the times, the entire repertoire of which was available to playwrights and dramatists beginning to put up their productions on the modern proscenium stage by the mid-nineteenth century. It will have to be seen if these forms found any continuity in modern drama that was to become increasingly popular from the mid-nineteenth century in Maharashtra.

Pre-colonial Dramatic Forms

Rudimentary dramatic performances, which are an integral aspect of religious and cultural expression, had existed for several centuries in the Marathi-speaking regions of the Deccan. Dramatic forms such as the *yakshagana*, native to the neighbouring region of Karnataka, also had a popular itinerant presence. Most of these forms drew upon well-known episodes from the two epics, the Ramayana and the Mahabharata, and stories from the Puranas or the *Bhagwata Purana*. The *dashavtara*, a dramatic presentation of the ten avatars of Vishnu; the *lalit*, which dramatised deities and their miracles; and the *bahurupis* which were impersonations of secular characters—many of these performances were torch-lit, night-time affairs celebrating specific festivals, as were the puppet shows which find mention in the works of Dnyaneshwar (Kosambi 2015: 9).

The Varkari sect, which worships the Vitthal deity in the Pandurang temple at Pandharpur, started gaining a presence in the cultural life of Maharashtra from the late twelfth century. Soon it was to become the most significant religious and literary movement of Maharashtra, drawing large numbers of devotees from all walks of life. The *kirtan*, a prose discourse punctuated by music and devotional songs which takes place in and around temples, has a familiar cultural presence in most parts of the country; in Maharashtra it is a performance practice closely associated with the Varkaris. Some of the greatest saints of this movement—Namdev, Ekanth, Tukaram—are spoken of as *kirtankaars*. The kirtan is quite clearly a precursor to the mythological play. As a part of the repertoire of songs and narrative compositions known as the *akhyan*, a kirtankaar also used the *bharud*. The bharud is a drama-poem, generally dialogic in nature, pivoted upon a metaphor. The metaphor is meant to carry a moral or religious message and works by way of allegory. While all Varkari saint poets composed bharuds, Eknath has the distinction of having composed the largest number. Most bharuds are short pieces; only a few are very long and extended. The most famous of these is the *Hindu-Turk Samvad*, which takes its audience through an extended argument/dialogue between a Brahmin and a Maulana, where the two characters representing opposing religious beliefs spar, with a generous infusion of mutual abuse, on a number of highly explosive issues, only to arrive at an understanding of a spiritual ethic common to both religions (Zelliot 2003[1982]; Mokashi-Punekar 2012). Bharuds were often performed en route the *vari*, the bi-annual pilgrimage on foot to Pandharpur when walking groups of devotees in the *dindi*s rested for the night.

*Gondhal*s are song and dance narratives performed as a special prayer to a specific goddess. As events that mark the culmination of social occasions such as marriages, gondhals are performed even today, especially in rural areas. From the seventeenth century, *shahir*s, who composed and sang heroic ballads known as *powada*s, travelled across the region, offering imaginative narrations of historical events and heroic acts of valour. These ballads extolled the heroism of Shivaji; with the passage of time the powadas also praised other Maratha kings and the Peshwas. Shahirs had a substantial role in knitting together the Marathi-speaking region through songs that sang of heroes and their exploits (Mokashi-Punekar 2017: 55–56); in effect they created a common pool of heroic memory. Not surprisingly these songs were often commissioned by the royalty in power. Another source of secular performance was the *lavani*, which was a song and dance performance generally celebrating romantic or erotic love. Though occasionally the Peshwas in Pune patronised the lavani, it was a well-known performance practice that was popular all over Maharashtra. The *tamasha* (from the Urdu word for a performance) is a series of performances strung together as a sort of 'variety entertainment' which also includes the lavani. This largely secular form is said to have emerged during the time of the Peshwas, catering to regiments of soldiers quartered in camps, as well as to populations in towns and villages. There are also records of a tamasha taking place at the court of a Peshwa (Dandekar 1941: 38–39). The tamasha was a combination of an initial invocation to Ganesha, perhaps followed by songs about Krishna with his milkmaids, a few erotic lavanis, finishing off with a short prose-and-verse drama. While women did not perform on stage for a long time, the tamashas were an exception; here female impersonators very early ceded ground to women dancers, whose provocative movements were the main source of the tamasha's appeal. This was also the reason why tamashas were considered vulgar and less than respectable; quite ironically then the predominant audience for these performances was male (Kosambi 2015: 10).

However, such distinction between elite and folk forms of entertainment may have perhaps crept in at a later stage. Dandekar refers to a document describing the celebration of an extended Holi festival in the year 1783 at Shaniwar Wada in Pune, the principal palace of Peshwa Sawai Madhavrao (Dandekar 1941: 38–39). Amongst other items it lists wooden puppet shows, mimes, male lavani singers accompanied by dancing girls as well as boys in female dress, tamashas by different groups and performances on stringed instruments. It is not quite clear at what stage hierarchies begin to appear in the positioning of popular entertainment; literary references give evidence of the longevity of these forms of entertainment, frequently coinciding with explicit derision for actors (Kosambi 2015: 10).

It is significant to note, however, that despite well-established and popular forms of performance traditions and practices, no substantial dramatic composition was either written or performed in Maharashtra before the 1840s. Interestingly, in Tanjore district of present-day Tamil Nadu, where a branch of the Marathas ruled for around two centuries, mythological plays in Marathi were written and performed in the royal court. This theatre constitutes an independent and parallel tradition that existed unknown till the turn of the twentieth century when many play texts were discovered as well as documents detailing their performances. Of these some 20 yakshagana plays in Telugu and 22 plays in Marathi (eight of which are extant) are thought to have been composed by the Tanjore Maratha king, Shahuraje; there are more plays by his descendants including Ekoji and Sarfoji. Shahuraje spoke of his composition *Lakshmi-Narayan-Kalyan* as a *natak* i.e., a play, though it is basically a long musical narration by the *sutradhar*, the narrator who describes all the incidents in the story, announces the entry and exit of characters and explains their actions (Kosambi 2015: 11). Studies on the Tanjore tradition of theatre assert that it continued independently between 1680 and 1850, and may have had little connection with developments in Maharashtra where the main forms of secular entertainment continued to be the powada, the lavani and the tamasha, till the year 1843 when Vishnudas Bhave put up his *khel, Sita Swayamwara*, in the royal court at Sangli (Jog 1973; Dandekar 1941).

VISHNUDAS BHAVE: *SITA SWAYAMWARA*

Bhave's staging of his dramatic composition *Sita Swayamwara* in November 1843 broke fresh ground and created a new genre of performance, even as it continued to draw traditionally upon the epics for its plot and story. It is also important to note that his *khel* quickly adapted itself to the modern proscenium stage from 1853, producing ticketed performances. After enjoying more than a decade of spectacular popularity, spawning many similar commercial drama companies and troupes who performed all over Maharashtra, productions such as *Sita Swayamwara* had already become old-fashioned and had to give way to even more splendid theatrical forms such as the *sangeet natak* and the historical 'bookish' natak. Bhave was a Brahmin, as were the majority of Marathi playwrights who came after him, with the honourable and singular exception of Phule; it must be remembered, however, that Phule's play, which was neither published nor staged during his lifetime, did not see the light of day for more than a century. It may also be recalled that despite his declared pro-British stance, Phule's play was not conferred the Dakshina Prize award instituted by the colonial government.

It is rather strange that after centuries of command in warfare and in the administration of court, the Brahmins of Maharashtra should have turned to theatre as one of their primary modes of expression. In his insightful study of Marathi drama, *Nataki Nibandha*, G. P. Deshpande suggests that,

> People who lost political power, turned to arts. Not only was it a silent protest against imperialism but it was also an attempt of the elite who had lost political power to find the spirit of their self in a new field...This seems to have been the case in the field of music too...I feel that the rise of Marathi theatre is an inseparable part of the process of the search of self-identity by the elite who had lost their political power. Birth of the modern Marathi theatre is a political event. (Deshpande 1999b: 8, cited in Sathe 2015: 23)

While Deshpande's conclusion that the elite of Maharashtra turned to the arts as a political assertion offers an interesting perspective, it must be acknowledged that the Brahmins and other upper castes also sought to position themselves in the matrices of the colonial government and did, in fact, wield a great deal of power.[3] As noted in preceding sections, with the introduction of Western education in the Bombay Presidency, the Brahmins made up for the loss of the earlier Peshwa-sponsored set of privileges by quickly inserting themselves into positions created in the fields of education, culture and later in politics. Western education and the opportunities it generated resulted in a wide range of employment avenues in the modern set-up. It created a burgeoning middle class that could assign to itself a self-conscious pre-eminence in the new social order. It is this power of the cultural and literary field that Phule hoped to access as a mode of empowerment since the institutional channels of colonial modernity, in the form of bureaucracy in various governmental structures, including the legal and educational, were denied to him and to fellow members of the lower castes, dominated as they were by the upper castes. Brahmins may have ceased to be the rulers, but they did command immoderate hegemonic influence.

The elite amongst these newly educated middle classes had their traditional Sanskrit learning and were also exposed to Western literature. Patriotic pride in their heritage coupled with the anxiety of aspiration for the modern led to a spate of translations from both Kalidasa and Shakespeare, in the process enriching Marathi language and literature. However, these changing paradigms of taste became the basis for devaluing traditional and folk performance practices. The tamasha and the lavani were no longer acceptable to this new Western-educated middle class. These forms were perceived to be vulgar and of questionable morals and taste. Even though a few upper-caste persons such as Patthe Bapurao or Ram Joshi managed some troupes, by and large there was an association of the disreputable with this form of entertainment which did not suit the new ideas of genteelness ushered in by colonial modernity.

We must come back, however, to the first commercial stage production in the history of Indian drama by Vishnudas Bhave, whose father held a position in the army under Raja Patwardhan at Sangli. Once the British had taken charge of administration after defeating the Peshwas, there was a respite from the interminable battles that had characterised the entire region under the Marathas, right from the time of Shivaji. There was peace, and with it the possibility for the arts to develop and flourish. It is said that a troupe of Bhagwat performers from neighbouring Karnataka visited Sangli in 1842, and the Raja who was present at this yakshagana performance was so impressed that he asked Vishnudas, who was his appointed storyteller-poet, to create a more refined version for the entertainment and edification of his own court (Gokhale 2000: 5). Vishnudas Bhave wrote, designed and staged *Sita Swayamwara* in November 1843 in response to the king's order. Called a *khel* by historians, Bhave's creation is exactly that: a play in the original sense of the term, rather than a play as drama. Quite clearly a progeny of the kirtan: something like the akhyan, it was a composition of dramatic poems based on stories from the Ramayana in which the sutradhar and his accompanists had the central roles. They sang the songs, and the masked actors enacted the contents of the songs, occasionally interspersing these with a few prose dialogues which Bhave himself had improvised during rehearsals. None of these dialogues was ever written down, unlike the Tanjore plays which were written compositions available in palm-leaf manuscripts (Gokhale 2000: 4).

Though a few historians question if Bhave's first composition is drama in every sense of the word, it cannot be denied that he was indeed the author of every word and action that was presented on stage even if not everything was actually written down (Gokhale 2000: 4). He even designed and made the masks and costumes worn by the actors—the requisite props and accessories: the crown and costume jewellery for the stage royalty, wigs for the 'women', false beards for the sages, extra arms for the gods, additional heads for Ravan, a peacock's head and plumage for Saraswati and a manoeuvrable trunk for Ganesh. The published dramatic poems for *Sita Swayamwara* are a series of songs in various classical ragas, encompassing the well-known mythological events surrounding the story of how Rama won Sita in the *swayamwara* organised by her father, Raja Janak. The published verse narrative sketches the bare outlines of the story, but must have formed the basis of a night-long performance; how it was embellished by action and prose dialogue can only be imagined today (Kosambi 2015: 35–60).

Predictably, this play faced opposition from the Brahmins at court, even as Raja Patwardhan, also a Brahmin, appreciated Bhave's efforts. He had desired refined entertainment and a kind of performance that was also removed from the putative vulgarity and crudity of the tamasha. Bhave had correctly interpreted the king's brief. Silencing the Brahmins by citing line and passage from the shastras that disproved their position on the sacrilege of Brahmins acting in costume, the Raja promised Bhave and his troupe land and royal patronage in return for regular dramatic presentations. Unfortunately, the king died before he could put a seal on his word, and as fortune would have it, the heir was a minor who had no power to carry out the order. Forced to fend for themselves, Bhave and his troupe obtained the required permission from court and decided to travel with their plays in search of livelihood (Gokhale 2000: 4–7).

In this way the first modern Marathi drama troupe was born. Bhave and his group of actors travelled the length and breadth of Maharashtra as well as the erstwhile Maratha princely states of Indore and Gwalior during the next decade. The troupe, which called itself Sanglikar Hindu Natak Mandali, and their extended repertoire of plays met with immense success wherever they performed; most popular amongst these were the ones based on Narasimha and Raja Harishchandra. Giving performances at every place en route, including Kolhapur and Pune, Bhave reached Bombay in 1853 where initially, as was their wont, his troupe performed in the compounds of private bungalows or similar places. However, a visit to the Grant Road theatre, built a decade earlier in 1842 by Nana Shunkershett (a great patron and the doyen of modern movements), where Bhave watched an English play, changed the course of his career. He was impressed by the theatre's clean orderliness, its seating arrangement, curtains, scenes and the stage, and it triggered in him an ambition to present his own play there. While his first play at the Grant Road theatre was staged in March 1853, receiving appreciative reviews by the ruling class, it was the play *Raja Gopichand* which the troupe presented in November 1853 in Hindi, in order to make it accessible to wider audiences in cosmopolitan Bombay, which became hugely successful and earned for its troupe's dramatist-producer a neat Rs 1800, an enormous sum in those days (Gokhale 2000: 8).

Bhave worked from mythological material, drawing from a cultural reservoir of narratives common to him and his audience; his innovation lay in setting his dramatic poems to appropriate music, training his actors to sing, mime and improvise prose dialogues, designing costumes and props that were quasi-realistic and introducing battle scenes—which were traditional in Bhagwat *mela* plays but which must have had a special nostalgic resonance for his largely elite audiences, given their political identity. These battle scenes presented thumping melodramatic action and blood-curdling roars and stretching as they did for sometimes over half an hour, could present the grand finale between the forces of good and evil, between the gods and the asuras. Bhave's dramatic efforts were immensely popular for more than a decade; they spawned several other traveling troupes who followed, more or less, a similar formula of dramatic presentation. There were at least four more Sanglikar companies, besides several other competing companies from Ichalkaranji, Kolhapur, Bombay, Pune and other places each of which took its name from the place of origin. From a dozen companies in the early 1860s, there were in a short span of a few years more than a 100 drama companies which testifies to the rage that these dramatic performances had become and the business they generated (Kosambi 2015: 35–60).

Soon, however, a newer and educated younger audience had come into being which was on the look-out for more refined sources of entertainment: colonial modernity had ushered in exposure to dramatic forms of the West as well as pride in elite native cultural heritage, as has been noted above. The stage had to be redefined yet again.

PROSE PLAYS: FARCES, HISTORICALS AND THE 'BOOKISH' PLAY

Colonial modernity in the form of Western education and the gradually emerging print culture led to a spate of translations from the mid-1850s. These translations were fed by the desire to induct into the Marathi language themes and forms which would enrich its literature; often writers expressed their feelings of inadequacy regarding the resources of Marathi and hoped that translations would serve to strengthen its volume and quality (Chitale 1877[1871]: i). Through means of the support provided by the Dakshina Fund (see p. 7), the Brahmin literati were in a position to exploit their traditional expertise in the classical language and embark on translations from the Sanskrit; many of their efforts were also published by the Dakshina Prize Committee. Kalidasa in particular and classical Sanskrit drama in general (in the wake of the Orientalists' discovery of these), were translated in profusion: not only did these translations recuperate ancient Sanskrit texts and help build the base for an incipient cultural nationalism, as discussed earlier, they also formed educational material in the new curricula of higher learning. In the mid-1850s translations of Kalidasa's *Vikramorvshiyam* and *Abhijnana Shakuntalam* were serialised in monthly magazines; between 1857 and 1872 one each of six major Sanskrit playwrights from Bhavabhuti to Shri Harsha were translated by Parashurampant Godbole. It is not surprising therefore that the tradition of *sangeet natak* founded by B. P. Kirloskar was inaugurated with a Marathi *Shakuntala* in 1880, followed by similar plays by other dramatists such as Deval (Kosambi 2015: 66).

Like Kalidasa from Sanskrit literature, Shakespeare dominated translations from English. Around 26 of his plays had been translated by 1913, some more than once (Majumdar 1913). Not only did these translations contribute to the body of Marathi literature, they were also in demand from theatre companies that specialised in the productions of Shakespearean plays in translation. Literal translations posed problems of cultural transfer in a language culture completely unacquainted with European cultural mores. Soon literal translations of Shakespeare gave way to adaptations, not only of this bard but also a host of other English playwrights and novelists. Adaptations, however, meant a move away from careful translations to a more populist 'lifting' of a plot or theme in the service of prose drama, which may have suited the needs of theatre companies in search of good material, though these invariably lowered the quality of the resultant productions.

Farces

Marathi prose drama in the initial years emerged in the form of farces. Even during the heyday of mythological performances typical to those created by Bhave and others, the competition between the several theatrical troupes/companies gave birth to innovative dramatic strategies in order to draw audiences. Though the farce may have emerged in Marathi theatre as a strategy to inveigle audiences, there must have been some degree of familiarity with this form: English plays offered spectators amusements such as farces in their amateur performances in India. The fact remains that in this early period farces were connected intimately to the musical mythological performances, perhaps as a way of adding a touch of realism and social critique in an appendage to a performance wholly given over to the mythological and fantastic. In his work on social drama in Marathi theatre, Dandekar refers to an interesting episode during the staging of a mythological play in Bombay. During the interval an old man ran up on the stage, shouting for the manager and bemoaning the seduction of his fifteen-year-old wife, who he alleged had been brought to see the play by her handsome seducer. The errant eloper was 'discovered' in the seats reserved for women, dragged onto the stage and restored to her husband; the manager then embarked upon a sharp homily on the evils of marriages between partners so unequal in age, revealing as he ended that all the people involved in the skirmish were actors, and the little scene had been enacted for the edification of the audience (Dandekar 1945: 11–13; Kosambi 2015: 69, n.21). The ruse was an instant hit: it was arguably one of the earliest instances of a carefully scripted 'reality' event. Soon the farce was an invariable appendage to a mythological play, its popularity stemming from its compactness, realism and humour.

However, the nomenclature 'farce', in a case of classic mistranslation (also apparent in the term 'bookish play', which will be discussed), began to be applied even to serious and tragic historical skits: a Shakespearean comedy in translation or a serious short play could both be considered under the genre if only they were performed after the conclusion of a long mythological play. Farces enjoyed extensive popularity between the 1870s and 1890s; from the 1890s they graduated to the serious social or historical play.

The earliest farces were rather impromptu performances, based at the most on written down dialogues given to actors. Even if published as a series of dialogues, they tended to be anonymous. As farces evolved to encompass short plays based on serious and historical themes, it was possible to make a clear distinction founded on their content: farces intended for rather low-brow entertainment and short prose plays with historical or social content. The latter generally merged into the category of prose drama known as 'bookish plays'.

The 'Bookish' Play

Named with equal proportions of inaccuracy and nonchalance by an elite class aspiring for 'the most desirable form of dramatic text—namely, one that was structured like a Shakespearean or a Sanskrit play' (Gokhale 2000: 11), the bookish play was simply a text written and published before it was performed. It is generally believed by Marathi literary historians that *Thorle Madhavrao Peshwe* (1857), written by V. J. Kirtane while still a student at Elphinstone College in Bombay, was the first bookish play. Recently, however, beginning with studies on the subject by Bhagat (2001) and continuing with Sathe (2015) and Kosambi (2015), opinion on this has shifted. These more recent studies locate Phule's *Tritiya Ratna* (1855) not only as the first bookish play, but also as the first modern Marathi play.

Thorle Madhavrao Peshwe inaugurated a trend in mainstream Marathi theatre of a non-musical historical-nationalist drama that mined the intense public interest in Maratha/Peshwa history. Kirtane exploited this for contemporary political relevance, making a direct comparison between the real durbar of the Marathas with the puny power of present-day kings who like 'mere caged parrots' are under 'the orders of inhabitants of a foreign island' (Kosambi 2015: 79). The play was acclaimed by the young university-educated audience for its depiction of Madhavrao Peshwa as an able ruler and statesman, who also seemed very modern in the portrayal of his relationship with his wife Ramabai; it was acclaimed as well for its employment of classical dramatic conventions, drawing from both Sanskrit and Shakespearean drama. Most studies also mark the depiction of Madhavrao's death on stage (in contravention of Sanskrit dramatic conventions), the subsequent *sati* (the immolation of the living widow on her dead husband's burning pyre) by Ramabai and the overwhelming response of the audience to the latter.[4] The play, first presented by Ichalkaranjikar Company in the 1860s, played upon the emotions of its audience by having, in a show of common sentiment, some actors impersonating females standing around the male actor playing the role of Ramabai dressed all in white about to enter the burning pyre. The manager invited some eminent local women in the audience to come up on stage and be a part of the ritual of filling with sindoor the forehead of the widow about to immolate herself, and the giving of the ritual coconut and grains of rice and wheat according to the custom that was said to bestow upon these women great religious merit. From the next show onwards, it is reported that large numbers of women from the audience queued up to do this honour, so much so that the show had to be stalled sometimes for more than an hour (Kosambi 2015: 60). Most historians note this response as a rather quaint sample of audience identification in times when modern Marathi drama was in its incipient stages. However, the enthusiastic and unequivocal identification of the audience with the scene depicting sati in a theatre and a stage that was largely espoused by the upper castes must be located within times that saw raging debates on the question of women's position in society and their reform. It speaks volumes of the upper castes' complicity with and active, uncritical support for regressive systems and values. This detail acquires immense significance in the context of Phule's *Tritiya Ratna* and the radical interrogation his play makes of Brahmin cultural hegemony, implicitly critiquing its treatment of women, which will be examined soon.

Thorle Madhavrao Peshwe elicited considerable critical approval and paved the way for several historical plays based on Maratha history. Concurrently there also began a stream of social plays pivoted on the question of reform; these plays attempted to exploit theatre as an effective means of propagating reformist ideas on questions such as child marriage and widowhood. While M. B. Chitale in *Manorama Natak* made laudable efforts in this direction, since the issues revolved around the concerns of the upper caste, the backlash from the conservative sections was not slow in coming. Plays such as *Swaira-sakesha* by R. S. Abhyankar, N. B. Kanitkar's *Taruni Shikshan Natika* or *Mor L.L.B Prahasan* by N. H. Bhagwat took up positions that mocked the reformers and legitimised orthodoxy. These plays lampooned all attempts at reform and presented the reformists as ineffectual and quite literally, impotent. These plays again offer a strong basis of contrast to Phule's depiction of the necessity of radical reform that was articulated from a non-Brahminical subaltern position.

Even as there was critical acclaim for some of the playwrights discussed above, prose plays rarely received the sort of popularity that the mythological plays did. The lack of music in these plays and the preponderance of dialogues could not appeal to an audience brought up on a theatre geared towards musical entertainment. The stage was now set for a musical play that was more refined and sophisticated than the mythological play, which combined modern dramatic conventions with traditional themes and also offered some splendid novelty in the form of musicality.

The *Sangeet Natak*

Kirloskar's musical play, the *sangeet natak*, was the new genre that achieved an innovative synthesis of Bhave's mythological play with the bookish play. In the words of V. D. Kulkarni, who rightly emphasised its close affinity with the prose play, it was 'the first musical bookish play', since it welded together Bhave's musical with the Western prose play (V. D. Kulkarni 1974: ix). As such it was a composite of Indian and Western dramatic traditions, offering its upper-caste audience a mesmerising blend of cultural continuity through its mythological/historical themes and modernity through the new dramatic possibilities inherent in the modern stage and its conventions, this blend made possible through the novelty of a broad range of musical styles (Kosambi 2015: 84). The influence of Parsi theatre was clearly perceptible in the lavish productions that these plays put up, in the spectacle and the pivotal importance of music, even though the Marathi *sangeet natak* brought in styles closer to Hindustani classical and other traditional musical varieties (Kosambi 2015: 84–85; Sathe 2015: 121–124). Kirloskar specialised in writing lyrics: the original Sanskrit *shloka*s were rendered in the form of lyrical Marathi songs that were set to varieties of music. *Shakuntala* had around 209 songs spread across seven acts; more importantly all the characters spoke dialogues and sang songs, expressing their feelings through them. This was the major difference between Bhave and Kirloskar: Kirloskar's plays attempted the etching of character through dialogue and song, responding indeed to changing notions of the individual within society. Like Bhave, Kirloskar too formed his own company and was hugely successful: the public sphere of Maharashtra was dominated by musical theatre for almost half a century. It validated a particular form of music as a mark of refined taste and respectability, thereby defining a form of colonial modernity both rooted in tradition and secular in its aspiration. Kirloskar enabled the transformation of Sanskrit plays such as *Shakuntala*, or well-known stories from mythology such as the story of Subhadra in *Sangeet Soubhadra* into a kind of secular social drama infused with music. After Kirloskar, musical plays enjoyed immense popularity in the hands of the significant dramatists who followed him: Deval, Kolhatkar, Gadkari and Khadilkar, each of whom redefined the musical play through mythological or social themes or plots, but kept alive the connect of Marathi theatre with music till the first few decades of the twentieth century. It is quite clear, however, that the predominant worldview, substance and style of these plays represented the concerns of the upper castes, the Brahminical elite of Maharashtrian society.

The foregoing sections have attempted to trace the beginnings of modernity in Indian theatrical practices as a whole, the development of modern Marathi drama and the deepening of its hold on the imagination of its largely upper-caste audience. They have focused on the development of the early mythological play and its commercial success, the quest to refine dramatic craft and the thematic range which defined the bookish prose play and finally the marriage between the two earlier forms that created a new genre in the form of the *sangeet natak*, the musical play. Even as later dramatists deployed mythology and music to encode strong political critique based on resurgent Hindu nationalism, Marathi theatre remained until the early decades of the twentieth century the exclusive domain of Brahmins and other powerful elites.[5] From the next section we move on to discuss the lone subaltern playwright, Phule, and his first work, *Tritiya Ratna*, a play astonishingly original in its theme and craft.

TRITIYA RATNA: THE TITLE OF THE PLAY

Of the three manuscript copies of the play that have survived (discovered in the private papers of Phule's first major biographer

P. S. Patil, as noted in the previous chapter), two were titled 'Tritiya Ratna' while a third had the title 'Tritiya Netra'. This apparent discrepancy in the title opens up a whole new area of fertile interrogation. In his introduction to the first publication of the play in 1979, while noting the difference in the two titles, both given by its author, Raikar attributes this second title to the influence of Lokahitwadi's pronouncement that English education had opened the third eye of knowledge for Indians. This is a reference to the well-known Hindu mythological narrative about the third eye of Lord Shiva, located in the centre of his forehead. Shiva's third eye is expected to flash fury and rage on the rare occasions that it opens. Raikar suggests that Phule must have been influenced by Lokahitwadi's assertion (Raikar 1979). Studies in English generally use *The Third Eye* as the title when they refer to Phule's play. When the rage and passion cross the threshold of tolerance, it is believed that Shiva or Shankar opens his third eye. This eye has the power to reduce to ashes all that is before it. Did Phule wish the title to indicate the potential rage of the lower castes once their consciousness is aroused? The title may point to the certainty of the raising of consciousness symbolically seen in the opening of the third eye and setting ablaze the slavery enforced by Brahminical constructs: this could very well be a possible meaning of the title 'Tritiya Netra'. However, if one considers Phule's philosophical framework it seems a little out of character that he would readily title his works with any word or term that implied association with any of the Hindu gods.

The accepted title in all subsequent Marathi editions has been 'Trutiya Ratna', which refers to another well-known mythological story. Datta Bhagat puts forward the interpretation drawn from the story of the churning of the ocean (*samudramanthan*) and how this churning gave forth successively a series of gems (Bhagat 2001: 58). Of these, the third gem was Lakshmi and the fourteenth was 'Aasud', which means a whip; as we know Phule used the word 'Asud' in the title of one of his later prose works. Phule's lifelong mission for which he struggled hard was to ensure that the Shudras had access to education. He believed that through education it would be possible for them to obtain wealth and prosperity. Shudras were oppressed because they were poor and their poverty was the result of their ignorance. Therefore, the third gem or tritiya ratna, which connotes money, glory and wealth, is actually Lakshmi. In the play the Kunbi couple decides to join Phule's night school, realising the necessity of education. Bhagat suggests that there is a correlation between their realisation of this truth and the title of the play.

The interpretations of the two titles offer interesting possibilities of understanding the central focus of the play as Phule saw it. They also confront a translator with the tantalising, though tricky, choice of how to translate the title of the play. Should the translation of the title read as The Third Eye or The Third Gem?

The first interpretation suggesting the destructive though cleansing anger of the lower castes has the advantage of contemporary resonance. For instance, the title of D. R. Nagaraj's well-known work *The Flaming Feet: Dalit Movement in India* also evokes the simmering anger of the Dalits and the ensuing violence in society in the clash between the upper castes' continued enforcement of traditional hierarchy and the Dalits' resistance to this oppression, and their assertion of modern rights. Nagaraj's title refers to the *Purusha Sukta* in the Rig Veda that describes creation and the origin of the different castes, ascribing to the Shudras the 'lowly feet' of the Purusha (the Cosmic Being) as the source of their origin. We must remember that Phule uses this creation myth and constructs upon it a dialogic polemic with devastating satiric effect in his prose text *Gulamgiri*; this text is also founded on the rebuttal of the mythology of the Vishnu avatars. In this sense, then, Phule does engage with Brahminical mythology only, of course, to deconstruct and dismantle it.

However, Phule's preoccupation with the social status of the Shudra as reflected in the second interpretation advanced by Bhagat: Tritiya Ratna as The Third Gem echoes in the epigrammatic prose poem with which Phule begins *Shetkaryacha Asud*, a text which examines the conditions of the peasantry. This little epigram, though denoted in the prologue of the book as a prose paragraph and not a stanza, follows the metre of the devotional abhang, which, as noted earlier, Phule renamed as the akhand and deployed for secular and didactic purposes. This is perhaps the most quoted of Phule's lines and may be translated as follows:

Without knowledge, discernment was lost.
Without discernment, there could be no rectitude.
And without rectitude, no talent or dynamism was possible.
Bereft of dynamism, there could be no wealth,
Thus through lack of means the Shudra sank:
Ignorance is the sole cause of so much wretchedness.

That Phule weighed both these potential meanings as possible options is indicated in the two separate titles inscribed in the handwritten manuscripts.

In deference to the standard practice followed by all editions of the play published so far, the present translation is also titled Tritiya Ratna, in English transliteration. Following, however, the standard form of alluding to the play in discourses in English, the subtitle in English translation (referring to the second title used by Phule) is The Third Eye. As a translator, I am aware that the transliterated title and the title in English translation are mismatched. However, since they are an accurate representation of the two titles Phule himself indicated and, moreover, since they follow the standard form of referring to his play in Marathi and in English, this translation retains both the titles.

Story and Plot

Phule wrote the play *Tritiya Ratna* even while he was fully occupied in running his schools for lower-caste children and working adults in Pune, struggling to keep them functioning in the face of a strong backlash from society. We have seen earlier that he set up his first school for girls of the Untouchable castes in 1848, an extraordinary act of affirmative reform by an individual, perhaps the first of its kind in the history of the world. This affirmative action by Phule encoded within itself an understanding that Brahminical Hinduism was a man-made construction that ensured the perpetuation of the powerful, and that the deprivation of the lower caste was a product of this construction. The theme of the play is based upon this very modern and radical understanding of religion and society. It focuses on an ignorant lower-caste couple, whose superstition makes them totally dependent on the counsel of a crafty Brahmin priest and leads to their exploitation at his hands. They gradually come to an informed understanding of their situation through means of a discussion with a Christian missionary, who becomes through this process a Socratic figure, someone who enlightens the couple and the audience. Even as it presents Hinduism as an oppressive ideology, which results in the material and social impoverishment of the lower caste, the play connects this to the larger political context of colonial rule and administration. It attempts to connect the new British policies of education and literacy, which though excellent policy initiatives in themselves, conferred enhanced power on elite social groups, leading to a virtual monopoly of the Brahmins in the new administrative, educational and judicial institutions of the colonial government. The play therefore is also a plea to British officials to understand the connection between the traditional religious prerogatives of the Brahmins and the extension of these in the secular spheres of political power. Primarily, however, it aims to raise consciousness amongst subaltern groups presenting the significance of secular education as a means of ending their servitude to the Brahmin.

The plot of the play is straightforward and uncomplicated, with a small cast of characters who seem to be for Phule, considering how they are named, representative in nature. The cast consists of a poor cultivator, a Kunbi and his wife Jogayi, a Brahmin priest, Joshi and his wife, a Christian missionary, a Muslim and a commentator in the form of the character of the Vidushak: who offers his opinion on everything that takes place on stage. This figure is not a sutradhar, the narrator in Sanskrit drama who weaves together the different events of the drama as well as the various characters, but a Vidushak, also a stock character in Sanskrit theatre. We will, however, discuss a little later the reasons why Phule introduced the Vidushak. We will also examine if Phule's characters remain representative in nature or if he has, unknown to himself, been successful in creating fairly complex and rounded personalities.

The play opens with the pregnant wife of the Kunbi alone at home. The wily Brahmin stops by her door, knowing she is alone, and warns her of the disastrous consequences that a conjunction of the stars and planets may have on her child. Having first scared her and then gauged her readiness to be guided by his advice, he sneaks in the proposal that she and her husband perform a set of rituals to propitiate the stars, which include a feast to a specified number of Brahmins. Playing on her ignorance and fear, he dupes her, and as his greed grows, he extracts grain, money and gifts of clothing from the hard-pressed couple. The young couple meekly agrees to meet his extractive ploys, taking recourse to the moneylender to pay for all the ceremonies.

The cunning Brahmin plots with his wife to further his own ends, even getting the couple to help them with much of the labour involved in providing for the feast, for which it must be noted, they have also paid. During the feast the Kunbi and his pregnant wife are made to wait in the sun outside while the Brahmins eat to their hearts' content. The Brahmin drops some leftovers into the Kunbi's hands as *prasad*, with which he and his pregnant wife have to satisfy themselves. Later in the temple where they all go for the final ritual, the Kunbi husband and wife happen to hear a Christian missionary near the temple and begin a discussion with him. Phule quite clearly did not intend his play to be propagandist: the missionary makes no attempt to proselytise the couple. He reasons with them, encouraging them to think on their own about the existence of God and his relation to the stone idol and, indeed, to the ascribed powers of a Brahmin. Slowly realising that he, and generations of lower castes before him, have been duped and exploited in the name of Brahminical religious authority, the Kunbi is enraged and wishes to physically smash the stone idol that has become for him the symbol of his oppression. However, the missionary remonstrates with him: what must be destroyed, he persuades him, is centuries of false knowledge enshrined in the sacred books of the Brahmins, which is possible only through education. The couple determines to educate themselves and the conclusion sees them eating their evening meal together at night, before setting out to join Phule's own night school for working adults. Only modern education, the play shows, can free people from exploitation and lead to a true understanding of the world and of God.

Dramatic Action and Conflict

From the above it is clear that the plot of this play is simple and straightforward. There is not much action; indeed, it is not action but ideas that move the play forward. The basic idea is this: Brahmins continue to perpetuate the religious and social system which keeps Shudras and women in ignorance and penury, enslaving them in the process. Phule's fervent advice is that only modern secular education can be the means of liberation. Since the theme of this play is focused on ideas, it is but natural that discussion and debate are central to it.

As Makarand Sathe suggests, the structure of the play is similar to Plato's dialogues (Sathe 2015: 34). In his attempt to debate ideas, open up the space for reflection and persuade his audience, Phule ensures that the dialogues are simple (spoken as some of them are by characters who are unlettered) even as they are marked by reason and logic. They also reflect social and political undercurrents of the time. The commentator of the play is the Vidushak, who clearly seems to represent Phule's views, ventriloquises his politics and has frequent asides throughout the play. His short interjections, in particular, extend the implications of the characters' views as articulated in their dialogues in response to larger political and social questions. Written almost seven years after he began his first school for girls in Pune, Phule posits education as an effective counterpoint to the oppressive system of caste hegemony. As a play of ideas then, the action is pivoted on discussion. In the initial scenes the conversation between the Kunbi's wife and the Brahmin priest, Joshi, or between the husband and Joshi, is glossed by the Vidushak, whose analytic and satirical comments enable the reader/audience to understand the deeper implications of Joshi's ploys pitted against the couple's credulity. Through these interactions and the ensuing development of the story, the play reveals how typical structures of exploitation are created, and how Brahminical forms of domination are established.

Once the paradigmatic structure of Brahminical oppression is highlighted in the very mundane domestic and social reality that is presented to the audience, Phule raises fundamental questions of ideology and interrogates the practice of Brahminical religion through the character of the missionary. The missionary is an outsider to Hindu society, but this character dwells very little, it must be noted, on Christianity. Appearing midway through the play, the missionary is a typical Socratic figure who probes, questions and elicits truthful responses from the Kunbi. Reluctant and recalcitrant initially, the Kunbi becomes gradually more and more involved in the ongoing theological discussion with the missionary. The Vidushak's interventions, grounded in local cultural and political detail, add complexity to the conversation. Phule deftly sketches the different phases of the discussion and the increasing depth of its radical questioning of Brahminical ritual and the resultant exploitative practices followed by Brahmins. Its dramatic intensity emanates from the central conflict presented between spirituality and superstition, divinity and dogma, dead exploitative tradition and blind faith seen in the clear light of reason. One must note Phule's technical and stylistic improvisations and thematic modernity in the creation of the character of the missionary and the construction of this literally iconoclastic discussion. The Kunbi couple slowly realises the truth of their situation and wakes up to the fact that they are being duped in the name of a false god.

Though Marx and Phule were coeval, the latter had no means of knowing or accessing the fundamental tenets of Marxist thought in the 1850s when this play was written (Deshpande 2002: 18). However, the progression of this little discussion in the play does tend in the general direction of an understanding of Brahminical Hinduism as false consciousness, even if it is a Christian missionary who paradoxically guides and nurtures the debate. As the Kunbi realises the deception, his rage directs itself against the stone idol in the temple which he is ready to break into smithereens. However, the Kunbi's recognition of the problem is not the resolution of the play; it has to pass to the next stage which is the assertion of the Shudra's basic right to access education, which alone can lead to an enlightened understanding of the system. The assertion sets the stage for conflict. The restriction posed by the Brahmins by creating hurdles in their path is a denial of Shudra aspirations. British rule and Christian missionaries, it is asserted, have supported the Shudras and given them alternate worldviews, and through this function the English may have bettered their lot. The Brahmin expresses his apprehensions regarding the possible change in the old order and the threat of religious conversion. The conflict dramatised in the play emerges from caste oppression, from the valourisation of the modern against the traditional, reason against ritual, and also from a nuanced position on the issue of gender. Not only is there a direct comment in the play that speaks with a macabre impact referring to the Brahminical marks on the bodies of widows and their position in general in Brahminical society, Phule ends his little play on a scene that has not received the attention it deserves. The Kunbi couple decides to enroll in Phule's own night school for working adults; getting ready to go to school, the husband invites his wife to sit down with him and together partake of the evening meal. This tender little scene quite clearly mirrors the relationship of reciprocity between Jotiba and Savitribai. In mid-nineteenth century India, this is a path-breaking assertion of equality between the sexes. We will examine the question of gender at greater length in a later section.

There is no doubt that the central dramatic conflict in *Tritiya Ratna* derives from the articulation of radical ideas; the interest is on the progression of argument and the resulting discussion is divided among the whole cast. It may also be seen, in Marxist terminology, as a proletarian play: not only is the protagonist a member of the exploited working class, the intention of the dramatist is to awaken consciousness and change it. The agit-prop play aiming to stir up protest and revolt was a product of the early twentieth century in Europe. The drama of ideas, in the hands of Ibsen and Shaw, had come into existence a couple of decades earlier, from the late 1880s. In India socially realistic drama based on social issues started as a wave during the 1930s or so, as seen in the first section of this introduction. Written decades earlier during the time when Bhave's mythological *khel*s were received by audiences as an exciting innovation, *Tritiya Ratna* appears as a stellar one-off literary event: on dazzling display are Phule's thematic prescience and his creative inventiveness in conjuring up a set of dramatic conventions in times where he had nothing in Marathi literature or drama, or indeed, despite the obvious influence of Western dramatic traditions on his play, in European drama, to guide or inspire him.

We move on in the next section to a discussion of the characters in the play which are figures through whose thoughts, words and actions Phule's revolutionary ideas are presented on stage. Do these figures function merely as vehicles of their creator's philosophy? Or do the characters, in the capricious manner typical of complex fictional creations, acquire a life of their own?

Characters or Types

Modern Marathi literature was highly influenced by Sanskrit poetics on the one hand and by Western sensibilities on the other, as discussed earlier in the context of the evolution of Marathi drama. Modern Marathi poetry and prose was influenced by Western romantic and modernist schools. Phule's approach differs markedly from both traditional Sanskritic and romantic approaches. The presence of social realism, the representation of the mundane and the everyday in his work, goes completely against the trend of presenting the mythological, fantastic or the historically heroic during his times. As seen in the preceding section, Phule anticipates by several decades the drama of ideas and discussion which Ibsen and Shaw were to practise from the late nineteenth century; he is also one of the first playwrights to have on stage a lower-caste husband and wife as protagonists, and indeed have them engage in an iconoclastic discussion on vested constructions of divinity. One can clearly see Phule's position on the literature produced by his contemporaries and its connection to social privilege in a letter written to Justice M. G. Ranade, turning down the latter's invitation to preside over a plenary session of a conference on Marathi literature in 1885 (CWMP 1991[1969]: 353–356).[6] It is clear Phule forged a solitary path marrying his social cause to literary forms in an effort to speak truth to colonial and elite power and to reach out and mobilise lower-caste groups and women. We must examine the characters in Phule's play keeping this background in mind.

Characterisation used to be a typical topic of discussion in critical studies of literary works a generation or two ago. With the onset of structural and post-structural theory in contemporary literary and critical discourse, the focus on the traditional markers of the well-made text—narrative, plot and character—has shifted. In their attempt to read texts against their grain, as it were, critics tend to engage with representations of social and political structures in a given text. This change in the critical lens is actually a shift of emphasis which Phule's works deserved to find during his lifetime, and never really did. In this sense, then, *Tritiya Ratna* can be seen, as will be examined soon, as one of the earliest literary texts focused on subaltern theme and characters, since it is concerned with presenting not only the subjectivity of the exploited lower caste caught in oppressive caste structures but also with presenting the possibility of liberating the consciousness from enslavement.

All the characters in *Tritiya Ratna*, on a first cursory look, seem to be representative in nature as Phule gives only two of them their proper names. Common nouns denote the few characters: woman, woman's husband: the Kunbi, the *padree* (Christian missionary), and the Brahmin's wife. Even if the Brahmin is called Joshi, which is a surname, it is also a common noun for an officiating priest, which is what he is in the play. In the excellent and comprehensive introduction to his edition of *Tritiya Ratna*, Datta Bhagat suggests that Joshi is an occupation in rural Maharashtra, which could be performed only by one born as a Brahmin (Bhagat 2001: 70–71). Therefore, Joshi too is a representative noun. Bhagat points out that the only character who is denoted and referred to in the dialogues by a proper noun is Damu, Joshi's younger brother, and perhaps he is called by his first name only to distinguish between the two Joshis.

Tritiya Ratna is a play of ideas and Phule's predominant emphasis is on communicating these; it may be fair to assume that since the characters appear to be representative in nature, they figure only as vehicles for their creator's ideas. However, surprisingly enough, when one reads the play closely, the characters seem to have a fund of energy, thought and emotion that allow them to transcend themselves as mere tokens. The problems that they are up against, their struggle and turmoil form the plot of the play: since Phule's characters are seen confronting obstacles, they seem alive and not merely representative. A close examination of the events reveals that these are flesh and blood characters (Bhagat 2001: 70–71).

The play begins with the Brahmin Joshi going to the Kunbi's house and expressing his displeasure at the amount of grain the woman is able to give him as alms out of her meagre store. To this she responds, 'Oh you Brahmins, we can never shake you off! How long must we care for your stomachs? Why don't you people take up an occupation and earn a livelihood?' (p. 77, this volume). It is true that this outburst is from a poor, ignorant, lower-caste woman who is being imposed upon by a Brahmin; yet, she does not succumb to his pressure without a spirited rejoinder. Though her vulnerability is a result of the social and religious context, she reacts in her individual capacity.

However, her distress increases when Joshibua questions her as to who would ward off the influence of the maleficent planets on the baby in her womb if she did not satisfy him. Afraid now, she pleads that he should tell her the total expense. When he gauges that she is ready to spend as much as he tells her, he begins to expansively list the expenses for the rites.

The little incident sketched above does not figure only as an exercise for the intellect: it is also meant for the audience to find reflected an everyday context of exploitation. The wily Joshi devises a scheme to demand the expenses for a meal for 23 Brahmins. It is possible through this to understand the extent of impoverishment that prevailed in mid-nineteenth century Deccan; the most a Brahmin can extract from a gullible lower-caste couple is a free meal and a paltry dakshina. Clearly, this Brahmin is not wealthy. Amongst the 23 Brahmins, he also plans to include his own brother and the brother of his wife, which pleases Joshibua's wife. He arranges to have his brother do the rite of *jap* (telling the rosary) instead of inviting another Brahmin to do so. On this his brother Damu says, 'Then somehow contrive to have it done for eight days in all; my dhotis are all in tatters and I can demand a new pair of dhotis then' (p. 87, this volume). Even as Phule, through a swift aside by the Vidushak, communicates to his audience Damu's real intention in demanding the money for dhotis (because he is itching to see a lavani), this is a telling piece of dialogue which reveals the Brahmin's economic condition. From this it is possible to discern the destitution of those sections lower down in the caste hierarchy. It is at such points in the play that a reader may also question why Phule does not make the connection between British colonial rule and the impoverishment of the Indian countryside. The poverty and the economic malaise of the Deccan in the nineteenth century was a result of policies that systematically siphoned off wealth and resources from the region and India as a whole. While the Brahminical class continued to exploit castes lower down in the hierarchy, the overall economic condition of the majority of the population was abysmally poor. That the British had a significant role to play in this impoverishment is a connection which Phule did not choose to make.

Coming back to the play, however, one may also note at such junctures in the play, the conflict between Phule the artist and Phule the reformer. Damu's dialogue noted above shows how clearly Phule understood the living conditions of the Brahmin and the Shudra. However, as a reformer Phule's ire was directed against the Brahminical class; he would not want his audience to sympathise with the Brahmins. Bhagat asserts that at points such as this, we find Phule's characters slipping away from his grasp and struggling to come alive. They do not exist in the play merely as vehicles of his thoughts (Bhagat 2001: 70–71). Towards the close of the play, the Kunbi realises that they have been duped in the name of the god Maruti. He says,

> Saheb, it may not be seemly for you to say it, but my mind has become certain and I have now understood that this lump of stone is certainly not worth worshipping, and that it must be smashed to smithereens and mixed with the earth so that another ignorant fool like me will not be deceived by the Brahmin's ploy and be reduced to a debtor. The other thing is that unless this deceiving rock is broken, the real God will never be understood or recognised by our people. (pp. 98–99, this volume)

A dramatist content only to critique may well have stopped with this little lecture by the Kunbi, but not Phule. The missionary's response here is crucial. He says, 'Have they really deceived you in the name of Maruti? Because they too are, like the rest of you people, totally ignorant. Just like their ancestors treated your ancestors, they also treat you in the same manner, and that is why these people (indicating the present-day loud-mouthed Brahmins) really have no understanding!' (p. 100, this volume).

Speaking through the missionary, Phule does not directly implicate Joshibua, but affirms merely that he is blind to the perpetuation of the ongoing system of oppression. We realise therefore that Phule points his audience's attention towards the system that enslaves people, which is very similar to the story 'When I Hid My Caste' by Baburao Bagul (Bhagat 2001: 77). Bhagat cites Bagul's story in order to illustrate this idea; the hero is beaten up badly by upper-caste people when they come to know of his caste. When his friend tells him he should lodge a police complaint about this atrocity, the hero responds, 'Arrey it is not they who beat me up. It is actually Manu who did this.' Speaking for Phule, the missionary, like the hero of Bagul's story, indicts the system of caste hierarchy itself as a whole. The artist in Phule is able to present the Brahmin, despite his manipulative cruelties, as a vulnerable human being, a mere cog in the machine of caste oppression.

THE ROLE OF THE VIDUSHAK AND THE INTENDED AUDIENCE

We must now examine the role of the Vidushak, and why Phule thought it was necessary to deploy this figure. In the preceding analysis of the central conflict in the play, there does not, apparently, seem to be a great need for this character on stage. The character of the missionary accurately represents the author's point of view, and therefore we must ask why Phule felt the need to create the Vidushak in *Tritiya Ratna*. Moreover, traditionally the Vidushak is a stock character of Sanskrit drama and theatre; indeed, he is almost always a Brahmin or a member of the elite classes. In a play devoted to interrogating oppressive social hierarchy, it is interesting that the character of the Vidushak, who is usually a male Brahmin figure, ventriloquises Phule's radical perspectives on caste and gender hegemony. There is also a great degree of ambivalence regarding the social position of Phule's Vidushak; though he is named generically, the target of his many asides are the Brahmins. His primary job is to highlight their many petty and cunning ploys. He never indicates his jati or his affinity with any particular community, though we must remember that when he finally exits the stage, the playwright has him salute the audience with a 'salam alequm' that flies in the face of all standard modes of expected appropriate behaviour that characterise a Brahmin Vidushak.

Intrinsic to the question of why Phule chose to employ this figure, and to the larger discussion of the play, is the composition of the audience that the playwright must have visualised while writing the play. This question is connected viscerally to the character of the Vidushak, for in *Tritiya Ratna* it is he who interjects comments on the proceedings on stage for the benefit of the audience, in the process lending urgency and immediacy to the developments unfolding in the plot. His observations, often acerbic and ironic, in ways present the playwright's point of view, directing his audience's attention to nuances of meaning, in the process nudging them to perceive and to evaluate the different personas and typical predilections of his characters. It is through the Vidushak's asides that Phule clearly hopes to manoeuvre the reasoning and nurse the resultant emotions of his audience. So who exactly did Phule imagine would be his audience?

Studies on Sanskrit drama suggest that the Vidushak in Sanskrit theatre must have been, along with the hero and heroine, an old member of a dramatic troupe, since he is said to receive divine protection in a stage performance. If, for Bharata, the main objective of dramatic performance is entertainment and uplifting the soul through an awareness of the noble and moral life, the value of the Vidushak as a figure who evokes laughter is obvious. Secondly, laughter, according to Bharata, is a phenomenon closely associated with love: as the close friend and companion of the hero, the Vidushak has an important function in a comedy of love. While Bharata mentions four types of Vidushaks, each of these stock dramatic figures—whether as the companion of a royal hero, or the employee of a minister or merchant, or the student of a Brahmin preceptor (depending upon the nature of the play)—is invariably a member of the elite class even as he is a source of the comic (Bhat 1982). Perhaps the type of Vidushak most well-known and loved by the theatre-going elite of nineteenth-century Marathi drama was the one integral to the comedy of love, where he figures as the Brahmin companion of the hero. Here he performs three kinds of functions:

the first is to match the pair of lovers or the couple in marriage as the case may be; the second is to entertain his audience through antics where the jokes are often at his own expense; and his third function is to comment on key events in the narrative by way of asides, in the process also ensuring that neither the pace of the play nor the audience's attention flags.

In Phule's *Tritiya Ratna* the Vidushak has almost continuous interjections meant for the benefit of the audience. However, Phule does not use the Vidushak for any of the functions which he is traditionally assigned in Sanskrit theatre, and this is the specific difference in Phule's deployment of the character. As a 'bookish' play *Tritiya Ratna* was quite clearly meant for a literate public sphere, even as it differed substantially in its purpose and content from other such plays written by and for the upper-caste elite. Secondly, by submitting his play to the Dakshina Prize Committee, whose members were Brahmins and the British, Phule was quite consciously and deliberately signalling his work as a form of structured and dramatised protest. Even if there had been a performance of the play, of which there is no evidence, his audience would, given the nature of the public sphere of Phule's times, be largely constituted of the elite classes. Therefore, the many asides and interjections of the Vidushak are patently addressed to the ruling elite, including the British. We can substantiate this claim through many of the Vidushak's anti-Brahminical comments; some of Phule's stage directions emphasise how and in which direction these comments are to be made. There is one instance that stands out, towards the end of the play, when the Vidushak turns his head towards the 'sarkar'—a clear sign that Phule had in mind an audience, whether as readers or people in the theatre, comprising British and Brahmin functionaries. Taken together with the policy prescriptions which the Kunbi lists out, there is no doubt that Phule aimed these to reach the British government.

However, even as Phule hoped to reach out to the colonial government and the Brahminical class, it is also quite implicit that just like his other texts, which were read out in many of the Satyashodhak Samaj meetings or set to music and sung aloud depending upon their form, there must have been an intent to circulate/perform *Tritiya Ratna* within the Shudratishudra constituency. In these hypothetical circulations we may only surmise the empowerment which the Shudratishudra may have felt on seeing a Kunbi character speaking up to the Brahmin Joshi or discussing the truth of the divine with the missionary on stage, or even noting the interventions of the Vidushak making fun of the Brahmins. We have of course no documentation of any such performance of *Tritiya Ratna*. We must also note that there is a gap of about fifteen years between the writing of Phule's play, which is his first work, and all the rest of his works which were written from 1869 onwards. We have no evidence that this early work was ever circulated except for the fact that its discovery in three manuscript copies indicates that it may have been read at least amongst a circle of Phule's associates. However, histories of Marathi drama document the Satyashodhaki *jalsa*, which was a type of 'variety entertainment' comprising verses, songs, akhands, short plays and dialogue exchanges: all of which attacked Brahminical hegemony (Sathe 2015: 224–225). This form of entertainment was begun by Phule's followers after his death in 1890, and these jalsas were performed in villages and in the remote hinterland. In simple language and with humour, they not only depicted caste discrimination but also addressed injustices done to women and their exploitation in a caste-ridden and patriarchal social order. One important continuity that can be established from *Tritiya Ratna* to the Satyashodhaki jalsas is the deployment of the clown. If Phule employed the Vidushak, the Satyashodhaki jalsas, catering as they did to the largely unlettered and rural audiences, used the figure of the *songadya* from the folk performative tradition of the tamasha.

At this point we must bring the discussion back to Phule's Vidushak in *Tritiya Ratna* and note the changes he introduces in this figure. We may be able to trace in these the influence of a figure who belongs to the tamasha. The ensuing analysis refers from time to time to Bhagat's discussion on the Vidushak in his 'Introduction' (Bhagat 2001: 66–70). The Vidushak-like character is also an essential part of Marathi folk theatre; only here, he is known as a songadya (or the imposter/clown). The songadya is seen performing intermittently all the functions that a Vidushak is made to undertake in Sanskrit theatre. However, he also has an additional function: the composer of the tamasha employs him to offer observations on the emotional status of the characters, the incidents and the time frame of the narrative. To audiences watching the tamasha, the songadya's gloss on events embraces their contemporary time, their history, past and future, enabling the tamasha composer to play on all of these, if need be, with satire and irony. The songadya often connects events on stage with a topical references to sharpen the irony implicit in a situation. Even on the proscenium stage, because of the presence of the songadya, who hails from folk dramatic traditions, borders between the time and space of the theatrical characters and the audience are blurred.

The composer of the oral tamasha aims to have his audience completely involved and immersed in the play. Therefore when the songadya speaks, his interjection is not really an aside—his speech is simultaneously connected to the characters in the narrative and cued in to his audience. Does the songadya-like Vidushak in Phule's play connect with his audience? The answer, Bhagat asserts, is not really in the negative. By means of his asides, he succeeds in imperceptibly establishing a dialogue with his audience. The Vidushak in *Tritiya Ratna*, like the songadya in folk drama, provides commentary as per authorial intent and has a near constant presence in order to aid the audience to reflect and introspect deeply.

The songadya of the tamasha and the Vidushak of Sanskrit drama appear in the plot-narrative out of a certain necessity. They perform all the functions earmarked for them. Phule's Vidushak does not have any intrinsic link with the story; we find that he enters and exits scenes according to the author's requirements, and it must be noted here that Phule incorporates stage directions to indicate his entry and exit, as will be discussed.

Here we come back to the question raised at the beginning of this section: In his very modern play with a modern theme and modern Western dramatic conventions, why did Phule find the need to employ the Vidushak, who may seem alien to these conventions? Barring a few exceptions, Sanskrit theatre was primarily focused on entertainment. Folk drama too works towards entertainment; however, at times the songadya may also be deployed to suggest a meaning or a moral. A related question is why did Phule not use the songadya for his purpose, going back in the process to a more native and arguably more subaltern dramatic form? Why did he deploy instead the Vidushak?

Within Western dramatic conventions, the playwright has no available tool or device that can be used to communicate a message or moral, since Western theatre traditionally works towards establishing an illusion of reality on the proscenium stage. At best the dramatist may employ one of his characters (overtly or subtly) to suggest his own point of view. The missionary in *Tritiya Ratna* embodies Phule's ideological stand. When Phule already had a character for this purpose, why did he also deploy the Vidushak? Bhagat thinks that we must also interrogate the nature of dialogues given to the Vidushak and examine just who are the intended recipients of his interjections.

A close reading of some of the scenes may throw up an answer to this question. A commonly held belief of the times was the Brahmin's power to read the future, and the Kunbi couple has faith that Joshi would ward off any impending disaster from their household if only they paid him his dakshina. Bhagat demonstrates how the Vidushak intervenes by telling us in an aside: 'Well if Joshi can indeed tell the future, where had these skills gone at the time when the Peshwas lay dead?'

Bhagat points to another occasion when the Vidushak reveals Joshi's cunning. The Kunbi woman is named Jogayi. Joshi and Jogayi share the same first syllable 'Jo' and, therefore, logically some of their planetary positions must be the same. Yet the stars seem to be aligned against Jogayi and hence the Vidushak says:

> The portents from planetary signs are just nonsense! Joshi's own words are proof of this. It is like this: both Joshi and Jogayi must have the same moon sign since their names share a common first letter. But the position of Saturn dictates that Jogayi should serve ghee rotis and that Joshi should polish them off! (p. 81, this volume)

His aside, Bhagat shows, voices Phule's perspective. Stage asides are not meant to be heard by characters on stage; they are intended only for the audience. So, not only does the audience watching the play realise how Joshi is deceiving the Kunbi couple, it also simultaneously notes that this is a dramatic convention, a function the Vidushak is meant to perform.

According to Bhagat, there are two levels of conflict in this play. The missionary is meant to reveal to the Kunbi couple that Joshi is deceiving them. However, in the larger framework of the Brahminical system, Joshi is but a representative of all such conniving Brahmins whose job is to trick every potential client. Had the play been a reflective or polemical work, Phule may have concluded it with an analysis of the mode and structure of deception and left it at that. Phule's challenge was to present the entrenched system of caste exploitation through the medium of a play. It is to meet this purpose perhaps that Phule creates the Vidushak. Phule knew that the theatre-going audience in the nineteenth century belonged largely to upper-caste, orthodox and conservative sections of the population. Not certain how well this audience would grasp or appreciate the import of his play—that the defrauding of the Kunbis was but a reflection of the larger reality of caste oppression—Phule may have decided to introduce the Vidushak to perform this role. A shrewd estimate of his audience made it necessary to have a familiar stock character such as the Vidushak to articulate precisely such assertions that could set off a disturbance and turmoil within their minds.

Dwelling on the difference between the proscenium stage and the open ground of folk drama, where the audience is an intrinsic part of the performance, Bhagat asserts that the songadya in a tamasha takes both his audience and the characters of the play through the time zones of the present, the past and the future. However, his interjections tend to be facetious and he cannot therefore get the audience to reflect deeply enough. The proscenium stage on the other hand does not involve the audience. Attempting to overcome the limitations of the Vidushak of the proscenium stage and the songadya of folk theatre respectively, Phule must have conceived, says Bhagat (2001), the very different form of Vidushak for *Tritiya Ratna*. Like the songadya in the tamasha, Phule's Vidushak erases the boundary between the stage and audience; however, so that the audience should not laugh away the issues and troubles presented on stage, he makes the Vidushak interact closely with the audience by deploying asides. Taking a dramatic convention from folk theatre, Phule married this to conventions of classical theatre, thereby experimenting with a very unique creation. Historians of Marathi theatre, says Bhagat (2001), have not seen this experiment with the interest and attention it deserves. There was no such tradition or theatre in Marathi that offered itself as a model or from whose dramatic conventions Phule could draw and experiment. He more or less single-handedly forged his own path, finding a voice and a form to express his own unique perspective on social hierarchy and its oppressive structures. While Phule has not received the critical attention he richly deserves for his literary innovations that are as radical as his views, his efforts in creating stage conventions unique to his dramatic experiment must be recognised—it is a singular achievement.

STAGE DIRECTIONS

To sceptics who question if *Tritiya Ratna* is a play and not a simple dialogic text, Phule's incorporation of stage directions constitutes proof that it is indeed a play. While stage directions are an inalienable and intrinsic aspect of modern drama, Sanskrit drama had no tradition of stage directions; quite certainly there was no question of folk dramatic practices, being oral in nature, having any stage directions. Phule must have obviously relied on English plays as possible models of composition. The following examination of stage directions in *Tritiya Ratna* is based to a large extent on Bhagat's excellent discussion in his 'Introduction' (Bhagat 2001: 62–64).

Joshi, an important character in *Tritiya Ratna*, marks the beginning of the first scene of the play; the playwright indicates how the entry is to be made: 'Finding an opportune moment when the pregnant woman's husband is not around, Joshi presents himself at the woman's doorway, intending to pronounce the date, the day, the star and other details of the planetary position' (p. 77, this volume). He is not content with the amount of dakshina that the poor Kunbi woman offers as fee for his services. Here Phule indicates the emotion with which the woman must react to his demands: 'tired and exasperated'.

'With a lot of urging', 'Appearing to think a little', 'with great anger', 'shaking his head', 'she said, lifting her chin, with eyes flashing', 'averting her face', 'turning her head towards the Kunbi, she said', 'looking to the five-faced figure of Maruti, she said': all these directions indicate what Phule had in mind regarding the portrayal of his characters, their movement on stage and their interactions.

As noted earlier, the stage directions also show that Phule thought about the entry and exit of his characters. On the mythological stage during Phule's times, it was not always a given that a character exited after his/her dialogues/parts were finished. When such characters stood about in the corners of the stage, the audience had to understand that they were no longer part of what was being enacted. This is also the device adopted in tamashas. This is the practice in Sanskrit theatre as well, where the band of singers and musicians continue to sit on stage even as the characters perform their parts. However, Phule does not follow this customary feature of Indian theatre. He has his characters enter and exit at specific points of dramatic action. At the point where it is necessary for the character of Joshi to exit, Phule indicates: 'Joshi started on his way home soon as she said this.' One must note here that the entry and exit of characters is a stage device intrinsic to modern Western drama.

Spatial Representation

A related point concerns spatial representations. Phule had imagined a place: a location where the play could be produced and staged. This is the reason he notes details at the very beginning of the play. The woman goes inside to bring a small quantity of millets but fears that Joshi may leave; therefore, 'sounds of the clattering of pots are heard from within as she calls out loudly'. Phule provides this stage direction to indicate the space he has in mind: it is an imagined space; it also implies that the space where the actual dialogues take place is the veranda of the Kunbi household. A door connects this to the interior of the house. There is a little yard in front of the veranda and close by, in the neighbourhood somewhere, is a temple of Panchmukhi Maruti. These are suggestions relating to the spaces behind the scenes written for anyone who wishes to stage the play; such stage directions are intrinsic to English theatre. While Bhave brought in painted curtains/screens for his plays, and Marathi mythological theatre during the nineteenth century still followed the practice of painted scenery, Phule preferred to incorporate the backstage devices of the English proscenium stage.

The play appears, on a cursory reading, to be a one-act play since directions are not always very clear. However, on closer reading it becomes clear that there are several scenes, though the play is not divided neatly into its scenes. For instance, when the Kunbi reports to his wife, 'Everything is almost done now. The two of us only have to go to the temple and take their blessings, and then it is all over' (p. 94, this volume), Phule seems to assume some of the scenes in his mind, and in places such as these the narrative simply encapsulates the spatial movement in the plot.

Even as stage directions regarding acts and scenes are not uniformly present in the work, the play has a basic plan for a diversity of scenes. We have seen that the play opens in the exterior of the Kunbi home; though Joshi visits it, he can only call from without, and the woman stands on the doorstep to talk to him. Rules of pollution and laws surrounding sacrality pose their own peculiar restrictions on the physical proximity of different characters. As a realistic play about social issues, one must note how astutely Phule plans his various scenes so that his characters from high and low castes can inhabit common spaces.

Bhagat gives instances from the play to show how Phule indicates the manner of its staging. In the first scene, Joshi tells the Kunbi woman as he is leaving that she must talk the matter over with her husband and confirm to Joshi if they will indeed have the rites for the baby's wellbeing performed. The woman discusses the issue with her husband. It is not fitting for the development of the plot that Joshi be present during this discussion; therefore, Phule has him exit the scene. However, after their little talk, since the matter has to be discussed with Joshi, it would have been necessary to have another act with Joshi in it. In order to avoid an additional act, Phule makes Joshi enter the scene again, and to make his second entry seem natural and realistic, he makes use of a device, a ruse: Joshi has lost his little snuff box, and to check if he has dropped it somewhere in front of the Kunbi household, he comes back. In a realistic play, the playwright has to make provisions for every such lifelike eventuality in the plot. Phule, says Bhagat, ensures that his play is schematically cohesive and organised (Bhagat 2001: 62–64).

Some scenes take place in Joshi's home: here the Kunbi can be permitted inside only up to a point and only because his help is required to bring in the heavy load of goods for the ritual feast. When the ritual and the Brahmins' feast take place within the household the next day, the Kunbi couple cannot be allowed inside, but must wait in the street outside. The stage directions for the scene after this indicates that it takes place in an open ground close to the Maruti temple; since the inevitable meeting between Joshi and the missionary should appear realistic, the most probable location for it is an open space. Since neither the missionary nor the Muslim, who appears in a fleeting role, can step into the temple, their meeting has to take place in an open area that does not carry any ritual or religious significance.

Phule, who consciously makes use of all the devices seen above, does not extend the number of acts/scenes unnecessarily. Instead he inserts details of place, location and time into his characters' dialogues, thereby imparting necessary information to his audience about events that have already taken place. Additionally, he also takes pains to ensure that the entry of any character on stage contributes meaningfully to the progress of the play. Bhagat asserts that *Tritiya Ratna* is an excellent example of the creative inventions of dramatic conventions (Bhagat 2001: 62–64).

Bhagat also examines the minute textual suggestions that help build a sense of living reality. As a play of ideas and discourse, considerable thought must be given to depiction of the movement and behaviour of characters and their interactions on stage. Phule meticulously provides suggestions for such stage depictions, and in remarkable detail. One may take, for example, the sack of grain that the Kunbi carries on his head to Joshi's house. Since the sack of grain is very heavy, Joshi's wife tells her husband to help the Kunbi lower the sack onto the ground. While helping the Kunbi lower the burden from his head, Joshi also enquires if he has been able to arrange for his dakshina for performing the rite—all these are directions for simultaneous action. Likewise, Joshi's ritual imbibing of water from his palm after finishing lunch, hanging his ritually 'pure' dhoti on the peg after the puja, wearing the upper body cloth even as he walks—all these are directions given within the body of the text, detailing onstage character movement and interaction.

The Christian missionary is an Englishman who has considerable mastery over the Marathi language: he actually manages a fluent discussion on metaphysical and logical issues. However, he has little knowledge of Hindi; as a result, when he speaks to the Muslim character in Hindi, his very typical accent and speech is reflected when he addresses the Muslim. For example, words such as '*tumku*', '*tumare*' are denoted with a hard 't'. This linguistic aberration, says Bhagat, was used later in many Marathi plays for comic effect. Phule, however did not use it for purposes of comedy: he must have aimed at creating a more realistic representation of the discussion amongst these characters coming from widely different linguistic and cultural backgrounds.

It is clear that almost all the dramatic conventions used in *Tritiya Ratna* are derived from English theatre, but adapted to suit the theme and cultural location of the play. We have examined in the preceding section the role of the Vidushak and how Phule found it necessary to marry conventions from Sanskrit drama to local dramatic practices and create a figure to help make his play more impactful. These are indications of Phule's ability to adapt, improvise and create a novel form that could contain and shape his modern perspective on a traditional, exploitative social order.

Dialogue

Neither a domestic play (though it might give the impression of being one, given its focus on the mundane affairs of a married couple), nor a study of character, *Tritiya Ratna* is a play of ideas, pivoted on discussion as noted above.

In the period this play was written, there was only mythological theatre in Marathi. Not surprisingly Phule found the existing dramatic devices completely unsuitable for the very modern and radical theme he had in mind. As seen earlier, in Bhave's mythological khel, the sutradhar was the main character who not only narrated events through the medium of songs, he also brought together characters that had very few dialogues, often improvised. Phule had to perforce depend upon the dramatic conventions of Western drama. However, as mentioned earlier, we must recall that even amongst the Western dramatic texts available to Phule, there was no theatre of ideas yet. The European drama of ideas in the hands of Ibsen and Shaw was to come much later. English drama in his times was character-centric and marked by ornate language, and Phule could not draw or even adapt in totality the dramatic conventions of this theatre. He had to cut a solitary way and forge a path all by himself. On the basis of episodes characterised by a spare, non-ornate language, he created his own theatre marked by satire, ingenuity and sharp verbal spars. Indeed, the strength and power of his play rests on its dialogues. In the discussion above on characters in *Tritiya Ratna*, it has been noted that though they seem to have been conceived as representative in nature, Phule's characters present themselves as sharply-defined individuals. This is possible because Phule distinguishes the speech of each of his characters on the basis of their social position in terms of gender, caste and religion.

A Kunbi couple, Jogayi and her husband are deceived by Joshi, who issues dire superstitious warnings in the name of religion; once they realise his cunning ploy, they start going to a night school for adults to educate themselves. Their psychological and ideological change is the central theme: it is a play about the transformation of consciousness. A careful examination of the simple plot reveals that it can, on the basis of its action, be divided into two parts: in the first, the couple is in thrall to Joshi; persuaded by means of his warnings and inducements they eventually agree to perform all the rituals he enjoins them to. Here the sly wiles of Joshi to persuade the woman and, through her, entrap the husband are presented with a refined ear for the entire trajectory of the process: initial wheedling, blandishments, the half-veiled threats in Joshi's dialogues to his later complacent notes of command and contempt in addressing the Kunbi. The couple is put to considerable emotional, physical and economic pressure in the process. The second part focuses on the tussle between their conflicted minds and their realisation of Joshi's manipulation, facilitated by the missionary, who enables them to see and understand the constructedness of religious practice by means of a sharp Socratic exchange. Phule's modern theme is elucidated through a rational dialogic process. The missionary convinces the Kunbi couple that the god in the temple is constructed of stone through human material intervention, deploying argument, logical reasoning and considerable wit, and succeeds in transforming their minds. In contrast to Joshi who manipulates, hoodwinks and deceives, the missionary endeavours to elicit the truth; he questions and debates and, through this process, precipitates reality for the Kunbi's knowledge and understanding.

Employing Irony and Satire

Even as this conflict ensues on stage, Phule has the Vidushak interject his asides into the conversation, demonstrating a capacity for experimenting with irony and satire. Some examples of these were noted in the discussion on the Vidushak. We could examine some more. Bhagat makes a number of important points in his discussion on dialogues in *Tritiya Ratna*, some of which are reflected in the ensuing analysis (Bhagat 2001: 81–82).

When the Kunbi couple fall into Joshi's ploy and decide to have the specified rituals performed, they have to incur a debt to pay Joshi's dakshina. Joshi then begins to scheme and calculate how his dakshina and the propitiatory meal for the Brahmins might benefit his brother and his brother-in-law. On this the Vidushak notes in a sly aside that this is what is known as being of use to one's kith and kin, '*looteche gahu ani babache shradh*': 'performing the manes with ill-gotten grain' and ensuring mutual benefits in the process (p. 90, this volume).

When Joshi gives his address to the Kunbi's wife, 'In the old market, up the butchers' lane,' the Vidushak swiftly quips, 'Is it to drive away the ill-effects of the goats' planetary positions that Joshi has chosen to live in the butchers' lane?' (p. 82, this volume).

Dalit narratives are replete with instances of how upper-caste teachers berate the children of the lower caste studying in their schools. One can only imagine the disdain and cruelty with which the lower castes, including women, were treated in the nineteenth century. Phule expands the experience of the oppressed in an inclusive solidarity by making the Kunbi protagonist narrate his own. We recall here that Phule's father had withdrawn him from his first school on the advice of a pantoji or Brahmin teacher. In the play when the Kunbi narrates to the missionary how his schooling was stopped by a pantoji, the Vidushak is quick to observe, 'Padreesaheb, if you persevere a little longer, you will see that the roar of all the Kunbis and Malis clamouring together for their rights will reach the steps of the government, since they are now beginning to understand a little, even though they inwardly fear the Brahmins' (p. 102, this volume). The Vidushak's comment shows up colonial administrative policies and procedures which held out the promise of a few gains to the subaltern classes while at the same time allowing them to be thwarted by coercive and corrupt Brahmins at the lower rungs of the system.

The Vidushak also delivers one of the most powerful lines in the play. At a point when the missionary, Joshi and the Kunbi couple are all present together on stage, the Vidushak poses a question: 'Did Manu take permission from the Kunbis and Malis before making his laws?' (p. 105, this volume) Given the times, this question, unsparing and critical, is like a bolt slamming home; hard-hitting, subversive and radical, the dialogues in *Tritiya Ratna* leave a lasting impact.

TRITIYA RATNA AS A POLITICAL PLAY: CASTE, GENDER AND THE NATION

In its interrogation of caste hierarchy and the hegemony of Brahminical constructs, *Tritiya Ratna* enables a radical, even Foucauldian, understanding of the relation between power and knowledge, and its manifestation in routine, everyday experience. *Nil Darpan* (as discussed earlier) was written and performed a few years after Phule's play. Though written after 1857, this play has fulsome praise for the Queen and the British government; its critique and ire are reserved for the white planters who oppressed the peasant. Both plays examine the plight of the peasant; like Mitra, Phule too reposes faith in the British government; however, his perspective on imperialism is shaped by his experiences as a member of a subaltern caste in a social order that had till recently witnessed the unmitigated clout of the Brahmins. *Nil Darpan*, despite its soft stand on British colonial power, enjoys the reputation of being counted as a political play, while Phule's *Tritiya Ratna* is restricted to the sidelines as a kind of a curiosity, a parochial outburst, so to speak, against the extension of Brahmin power in institutions of colonial modernity. The following discussion attempts to see how Phule's representation of power and authority stems from his prescient and sophisticated understanding of the dynamic relation between caste and gender hierarchies. It will also examine his perspectives on the ideas of the nation.

Caste

Neither the members of the Dakshina Prize Committee in 1855 nor scholars of Marathi drama during the later years after the play was published in 1979 thought that *Tritiya Ratna* fulfilled the required criteria to be considered a play. In the opinion of Marathi critics, it was a polemical text in the form of dialogue: the fact that Phule had structured his better-known work *Gulamgiri* in the form of an extended polemical dialogue must have been an added persuasion in the formation of this opinion. However, the well-known playwright and critic Datta Bhagat (referred to extensively in previous sections) categorically opposes such a view. Not only does he prove that *Tritiya Ratna* is a dramatic composition (as indicated by Phule's own reference to it in *Gulamgiri*) based on a discussion of its plot, characters, dialogues and stage directions, all of which work towards presenting the central conflict in the play, Bhagat argues that it must be, in all truth, considered the first modern play in the Marathi language and also one of the earliest texts in the fast growing body of work now categorised as Dalit literature. It should of course be understood that though Dalit literature emerged from the 1960s in the wake of Babasaheb Ambedkar's revolutionary politics, the fiery interrogation of the caste system presented by *Tritiya Ratna* more than a century earlier establishes its strong ties to a body of literature and a social consciousness that was yet to be born. However, the present discussion of the play, while noting the claims of Bhagat in seeing the text as a forerunner of Dalit literature, attempts to locate Phule's first literary text as an experiment in forging a subaltern solidarity amongst all oppressed sections.

Bhagat goes further in his submission that Phule, in addition to being the first modern dramatist in Marathi literature, is also one of its most significant playwrights who virtually created a new type of drama from scratch, experimenting with dramatic conventions which he evolved for this genre (Bhagat 2001). The play presents—for the first time in the history of Indian theatre—a vision and an understanding of caste oppression. Through the figure of the sturdy subaltern character who grows through a rational process of consciousness raising, whose position as an exploited victim transforms to that of a confident agent able to choose his destiny, the play expresses and propagates an awareness of caste identity and issues, and presents a severe indictment of Brahminical hegemony. Phule attempts to needle his audience, to get them to think and question entrenched social and religious categories. Even as the play attempts to work on the empathy of the upper caste and appeal to their sense of justice, Phule addresses a more basic issue: the consciousness of the Shudratishudra. Indeed, the play hinges upon the dramatised presentation of the consciousness of the dominated slowly coming to an informed realisation and reasoned understanding of the 'relations of domination and subordination hinged upon the knowledge of a dominant class' (Vendell 2014: 53). As seen earlier, if Joshi, the Brahmin priest, is an example of the old ritualistic, stagnant and rapacious practice of traditional forms of knowledge, the missionary embodies the faculty of rational enquiry into systems of domination. The Kunbi couple is representative of 'the capacity of a subaltern class to offer recognisable observations' about 'the experience of domination' (ibid.). Even as Phule indicates the awful unjustness of the system, he seems to nurse within himself the hope that this system will crumble and be dismantled when the Malis and Kunbis educate themselves. This is the hopefulness of an activist-reformer and the note on which the play ends. His guileless hope is a result of his role as an educator, wherein he rejects Brahminical forms of knowledge and questions colonial administrative structures and the manning of these by Brahmins who prevent the lower castes from accessing institutions of learning. While *Tritiya Ratna* recognises these obstacles, it does not attempt to unravel these knotty issues, which his later verse polemic 'Brahmin Teachers in the Education Department' does with devastating satire (Mokashi-Punekar 2016). Phule clearly intended his play to be performed and, through it, to reach out to the British government and the Brahmin elite on the one hand, and to working-class and peasant collectivities on the other, much as the Satyashodhak Samaj with its networks, its various institutions and its connections to urban and rural labouring groups was to do in Phule's later career as a reformer-activist. These ideological and interventionist aspects of Phule's thought inaugurate the first modern articulations of non-Brahmin and Dalit politics. It is in this sense then that *Tritiya Ratna* is one of the earliest and most radical expressions of subaltern literature.

Today it is understood and agreed that Dalit literature is an expression of Dalit identity. Laura Brueck calls attention to Dalit *chetna*: the consciousness of caste which marks the authenticity of the Dalit text and which implies a challenge to traditional aesthetics (Brueck 2006). Dalit textualities, whether literary or historical, are revisionist at their core; they seek to resignify 'the Dalit's negative identity within the caste structure into positive political value' (Rao 2010[2009]: 2). Even as we note the broad base of the oppressed which Phule attempted to mobilise through his writings and activism, we must pay attention to an intrinsic feature of *Tritiya Ratna* that Phule inaugurates, which was to become an essential feature of Dalit literature a century later: realism as the dominant aesthetic and form of expression. If Dalit consciousness is the structuring device of literature born out of protest against caste hierarchy and hegemony, its aesthetics are moored in realism. It is important to understand that realism has been the preferred mode of representation for Dalit writers since the 1970s, whether the genre be fiction or autobiography. In her excellent study on this topic, Toral Jatin Gajarwala asserts that the lineage of realism can be traced from the social novel, the novel of social reform and peasant literature in the hands of Zola, Tolstoy and Dickens, via Premchand and Mulk Raj Anand in India. However, in employing realism, Dalit writers have, in fact, attempted to 'revise realism's history of representational failures'. Dalit literature, she argues, 'is the space where realism now lives' (Gajarwala 2013: 3).

Though Phule precedes many of these writers, and developments in realistic fiction cannot be retrospectively fitted on his work, it is remarkable that he should have hit upon, so unerringly and in a cultural ethos so inimical to it, the realistic mode for his play. At several junctures in discussions above, it has been noted how Phule's first work is an attempt to focus on and represent quotidian reality; Phule's intention is to present the everyday and the mundane in order to highlight the routine structures of oppression in daily social and economic transactions between the high and low castes. Realism as the representational mode is therefore a conscious and deliberate choice exercised by the playwright. This choice quite patently dismisses the mythological themes of the contemporary Marathi drama of his times as irrelevant, claiming for itself the right to document the structural injustice, oppression and violence engendered by caste hierarchy. As a literary composition born of protest, the play addresses both ethnographic and historical categories, with a self-conscious intent to record, reveal and critique.

Gender

Phule's main thrust in *Tritiya Ratna* is to show up Brahminical Hinduism as an ideological imposition on the lower castes and also as a system of extracting an income for the priestly class through its insistence on rituals and ceremonies; education, this play advocates, is the only panacea to this systemic oppression of the caste structure. As discussed earlier, Phule's enduring faith in the power of education to liberate the lower caste is implicitly connected to his interest in women's reform; his first intervention, it may be recalled, was a school for Untouchable girls which he set up when he was only about twenty years old. Through this act he was challenging the orthodox Brahminical order strongly entrenched in Poona, which had debarred the lower caste and women of all castes from learning and made textual knowledge an instrument of power.

Though the link between the lack of education and the decline of a people was an argument central to the discourse of most nineteenth-century reformers, yet as Uma Chakravarti points out, there was a distinction in the rationale provided for female education:

> While for the upper caste or middle-class social reformer it was to provide fitting 'helpmeets' for the new class of men, for Phule education was the third eye—the instrument of a new mode of understanding social relations. Further, this was as essential for the low-caste women as it was for low-caste men. (Chakravarti 1998: 73)

Chakravarti cites a reference to a speech by Phule published in the journal *Dnyanodaya* where he accurately pinpoints traditional upper-caste attitudes to the position of women:

> In their opinion, women should forever be kept in obedience, should not be given any knowledge, should not be well educated, should not know about religion and should not mix with men… (Phule, cited in Chakravarti 1998: 74)

The intellectual space and potential which Phule's interventions opened up can be seen in two explosive pieces of writing by lower-caste women published in the nineteenth century. Muktabai Salve, a fourteen-year-old Mang girl in one of Phule's schools, wrote the essay 'Mang Maharachya Dukhvisayi' ('About the Griefs of the Mangs and the Mahars') a few years after she joined Phule's school.[7] Muktabai focuses entirely on the different manifestations of Brahminical hegemony and her experience of being at the bottom of the caste hierarchy, though she does not dwell much on the experience of being a lower-caste female. Yet her understanding of the political, intellectual and material dominance of the Brahmins and the implicit way in which this ideology creates hierarchy and fragmentation even within the marginalised castes is testimony to Phule's belief in the power of education to erase false thinking. Tarabai Shinde's *Stri Purusha Tulana* published in 1882 is an equally radical work that critiques patriarchal hypocrisy in an inventive style; it forms the only intervention by a woman in a contemporary case concerning a Brahmin widow, Vijayalashmi (O'Hanlon 1994). Tarabai's father was a member of Phule's Satyashodhak Samaj and a known figure in the non-Brahmin movement of the time.

Tarabai's polemic not only intervened in the immediate discussion surrounding this case and the issue of widowhood in general, but went far beyond to offer a stinging indictment of patriarchal double standards in Brahminical, as well as in Kunbi and other non-Brahmin caste societies. It caused a furore amongst leaders of the non-Brahmin movement since her work entered the public domain on a controversial issue and dared to take up a position that tore apart self-flattering, patriarchal assumptions. Phule fiercely defended Tarabai's stand against the onslaught she faced for her putative insubordination; he was the only reformer in nineteenth-century Maharashtra who defended both Tarabai and Pandita Ramabai in their indictment of patriarchy (Chakravarti 1998: 77). Even if Phule does not speak of patriarchy as a conceptual category, his interventions reveal how he perceived caste and gender as interwoven hegemonic structures in Indian society, which was arguably far ahead of his times (Deshpande 2002: 15).

Phule's complex understanding of gender as interlinked to caste is also seen in *Tritiya Ratna*. Like his male characters, the two women characters too are unnamed and generic (Jogayi's name seems to occur only as a ruse to consult the almanac). There is a marked difference in the representation of the behaviour and consciousness of the two women characters, given that they occupy different positions and stations in life within the caste hierarchy. However, even as Joshi's wife connives with her husband to extract the maximum gain from the poor Kunbi, the Vidushak delivers a stinging aside which is meant to remind the audience of the fate of widowhood which awaits Brahmin women.[8] Even if this comment does not find elaborate representation within the constraints of the plot of the play, Phule clearly intends his audience to see how Brahminical ideology oppresses both women and the lower caste.

In this context we must also note the radical and therefore startling gesture, referred to earlier, that Phule portrays at the very end of the play after the characters, and the audience, have been educated about the reality of the caste system and its oppressive structures. The Kunbi husband and wife return to their humble dwelling, having resolved to follow the missionary's advice, namely, to join Phule's own night school for working adults. As the wife bustles about preparing their meagre evening meal, the Kunbi tells her to sit down and eat with him before they both leave for school. This is a rare articulation of gender parity even if it occurs in a fictional context: a husband ensuring for his wife equal access to food and education. We may also note here a biographical connection to Phule's own relationship with Savitribai founded on profound reciprocity and mutual regard. This fact may be gleaned from several biographical incidents in Phule's life and in Savitribai's writings referring to her husband. The earlier sections have noted the conservative and often regressive opinion on the question of women's reform presented in mainstream Marathi theatre of the nineteenth century. That Phule could conceive and present social and gender relations based on modern ideas of equality which ensured the dignity of all sections of society is evidence of the radically progressive and redemptive quality of his very first work.

Anti-Imperialism and Nationalism

There is no doubt that Phule was deeply skeptical of the nationalistic sentiment, dismissing it as an upper-caste conspiracy aimed to wrest political power. Written only two years before 1857, *Tritiya Ratna* shows not the least interest in engaging with larger political developments that were taking place both in the immediate region of western India, or in the country as a whole. It also steers clear of either Hindu mythology or Maratha/Peshwa history as a way of representing issues of nationalism, which were soon to become the favourite themes of mainstream Marathi theatre, choosing instead to look inwards and address the pressing issues ailing Indian society. The nation as a political category, the emotional core on which it is based, Phule understood to be an upper-caste construct. Though the counter-history, which he proposes in *Gulamgiri* and a few other works, does assert that the Shudratishudra are the original inhabitants of the land which the conniving Aryan Brahmins invaded and appropriated, Phule never argued for an independent nation for the Shudratishudra (CWMP 1991[1969]: 119–201). Phule only ever asserts the necessity of a just social order that is premised on the equality of castes and sexes, where every individual is guaranteed equal access and opportunity to a life of her choice; this was his idea of an ideal society which he termed *Balistan*, referring to the just reign of the mythological ruler Baliraja. His last works, especially *Sarvajanik Satya Dharma Pustak*, elaborate on these ideas of a good society. The concept of a nation then, does not engage Phule; he is ferociously invested in the possibility of equality amongst a people.

A second related question is Phule's stand on imperialism. Perhaps the main reason why his interventions have not been considered with the seriousness they deserve by revisionist historiographers, in particular the research undertaken by groups involved in projects such as the Subaltern Studies initiative, may be his rather soft position on imperialism, colonialism and missionary activity. Is it possible that he did not see the connections between them, or that he did not wish to attend to the corrosive and exploitative ideology on which imperialist European nations extended their power to rule the world?

G. P. Deshpande observes that Phule does not connect the strong critique of idol worship which the Christian missionary makes in *Tritiya Ratna* to similar critiques made by the Marathi Bhakti saint poets, a cultural sub-stream with which both the characters of the play and its potential audience would be deeply familiar. Deshpande also notes that Phule's iconoclastic missionary does not refer to Christian icons (Deshpande 2002: 18). This seems to reveal a rather shocking bias and a fairly profound political incorrectness. Can it be read as Phule's partiality towards the missionaries? Can this partiality also be extended to his rather benign perspective on British rule, which he hoped would bring about an end to the hegemony of the Brahminical class and mark the beginnings of an egalitarian society founded on modern secular institutions? These questions seem inescapable as does the fact that Phule did not sufficiently recognise the devastating effects of imperialism. However, together with these questions one must remember how the Kunbi questions English officers and their turning a blind eye to the rapacious Brahmin teachers in villages and hamlets who obstruct the education of the lower caste despite the policies initiated by the colonial government. It seems clear that Phule reposes hope in the British rule, even as he interrogates the lacunae in their administrative capacity and will. Only British rule, in his view, holds the promise of the overthrow of the Brahmins and their duplicitous hegemony, understandable perhaps, given his social location and the times.

CONCLUSION

Keeping the fantastic and mythological steadfastly away, Phule attempts to represent quotidian reality in *Tritiya Ratna* in times inimical to such representations, given the governing trends in Marathi drama of the period. His focus is completely on the humdrum, everyday reality of subaltern existence; the play aims to represent the quotidian in realistic, naturalistic detail. By submitting this work to the Dakshina Prize Committee, he was attempting to enter and lodge his clear-eyed and searing depiction of caste relations in the public sphere of his times. Phule quickly threshes out the structures of its oppressive system, establishing these through ideas and discussion. Though he does not choose to dwell on the inherent pain and sorrow endemic to exploitative hierarchies, Phule's work is without doubt a literature of protest. Thematically and formally *Tritiya Ratna* was far ahead of its times and an early precursor to the body of literary texts today categorised as subaltern literature. Though Phule has found little acknowledgement as a literary figure in Marathi literature, his original and radical experimentations with literary genres and his seminal contributions to redefining the role of literature in society ensure that he has a unique standing in the history of literature, even as the oppressed discover continued relevance in his writings. It is to be hoped that translations of his works in various languages will only add to this momentum.

Notes

1. See, for instance, Datta Bhagat's 'Introduction' (in Marathi) to *Trutiya Ratna* (2001); and Sathe 2015.
2. See, for example, Bhatia 2004; Chatterjee 2004; and Dalmia 2006. Anthologies edited by Tutun Mukherjee (2005), and G. P. Deshpande

(2004[2000]), amongst several others, also locate the beginnings of modern Indian theatre in the mid-19th century.

3. I am greatly indebted to Christian Lee Novetzke for some of the points discussed in this section as well as in the rest of this chapter.

4. See K. A. Guruji, 'Natakanchi Sthityantare', cited in A. V. Kulkarni 1961[1903]: 65–67; Banahatti 1957: 200–204; Kosambi 2015: 60; and Sathe 2015: 47.

5. While several studies on 19th-century theatre in Maharashtra examine the connections between the early nationalist movement, Tilak and Marathi drama, Sathe (2015: 170–183) offers a perceptive and politically astute analysis of Tilak's centrality to mainstream Marathi theatre.

6. For a discussion of this letter, see Mokashi-Punekar 2017: 162.

7. Muktabai, 'Mang Maharachya Dukhvisayi' (1855), reprinted *in Dnyanodaya Centenary Volumes*, ed. B. P. Hivale (1942), cited in Tharu and Lalitha 1993[1991]: 215–216. For a detailed discussion, see Chakravarti 1998: 74–76.

8. The Vidushak acidly comments: 'Bai, it is true they are indeed a species, but remember this species is of the Brahmin caste! You are not yet aware, lady. You better check on some of the widows in your clan and ask them. Then you will know well what the signs of the Brahmin caste are—they will show you all its marks and imprints right on their bodies!' (p. 90, this volume).

The Third Eye[1]
(A Play)
1855

Cast of Characters

(*in order of appearance*)

Joshi: a Brahmin pundit
Woman: a Mali-Kunbi named Jogayi
Vidushak
Husband: a Mali-Kunbi, Jogayi's husband
Joshi's wife
Damu: Joshi's brother
Missionary
Muslim

No sooner does an infant of the Mali-Kunbi caste come to life in the womb of its mother than the Brahmin Joshi descends upon the poor woman and persuades her with his lies and falsehoods. I have written below an account of how he strips her completely of the family's meagre earnings.

Place

Finding an opportune moment when the pregnant woman's husband is not around, the Joshi presents himself at the woman's doorway, intending to pronounce the date, the day, the star and other details of the planetary positions.

On hearing his voice, the woman of the household comes to the threshold with a handful of grain for the Brahmin's alms.

JOSHI: (mighty vexed on seeing the small quantity of grain) Bai, is this all the alms you have for me, a Brahmin?

WOMAN: Maharaj, what now? What's the matter? Is this not alms? I am a poor woman; my husband earns barely four rupees a month.

JOSHI: Bai, who can say that this is not alms? But how is my stomach going to be satisfied with this much? And how then am I going to be able to think of your welfare?

WOMAN: (tired and exasperated) Oh you Brahmins, we can never shake you off! How long must we care for your stomachs? Why don't you people take up an occupation and earn a livelihood?

JOSHI: (thinking to himself, 'This is nothing new she says; occupation and livelihood are written upon our foreheads.') Yes, yes, that's right, that's right. But if you also face a loss, like your neighbour, then I won't let you complain afterwards, you know!

WOMAN: (as if reflecting a little) That woman's baby, it died because that was its fate.

JOSHI: Uh-huh, so you think it died because it was destined to?

WOMAN: What was it then if not its fate? Did it die because you were not given enough alms?

JOSHI: Even if it is a little, it must fulfill us.

WOMAN: Had she given enough to satisfy you, would you have saved her baby?

JOSHI: Can there be any doubt? Had she managed to satisfy me, I would definitely have got rid of all the misfortunes hovering over the baby, and wouldn't she have been the mother of a son today?

VIDUSHAK: (pointing to the audience) You can ask the Joshi about how he lets your children die.

WOMAN: I don't understand what misfortunes lay in wait for her son. Why don't you tell me about them?

JOSHI: Don't you know about the inauspicious signs of the planets? My dear, Lord Mahadev himself dived into the water in fear and hid from them! Who indeed is safe from their dreadful influence!

VIDUSHAK: (indicating the audience) It is true that Mahadev was simple! No wonder then that he listened to the Brahmin and was frightened of the stars!

WOMAN: (fearfully) Are those stars making trouble for me?

JOSHI: Not for you, but they hover over the life in your womb. I can't spell out how they may strike to end it all.

VIDUSHAK: If this Joshi can save human beings from death, then why doesn't the British government shove all the drugs and medical facilities into a corner, raze the hospitals and wait upon the Brahmins' tongue for every panacea?

WOMAN: (visibly frightened now, she opens her fist to cast the grain back into the *soop*,[2] then folds her hands and says beseechingly,) Maharaj, please tell me if there is any way out of this.

JOSHI: You are foolish. Are you capable of bearing the costs of a way out? Your husband barely makes four paltry rupees in all.

VIDUSHAK: Well, if the Joshi can indeed tell the future, where had these skills gone at the time when the Peshwas lay dead? Could he not have leaped beyond and informed their Sardars well in time to stop the events?

WOMAN: (wondering to herself how her husband is going to give the money) All that you say is true, but please be so kind as to at least tell me how much it is going to cost?

JOSHI: All right, all right, let me go now. We'll see about all these things afterwards. It's getting late, and I have to collect my alms.

WOMAN: (beseeching again) Oh, please don't do this Maharaj. I will give you enough grain for your alms.

JOSHI: You might give me the grain! But does it not need to be ground and rolled into *bhakris*? And then how am I to get some vegetables to go with it and some ghee? If I take back only your grain, shall we eat it plain or boiled?

WOMAN: Maharaj, I will give you all that you require now, but please do tell me how these planetary signs may be warded off. Please do suggest some way of doing this, and I will be so thankful to you.

JOSHI: Oh you Kunbi women! Will you ever keep your word? My dear woman, once your husband comes back, I know you will go inside and sit cozy, and to hell with me waiting outside.

WOMAN: Maharaj, can this ever happen? Because my husband often says: 'a Brahmin is of the highest varna and one's means are not reduced by gifting the Brahmin. But what to do? I have a low-paying job. If God can tell my master to increase my wages, certainly then I will be able to give the Brahmin everything he asks.' (Here Joshi smirks to himself, licking his chops.) And please don't hold anything against my husband. Because of his helplessness, he may complain to me a little within doors. But Maharaj, please wait a little till I go inside and come back. (So saying she darts indoors.)

VIDUSHAK: Joshi's crafty ploy has struck home like an arrow, hasn't it now?

JOSHI: Bai! No, no, let me go now. Enough of your idle talk.

WOMAN: (turning her head to answer as she hurries inside) Please trouble yourself to wait a little, Maharaj, I will be back in just a moment.

JOSHI: Ah, you won't let me go! What work do you have with me now?

WOMAN: (sounds of the clattering of pots are heard from within as she calls out loudly) I am trying to put together something for you. Please do not leave without it!

Moments later the woman returns with a basket containing a large measure of bajra and offers it to the Brahmin standing near the doorway.

WOMAN: Please take this grain—it is enough for you, isn't it?

JOSHI: (with a show of anger) Do you think we are like your husband, working with a sledgehammer and pounding away on iron and metal? Ho! ho! What impudence! Will we survive even three days on dry rotis? We are Brahmins; don't we need rice for one meal at least?

VIDUSHAK: Folks! Just see how the Joshi is scheming to extract rice from the poor woman when even a fistful of coarse grain was in doubt earlier!

WOMAN: Maharaj, don't be so impatient, I have contrived something about this too.

JOSHI: (sniggering a little) Unh! Unh! Is that so? Bai, you understand so much! (As he speaks, he fishes out from his waist a little box of snuff, and smoothing down his moustache inhales a pinch into his nostrils with great show as if he were indeed the scion of a wealthy businessman.)

WOMAN: (taking out a quarter tucked into the knot at her waist) Here take this, for some dal to go with your rice.

JOSHI: Hold on! Let me inhale my snuff first. You're always in such a hurry, woman!

VIDUSHAK: It was Joshi who was in a hurry so far; now he says wait, since he's been plied with riches!

WOMAN: Maharaj, you are satisfied now, aren't you?

JOSHI: (shaking his head) Well yes, but you don't sit around. Hurry up now and offer a paisa and a small betel nut to the almanac, and I can then tell you a way to ward off the ill portents of the planets on the infant in your womb.

Now the woman has no money of her own; she borrows a coin from her neighbour, takes out a betel nut tucked in her waist, lays down both offerings and herself prostrates at the feet of Joshi with utmost humility; then she sits a little apart, her hand on her forehead.

WOMAN: (pensiveness on her face) Please tell me, Maharaj.

VIDUSHAK: It is a hard thing to bear, Maharaj, the fire in the belly.

JOSHI: Bai, what is the moon sign which gives you your name?

WOMAN: My name? My name is Jogayi.

Joshi then spreads the zodiac chart before him and seems to be absorbed in it for sometime, his right thumb touching and dancing upon the tips of the rest of the fingers, muttering under his breath, then again biting his lip and clenching his teeth, at times appearing to glance at the Kunbi woman's face…

JOSHI: Bai, your name indicates that your sign is Capricorn. There is no way the position of Saturn in this sign is going to leave your baby unharmed; you should understand: this is absolutely certain. To stave off this baleful influence you must now, from this day onward, go to the Panchmukhi Maruti every Saturday and offer a garland made of cotton flowers or at the least a garland made of leaves. This will bring you some respite. Secondly, you must make a vow at the Panchmukhi Maruti temple saying, 'Victory to you Lord Maruti. Please protect my baby from all the evils of the planetary signs and I promise to feed 23 Brahmins a meal of ghee rotis this coming month of Shravan': this will ensure that your child is not harmed for some time.

VIDUSHAK: The portents from planetary signs are just nonsense! Joshi's own words are proof of this. It is like this: both Joshi and Jogayi must have the same moon sign since their names share a common first letter. But the position of Saturn dictates that Jogayi should serve ghee rotis and that Joshi should polish them off! Moreover, I think that the Brahmins have themselves invented these planetary positions, and therefore why would they ever trouble their own fathers and creators? Truly, I too wish that they never bother their fathers. However, if Brahmins are the creators of the planetary positions, then it follows that the ordinary folk should also be treated like their own offspring.

WOMAN: Maharaj, how many days is it to the month of Shravan?

JOSHI: It will start sixteen days from now.

WOMAN: Oh, then it is quite close. When my husband comes home, I will consult him and then start planning for it.

JOSHI: Bai, I will take your leave now; start planning and you won't give it a miss now, will you? It is only for your welfare that I have told you these things.

WOMAN: Please go if you must. But when will your worship come this way again?

JOSHI: Now what is the need for me to come here again? There is such a long list of jobs I have to do as it is!

WOMAN: Then will you not, at least, tell me where you live?

JOSHI: In the old market, if you go to the butchers' lane and ask anyone for Jairam Joshi, they will show you my house, because I live close by them, a little toward the northern side.

VIDUSHAK: Is it to drive away the ill-effects of the goats' planetary positions that the Joshi has chosen to live in the butchers' lane?

WOMAN: Now it is time for you to go, but when I send you a message within two or three days, please be so kind as to drop by again.

Joshi started on his way home as soon as she said this. Then Jogayibai in great hurry cooked their meal and sat on the threshold waiting for her husband. Soon her husband was home and she served him his meal. While he ate, she discussed the matter with him as narrated below.

WOMAN: Listen, do you think these planetary positions and the misfortunes they might bring are for real?

HUSBAND: My dear, how can they be anything else? Of course they are real! You know the Christian Padrees go around advising people that Brahmins are forever warning everyone about the planets and the misfortunes they bring: do you also think that the Brahmins are wrong?

VIDUSHAK: Is it not for lack of education that the Kunbi is more ignorant than his wife?

WOMAN: It doesn't seem wrong; that is why I am asking you. This morning Joshi Maharaj from the butchers' lane dropped by and said something terrible may happen to our baby.

HUSBAND: Terrible? How so? Speak, let me know at least.

WOMAN: (averting her face) You won't be angry now, will you? He has recommended a few things which are bound to be expensive.

HUSBAND: So what are these things that we need to spend on?

WOMAN: Oh, the expenses are nothing much, hardly anything in fact; but you will have to say yes. That's the first thing.

HUSBAND: What else can I do but say yes? We marry, run our households, and there must be some fruit from all of this. If it cannot be of any use to the children, of what use is it at all?

VIDUSHAK: What depths of ignorance among the Kunbis! Not seeing through the Joshi's scheming contrivances, they think his advice is genuine! Well, what is anyone to do if their destiny is in splinters!

WOMAN: Shall I tell you? Shall I? (she asks repeatedly). Our Joshibua said that since there is Saturn in the position of my moon sign, and because it mustn't pose a threat to our baby, he has told us to feed 23 Brahmins a meal of ghee rotis and take their blessings in the Maruti temple.

HUSBAND: Well, and what do you feel about this?

WOMAN: I am a woman. I understand but little! I will go with what you say. Won't this mean expenses? This is not just idle talk!

HUSBAND: What you say is true. How much money will we need?

WOMAN: How can you ask me this silly question? Don't we have wheat rotis on festivals too?

HUSBAND: Oh, why don't you understand? When we have rotis, don't we have them with jaggery water? But for the Brahmins, they must be soaked in ghee plentiful as our sweet water. Now can you or I estimate how much ghee will be required to do that? Now who is silly, you or me?

WOMAN: (crestfallen) All right then. I will go to Joshibua's house and find out.

HUSBAND: Do you know where he lives? If you do, I will go and find out; you are in a delicate condition. You don't have to go out in this hot sun.

Just then the Joshi landed up at their doorstep and called out for the woman; hearing his call the couple gladly came out.

WOMAN: (with her chin raised and eyes wide open) Now, why do you look so perturbed, Joshibua?

JOSHI: Bai, I came looking for my little snuffbox, which I must have mislaid here or somewhere else.

HUSBAND: Was your snuffbox an expensive one, Maharaj?

JOSHI: Baba, what do I tell you! A patron like you, charitable and pious, had given it to me. How would I know its price? But its cost in Mumbai must be at least four annas I guess.

HUSBAND: Please take this Maharaj. I have four annas with me. But don't be sad now.

JOSHI: (thinking to himself, 'If this man's wife has told him about the quarter taken earlier, then perhaps perceiving my trickery, he is now testing me,' and says as if startled) No, no, I don't want this quarter. How long can we torment you poor people? But what do I do? If I hadn't come to your house earlier, perhaps this poor Brahmin would not have faced such a loss.

HUSBAND: I understand, Maharaj, and that is why I am giving you this quarter. I am giving it of my own free will. Please don't think otherwise.

JOSHI: All right, may Ishvar always bless you. (Saying this, Joshi flicked the quarter off the Kunbi's hands).

VIDUSHAK: Did you see with what swiftness the Joshi palmed the Kunbi's quarter just now on pretext of his snuffbox?

WOMAN: Maharaj, please feel comfortable and give my husband an estimate of the cost of the feast. We have planned to go ahead according to what you have told us.

JOSHI: Well then, what objection will I have to this? We advise you, and you act according to our advice: our work is done!

VIDUSHAK: Joshi's work is so easy, isn't it? He has to just open his mouth, and everything is laid out for him, nice and easy!

HUSBAND: That is good of you, Maharaj. You would not have come trudging all this distance to advise us otherwise.

JOSHI: At least five rupees for the puja and the shradh will be necessary I feel. And then you know, as they say: the more jaggery you use, the sweeter the thing! The rest is up to your piety.

VIDUSHAK: Joshi has slapped this expense of five rupees on the poor Kunbi's shoulders: what piety is he speaking of?!

HUSBAND: All right, Maharaj, in a day or two I will somehow try to gather five rupees and place it in your custody; then you can arrange to have the feast for the Brahmins or spend it in whatever form you think best.

JOSHI: Have you taken leave of your senses, man? What is the meaning of saying do whatever you think best? How can you say such a thing?

WOMAN: Please don't be angry with his words, Maharaj. Do what we will, we are still the Kunbi caste; we live by the plough. How would we know the manner in which we must speak with you?

VIDUSHAK: Little does this plough-cutting Kunbi's wife know that if her husband had turned to learning a little while ploughing his fields, the Brahmin would have taken to his heels and run!

JOSHI: What you said is the truth, and nothing less. But Bai, tell me, if these five rupees fall short, am I supposed to sell the vessels in my house and pay for the feast?

VIDUSHAK: As long as there are vessels in the Kunbi's home, would Joshi ever sell his own?

HUSBAND: Maharaj, why do you say such things? It was my mistake! But please tell me the cost of the feast. If I take a loan twice, then it will mean a double payment to the scribe to note the transaction.

JOSHI: Oh all right, baba! Then go and draw a loan of ten rupees, and I can get someone to do the *jap* and pay off all the dues.

VIDUSHAK: In Joshi's book of accounts, as long as his own tummy is full to bursting, the Kunbi can go to hell.

HUSBAND: Please tell us clearly so that we comprehend, Maharaj. If you don't want us to speak then stop our ears. Now you should leave. Please come back again on the day of the dark moon, and we can immediately chalk out the next day's plan.

JOSHI: Your servant is on his job! Now leave and come back tomorrow: keep going back and forth.

WOMAN: Maharaj, please don't mind these trips to and fro; I will give you something more. Be sure that I won't be under your obligation.

On her saying this, Joshi started off for home. But listening to Jogayi's impulsive words, her husband, weighed down as he was, anxiously wondered who, apart from a usurer was going to lend him the money. And how in the world was it ever going to be paid back since all that he ever earned amounted to four rupees? He might as well, he thought, think of their soon-to-be-born baby as the harbinger of doom.

WOMAN: Oh, why are you so cast down now? Were you thinking we should not have offered to give anything for Joshibua's efforts?

HUSBAND: What is the point of my thinking? Will all this happen without payment for his efforts? But where are we going to get this loan of money? These questions bother me.

WOMAN: Oh, but why do you worry? Now go to the moneylender Babaji who lives by the black fields, and from him you can write down a loan of 12.50 rupees, which is 10 rupees at 1.25 rupees interest. It will be a burden, but we can pay it off little by little till there is nothing left.

VIDUSHAK: How can this woman not understand that the usurer will strip their home completely bare! What credulity is this!

In a few days' time the loan was written down, with Jogayi as witness and her husband offering himself as the mortgage; the money was obtained. The Kunbi went in search of Joshi's house and brought him home. Then, tinkling the coins, the couple showed him the money and said,

Now hurry up Maharaj.

JOSHI: Hurry up we must, but where do we find a Brahmin who will perform the jap with complete dedication?

WOMAN: Maharaj, can you not perform it yourself?

JOSHI: How many tasks am I supposed to do? What a nuisance all this has become!

VIDUSHAK: Does performing the jap involve any labour or any reflection at all?

WOMAN: Maharaj, please do as you think best. We have nothing to say on this: it should reach God through you. That's all we want.

JOSHI: That is why I am thinking about it. Stop, don't speak for a bit. Let me reflect a little.

Saying this, Joshi thought to himself: this job could be given to Damya, since he can yap away like a dog, explain things and take these idiots off my back. Hatching this plan, he said,

Listen, my younger brother will do this job with great sincerity. I can see this after some reflection.

WOMAN: Oh, it is best if your brother Damu can do this.

JOSHI: All right then. Now I will give you the list of all the puja items and the grain and cotton cloth you must buy; please be quiet and pay attention. (Saying this, he gave them a list of things which would cost about four rupees.) But we will get the ghee ourselves because you will surely not have the faintest idea of which sort to get.

(Then he went home and enquired with Damu,) Hey Damu, will you take on the jap tomorrow?

DAMU: Who is getting it done?

JOSHI: It is a Kunbi.

DAMU: And for how many days does he want it done?

JOSHI: Oh, it is all in my hands! They will do as I tell them, boy.

DAMU: Then somehow contrive to have it done for eight days in all; my dhotis are all in tatters and I can demand a new pair of dhotis then. But Dada, don't tell them to buy the dhotis. If you can get the money, I will go and get myself a pair from the right place.

VIDUSHAK: What does Joshi know of Damu's dreams, which have in them a *lavani* and a *baithak* with *pan* and *beeda*![15] He has no intention of buying any dhotis!

JOSHI: All right then.

He went back then and there to the Kunbi household, but the woman had sent her husband to the market to fetch the things. She was alone at home and Joshi had to cool his heels till her husband returned. When he came back...

JOSHI: Baba, some very useful arrangements have been made. Damu has agreed to take on the jap, and I did tell him about your straitened circumstances, but he says, it is true you have organised everything nicely, but Saturn is not going to be placated with only a day of jap.

VIDUSHAK: Damu accepted the job Joshi recommended for the sake of his dhotis. What an obligation he has conferred on the Kunbi!

HUSBAND: How many days of jap does he recommend then?

JOSHI: At least the eleven days of the lunar month. That is my view.

HUSBAND: There is no problem from my side, but will the money we have be enough for all these things?

JOSHI: How many more things are there to fit in? For your sake I somehow manage to scrimp and do everything thriftily; after all, one can only stretch one's legs according to the length of the bedclothes. Keeping this in mind, I have promised him only a pair of dhotis.

VIDUSHAK: Do you really believe that these stories of Joshi's frugality have no shade of deceit?

WOMAN: (clapping her hands joyfully) Maharaj, with your planning we don't need to worry about anything!

JOSHI: Then shall I go ahead and get him to perform the jap for eleven days?

HUSBAND: Yes, by all means. You organise everything the way you want with these ten rupees. You are the chief person here; you don't even have to come and ask us.

JOSHI: Well then, I will go now; but you must pick the wheat and rice clean; and be sure to grind the wheat into fine flour. (Saying this he went home.)

A few days later, the Kunbi took a few days leave from the merchant's shop where he worked. He made all the preparations himself. Just a day before the feast, Joshi brought himself to the Kunbi's house and standing on the doorstep, a hand grandly placed on the hip, said,

JOSHI: Baba, how are things? Is everything ready now?

HUSBAND: (hands folded) Maharaj, everything is ready from our side, but how are things on the matter of the jap?

JOSHI: Idiot, have you not realised this until now! For the past ten days Damu has been reciting the jap every day near the Panchmukhi Maruti temple! Ho! What blind ignorance!

VIDUSHAK: Can Damu have done any jap apart from 'How to destroy the Kunbis in ten days'!

HUSBAND: If this is the case, it is wonderful! But had you let us know, we would have gone to the temple to prostrate ourselves at his feet.

JOSHI: Now all of that can happen tomorrow. Why are you nervous? However, I think you should carry all these things to my house by evening today. We will sort out and organise everything in our house, bit by bit; for one thing, your house is very small, and secondly, you have very few vessels and containers here. (Saying this, he left for his home.)

VIDUSHAK: It is clear that the Pandit wants his own home to be the venue because he can claim for his use all the leftover grain and other goods, and see that it does not go to the Kunbi after the event, is it not?

Here, as per Joshi's orders, as Jogayi helped her husband heave the goods onto his head and shoulders, and as he walked heavily burdened to Joshi's house, the Brahmin and his wife were conversing. I reproduce some of it below.

JOSHI: My dear, do you know something?

JOSHI'S WIFE: What now? How would I know something if you haven't told me?

JOSHI: You know our Jogayi's husband is going to have a feast for 23 Brahmins tomorrow.

JOSHI'S WIFE: Uh-uh, whose job is it to invite these Brahmins?

JOSHI: It is my job; I am the main person here. I can invite anyone I wish.

JOSHI'S WIFE: Then please be sure to invite my brother as well as my cousin, and since you are the chief in this event, please ensure that they are given their dakshina along with the feast.

JOSHI: So be it! Now if we can't be of some use to our kith and kin during such times, then when will we do anything? I am going to invite them, but I thought I should get your opinion on this before doing so.

VIDUSHAK: During these times Joshi thinks he should be of some use to his relatives. This is what is known as 'performing the manes with ill-gotten grain' and ensuring in the process benefits to himself and his kin![4]

JOSHI'S WIFE: (tossing her head) Look at these men! What a species! You wanted to know my opinion! Is it possible that you are not concerned about your brothers-in-law?

VIDUSHAK: Bai, it is true they are indeed a species, but remember this species is of the Brahmin caste! You are not yet aware, lady. You better check on some of the widows in your clan and ask them. Then you will know well what the signs of the Brahmin caste are—they will show you all its marks and imprints right on their bodies!

Just then Jogayi's husband came staggering under the heavy burden of grain and flour on his head. He stood at the door and called out to Joshi,

HUSBAND: Please help me lower the weight from my head.

JOSHI: Arrey, I have just got into my ritual garments. Call out to someone walking on the road to help you lower it. If not, I will have to wear my street clothes and help you do it.

JOSHI'S WIFE: (squinting slightly) You haven't gone mad, have you? Some passerby in the street is sure to take pity on him and help him lower the burden. You get over and done with your *sandhya* now so that you are free to have your meal.[5]

VIDUSHAK: People passing by should take pity on the Kunbi, but this woman who is going to enjoy ghee rotis from his labour, should she not have any mercy?

HUSBAND: Maharaj, won't you help me lower the weight? I will have to throw this burden as I stand, because there is a crick in my head and my neck feels as if it is about to snap. What can I say about your sacral purity!

VIDUSHAK: It is written in the Christian *shastras*: 'You are weighed down by several burdens'. Do you not see it becoming true here?

JOSHI'S WIFE: (with great reluctance) Arrey, don't create a hullabaloo for nothing. I will help you lower it, but be careful now! Don't tip all the weight on me!

HUSBAND: Never, Baisaheb, help me just a little, balance the stuff on my back and I will lower everything myself. I will not allow any weight to fall on you. (Saying this, he finally lowered the heavy bundles from his head and shoulders.)

JOSHI: (from afar) Sit, sit. Rest a little. Was it too heavy for you?

HUSBAND: It's all right Maharaj. Labour is our fate. It will have to be borne as long as there is breath in our bodies.

VIDUSHAK: True, true! The Kunbi has to bear the Brahmin's burden!

JOSHI: Well then, do you have any Brahmin acquaintance that you would like to invite to the feast tomorrow?

HUSBAND: (opening his mouth joyfully to answer, but is just then interrupted by the Joshi's wife, who tells her husband)

JOSHI'S WIFE: Have you taken leave of your senses?

JOSHI: What do you mean? Why are you saying this to me?

JOSHI'S WIFE: If you are going to ask him to invite a Brahmin acquaintance of his, then tell me this clearly: is this a meal meant to feed the Brahmins or just any other feast?

JOSHI: (thinking that she has done well to save a place for her brother said) Wah, wah! This is quick thinking on your part!

VIDUSHAK: See with what cunning Joshi's wife has contrived to influence her husband for the sake of her brother!

HUSBAND: Maharaj, Tai has stopped you from letting me invite someone; I will also not eat in your house.

JOSHI: No baba, how do you say such a thing? The food that is left over after feeding the Brahmins you will have to take as the prasad.

VIDUSHAK: Rotis dripping with ghee for the Brahmins, and for the one who's paying for all this stuff, the leftovers as prasad! Joshi, you have surpassed yourself!

HUSBAND: All right Maharaj, let everything be as per your wishes.

JOSHI: Now you go. You will need two or three rounds to fetch the wood. See that you are done with this by evening. Once I finish my meal, I will go to Bhavani Peth and invite the Brahmins for lunch tomorrow, or else they might commit themselves to other invitations.

HUSBAND: Well then, make haste Maharaj.

Saying this, he slung his empty basket up on his head and hit the road. Just then Joshi ran behind him in a hurry, holding up the folds of his dhoti in his fist, and skidded to a halt behind the Kunbi.

JOSHI: Arrey baba! Why don't you do this? When you carry the second lot of things here, please bring with you carefully all the remaining money; then I can go today itself and get the pair of dhotis for the Brahmin doing the jap; we may not get the time tomorrow. But Damu had told me earlier to give him the money so that he can get them from a reliable shop. So I will ask him, and he can do as he wishes, take either the money or the dhotis. We should not have any problem from our side. He has already asked me a few times for the money.

VIDUSHAK: Joshi says Damu asked for it; will anyone say it is true?

HUSBAND: All right. (Saying this he went ahead.)

JOSHI'S WIFE: (serving food to Joshi) Listen, don't you think it was smart the way I stopped the Kunbi from naming his acquaintance?

VIDUSHAK: Won't it be better to call it duplicitous cunning?

JOSHI: Wah! That was a smart move! But then, whose wife are you? Of what use is it to be born a Brahmin and not scheme and trick!

JOSHI'S WIFE: Please be so good as to tell me when you mean to go to Bhavani Peth. I haven't met my mother for many days now, so please tell her to come and meet me tomorrow, no matter what. But you will have to hurry as soon as you finish eating; sometimes she sets off to listen to the puranas.

JOSHI: All right then, I will leave soon after my meal, but I will have to wait till he returns with the rest of the money which I asked him to get on the pretext of the dhotis. I think he seems a bit moody. How do I persuade him when he is not even our debtor?

VIDUSHAK: At least the usurer lends the money and takes it back in installments; see how Joshi instills fear, extorts and then grabs the money in haste?

JOSHI'S WIFE: You do one thing: you get a pair of dhotis from some tailor on a two-day loan just to show the Kunbi, and when he gets the money, I will ask him to give it to me, telling him that I will send it to you through somebody, that you waited a long time for him but had to go since it was getting very late and you had to invite the Brahmins, and so saying I will take the money from him and keep it with me. Then you can either give Damu Dajiba the money or settle the loan as per your wish.

VIDUSHAK: Bai! What knavery for the sake of a single stomach!

JOSHI: This plan is excellent, but don't hesitate in the least to get the money from him and keep it with you, understand?

JOSHI'S WIFE: Wah! Aren't I your wife? How can I let it go? As soon as he comes, I will confuse and startle him, if need be; I will take the money first and then help him unload the things, don't you worry about this now.

VIDUSHAK: She says she'll ease the money off him first and then help unload the burden from his head. Wah! What depths of limitless sympathy!

JOSHI: All right then, you are clever and I have no need to worry on that score. You will get the work done.

JOSHI'S WIFE: Listen! Is this Kunbi from a wealthy home? If he is, you can extract two or more feasts from him.

JOSHI: It is not like what you are saying. Had he been wealthy, I would have constructed a fine base and got him to sponsor five such Brahmin feasts. And what would have stopped me from telling him to have me do the Harivijay recital in his house? Well, perhaps if he repays this loan quickly, we can think on this subject later. But you tell him to sleep in our house tonight since we do not have a servant to scrub the vessels in the morning tomorrow. And also tell him this, that we would have hired someone to do the work, but we were not very sure if all this would be covered in the budget of ten rupees.

VIDUSHAK: Listen, all you Malis and Kunbis! If you listen carefully to this discussion, or read it, then you will be definitely in a position to declare: no matter even if a gang of robbers attacks your house, but don't even dream of depending upon a Brahmin or a Joshi![6]

JOSHI'S WIFE: Oh, you seem to be able to trot out a great many reasons and excuses.

VIDUSHAK: It is so much labour to give these excuses, isn't it? Doesn't it make the tongue wag and tire it out?

JOSHI: What else to do: how can we Brahmins survive without them?

VIDUSHAK: You people must have an occupation, baba. Only then will you get along well (without abusing the Mangs and the Mahars) in this world. Now give up this trickery and roguery because your future doesn't seem very bright to me.

Joshi finished eating. He slurped a little water from the palm of his hand to mark the end of the meal, rose to his feet and covering himself with his top cloth, he hung the sacral cloth on a peg, hurriedly pleated his dhoti, dragging on his vest even as he walked out on the street. Then he went to his mother-in-law, narrating to her in great detail all the doings for the feast, ending with his wife's injunction asking her mother to visit her the next day no matter what. He then got a pair of dhotis on loan and till 10 in the night spent time with a few friends and acquaintances. Returning home afterwards he checked whether his wife had managed to get the money from the Kunbi and seeing the man sleeping over, Joshi praised his wife and lying down upon his bed, slept like a log the whole night. The next day till about 10 in the morning he supervised the completion of all the chores by the Kunbi, the women, the children and all the other relatives. Joshi then said the following to the Kunbi:

JOSHI: Now go home, have a bath and return around 1 o'clock in the afternoon with your wife. In the meanwhile, I will see that the Brahmins are served their feast, after which we can all proceed to the Maruti temple for the dakshina. Thereafter I will arrange for you to be blessed by them.

Hearing these words, the Kunbi was very happy and reaching home started telling his wife the following:

HUSBAND: Everything is almost done now. The two of us only have to go to the temple and take the blessings of the Brahmins, and then it is all over.

WOMEN: Now my heart feels free of anxiety you know!

HUSBAND: Of course, it must feel relieved!

Just then hearing the cannon sound for 12.00, the two of them set to in a great hurry, and around 12.30 they started to walk to Joshi's house.

Here they found that the leaf-plates were only being laid out then for the meal. On seeing this, they made themselves as comfortable as they could in a little shade beside Joshi's house and were kept waiting in the heat of the day till 3 o'clock. Joshi and his retinue of Brahmins rose from their meal, had their pan and betel nut and rested for a while. Joshi then went within, and on a leaf-plate he packed some food, and standing over them said:

JOSHI: This is the prasad. Sit at ease a little beyond and eat it slowly. (So saying, standing as he was, he dropped the packet into the garments they held outstretched below.)

HUSBAND: (nodding his head) Well Maharaj, it's because of our good fortune that we have got this prasad.

Saying this, they sat down at a distance and polished off the food, and licking the leaf and their fingers clean, drank water till their bellies were full. Then they sat down under a little shade by the house.

VIDUSHAK: (turning his face to the Kunbi) Arrey, it is true that it is because of your fate that Joshi extracted from your wife, instead of the fistful given as alms, a large measure of grain, a quarter of a rupee, a small coin and a betel nut; and from you he's taken, on the excuse of losing his snuffbox, one more quarter: all these he has plucked from the two of you. Secondly, in thrall to this Joshi, you have taken four days leave from your Savkar, the shop owner; throwing away your earning of fifty annas, you have mortgaged yourself and your wife; for a loan of ten rupees, you agreed to take upon your head, a debt of 12.50 rupees; and toiling day and night like a slave for four whole days, you have made all the preparations for this feast. It is Joshi's good fortune that without so much as lifting his little finger, he extracted from you all the expense for the feast and arranged to take money for the dhotis of his brother Damu; he invited to the feast all his kith and kin, sat them down in rows for the feast, which they all finished long before you even got a taste of it. Yesterday, he was reluctant to even help you lower the heavy burden from your head and back. Moreover, without any self-respect you hauled all the heavy goods to his house and till this morning allowed him to wring from you all the labour for the feast, and later, on his instructions, you brought your pregnant wife here in the burning sun and sat beside her in the open heat of the day from 12.30 to 4.30 in the evening. Finally Joshi threw some food in your lap and told you to eat it at some distance from the house. From this it is clear: does anyone else in the whole world have the same misfortune as yours?! In a British government underpinned by Christian ethics, an idiot like you can be persuaded and duped by a Brahmin: this I don't see anywhere else in the universe apart from Hindustan. (Then he touched his hand to the Brahmin-run journal *Gyan Prakash* and said, 'Listen baba, don't you see your fellow-Brahmins, your *jaat-wallah*s, doing these things right under your nose? If it is true, you should write this up and publish it, shouldn't you? Don't feel too ashamed to do so!"[7]

Then, around 4.30 in the evening all the Brahmins set out for the temple, taking along with them the Kunbi and his wife waiting patiently outside. There all the Brahmins started to recite in loud stentorian tones in order to bless the couple. Meanwhile a Christian missionary stood close to one side of the temple and unseen to the others started giving advice to the Kunbi, even as the Brahmins stepped up their clamour, to which we shall now pay attention.

MISSIONARY: Why Patilbua, do you know anything about how many gods there are?

HUSBAND: Don't I know it! Are we godless like you people?

MISSIONARY: (with astonishment) What do you mean we are godless? Please baba, tell me what you mean.

HUSBAND: Is there any idol of a goddess in your temple of Mumma Devi?[8] See how our god can be seen plainly even with our eyes! (Saying this, he points his finger at the idol of Panchmukhi Maruti.)

VIDUSHAK: See Padreesaheb! Just see how the Brahmins have addled his brains and made him so completely ignorant that he can't even tell the difference between God and stone.

MISSIONARY: Patilbua, according to your understanding it is true that this is God, but if I ask you a few questions about God, will you answer without getting angry?

HUSBAND: Wah! What can be my objection in answering you? You ask and I will answer.

MISSIONARY: Patilbua, now your Maruti, of what is this god made?

HUSBAND: Why would one get angry at this? Our god Maruti is made of stone.

MISSIONARY: Well, well, and from where do you think this stone was brought?

HUSBAND: It must have come from the stone quarry, I think.

MISSIONARY: Well! But was this boulder in the quarry the only one that was there?

VIDUSHAK: Why do you ask these silly questions! Listen, the gravel strewn on roads, is it not made of the same stones? And does not the same gravel turn to dust after being trod upon by so many of us?

HUSBAND: Now it is known as a quarry; who would claim that this was the only boulder there? The quarry consists of such a big rock that the boulder from which the Maruti was made must only be a small chip or a shard of it!

MISSIONARY: Well then, is it possible for you to estimate the size of that original rock from which the boulder was broken and brought here? Any idea how big it must be?

HUSBAND: Saheb, my understanding is limited. I cannot possibly estimate how big that rock might be.

MISSIONARY: Well then, can you at least guess where it must be?

HUSBAND: This I can tell you. That rock is in the earth itself.

MISSIONARY: Well, if that rock is inside the earth, is the rock within the earth or the earth itself is within the rock? Let me see how this is explained.

HUSBAND: The rock? The rock is in the stomach of the earth—even a five-year-old could tell you this! What is the wonder of my giving you such an answer? And moreover, because the poor, gentle earth has borne the weight of the rock without a murmur all these years, it is not wrong to say that she may be seen as its mother!

MISSIONARY: All right then, how did the earth come into being? By itself or did somebody create it?

HUSBAND: (eyes half-shut, head a little lowered, turning his inward eye upon the whole wide world, said with a deep sigh) Saheb, I think someone must have created the earth.

MISSIONARY: Well done! Baba, well done! (With head upturned and in a soft voice) Our Father in heaven, you are the one who has created this world and all of us; you are all mighty, powerful and blessed! We must all serve you with one mind and purpose. God, you are all merciful, and all the Malis and Kunbis are now in your sight, and you will redeem and save them soon! (Turning to the Kunbi, he said) Patilbua, now should we worship the earth or should we worship the one that created the earth, please be so kind as to tell me this.

HUSBAND: Him! Indeed, him! We must worship him with all our devotion. Because he is unseen and invisible. I understand this clearly now after thinking about it; it flashed across my mind.

VIDUSHAK: Padreesaheb, please do go on with your counselling; don't be in a hurry to wipe your face with your handkerchief; otherwise these garrulous Brahmins will surround this Kunbi, fill his mind with far-fetched and fabulous ideas and who knows, under the flow of such thoughts they might even get him to doubt and to hate you. Surely you have experience enough to know how they connive to do this! It is not necessary that I should warn you about it.

MISSIONARY: Patilbua, you are sure of your thoughts, aren't you? I would like to ask you about something else, but only if you are agreeable to it.

HUSBAND: Saheb, please ask me whatever you wish, but ask me questions only about God, the creator of the universe, because at this moment I seem to have no taste for any other subject.

MISSIONARY: (pointing his finger at Maruti) Patilbua, is he the same God? And because he is invisible to the eye, does it mean that in his place this idol must be worshipped?

HUSBAND: (looking at Panchmukhi Maruti with sudden immense rage) Saheb, it may not be seemly for you to say it, but my mind has become certain and I have now understood that this lump of stone is certainly not worth worshipping, and that it must be smashed to smithereens and mixed with the earth so that another ignorant fool like me will not be deceived by the Brahmin's ploy and be reduced to a debtor. The other thing is that unless this deceiving rock is broken, the real God will never be understood or recognised by our people.

VIDUSHAK: I now leave it to you people to figure out the difference in the teachings of the Brahmin and the Padreesaheb.

MISSIONARY: (with great fearfulness) Patilbua please do not smash it now, at this point in time, because there are very few people who have your understanding. The others will file a complaint against you and the government will have you arrested. And it may well decide that you are a culprit and punish you.

VIDUSHAK: Padreesaheb, why do you fear so much? These Kunbis and Malis are hardly going to smash the Maruti idol! No sooner than this fellow reaches home, some Brahmin is sure to tell him that Padreesaheb's religion is false, and that will be the end of that! He is sure to listen to the Brahmin and censure you and your religion. Do they give him any leisure, any space, to reflect upon religion? As it is he has hardly a thought in his head; on top of that it is so deeply ingrained in him that the Shudra can never override the Brahmin's injunctions: for a long time now the Brahmins, through their writings and their power and arrogance, have imprinted this upon the minds of Kunbis and Malis. You only have to look at someone like Manu or Parshuram if you doubt my words, and then it will be established.

HUSBAND: What can I say, Saheb! These loud-mouthed Brahmins have so duped and beggared me in the name of this dratted Maruti, that if I were to tell you everything right from the beginning, you would see my helplessness and declare some punishment for these Brahmins too, even if we were to set aside the smashing of the Maruti idol.

Just then a Muslim who had been standing there, listening to the entire conversation, extended his hand and said in Dakkhani Urdu,

MUSLIM: Padreesaheb, during the years gone by, our Badshahs had demolished so many big idols of these Hindus; we can say they did a good thing, can we not? What a pity these people grumble so much against them!

MISSIONARY: (in English-accented Dakkhani Urdu) You don't know, my sahib, that your Badshahs broke these people's idols. It is true that it was a good thing. But it was not good that these people never made a case of their own against their own religion and smashed their idols themselves.

HUSBAND: Saheb, what is it that this Bhai is saying?

MISSIONARY: He is saying that it was a good thing that one of their Badshahs demolished the idol in the temple at Sorati Somnath. I told him, however, that had his people, i.e., the Muslims, tried to make the Hindus understand, as we try to do, and persuaded them to smash the idols on their own, then perhaps the Hindus would not now feel resentful against the Badshahs.

HUSBAND: Bhai saheb, please do not interrupt us. Let Padreesaheb speak to me a little more, because what you are saying and Saheb's words are all beginning to sound very true to me now.

MUSLIM: (in Dakkhani Urdu) Padreesaheb, this Patel is very happy talking to you. Please carry on. I will also stand by and listen to you.

MISSIONARY: Have they really deceived you in the name of Maruti? Because they too are, like the rest of you people, totally ignorant. Just like their ancestors treated your ancestors, they also treat you in the same manner, and that is why these people (indicating the present-day loud-mouthed Brahmins) really have no understanding!

HUSBAND: If you say this Saheb, then who can ever shut them up? Because what this indicates is the son can live a life of ease on the father's earnings. But the son has no compulsion to pay any taxes on this income. That is, just like his ancestors, he can happily eat the ghee rotis made from our sweat and blood, but the expenses of this must be borne by us Malis and Kunbis, and if we have a mind, we may scout around hunting for their ancestors, is that it? What a farce!

VIDUSHAK: Who would want to let go of that which is within grasp and run after that which has escaped!

MISSIONARY: Patil, don't be so angry now, calm down a bit and talk to me. Are you able to read?

At this, all the Brahmins look at each other, startled, even as they continue to bestow blessings.

HUSBAND: What is the use of my getting angry, Saheb? What effect am I ever going to have on those Bhats? But no, I cannot read.

MISSIONARY: Why! Why can't you read?

HUSBAND: Saheb, when I was little, my father lived in a village and it's true, he put me into a school so that I could get some learning, but the teacher used to beat me up. And so my mother took me out of school and made me herd the cattle.

VIDUSHAK: (turning his head to the government, says)[9] What the Kunbi said just now is the absolute truth; it really happens like this, you know!

MISSIONARY: Why did the teacher beat only you? Did he not hit the other children? Were you perhaps naughty?

HUSBAND: I may have been a little naughty perhaps. But is it possible that every child of the Malis and Kunbis was naughty like me? At least in that village, all the Kunbis kept their children at home. Now you might say that all the Malis and Kunbis are ignorant clods. What taste do they have for reading or writing? Therefore, they must have kept their children at home!

MISSIONARY: That's right; (from what the Brahmins say) my opinion is the same.

HUSBAND: Saheb! When mamledars[10] and other Brahmin officers, who have obtained education similar to the English people, and having now become so grand and important, show off to the world, do you think that there is no desire in our hearts to be educated? No, no! We often feel that we must also be educated and become at least a police or revenue official, but what do you know of the contrivances and shenanigans these Brahmin school teachers employ?

VIDUSHAK: Saheb, you Padrees must also reflect on what the Kunbi has said just now.

MISSIONARY: What you are saying is true enough, but now things are changing. Because the merciful Candy Saheb has recently gone on a drive on this matter and after training new school teachers has sent them on an urgent basis to many villages.

HUSBAND: Saheb, I think what you said projects your own weakness. I have also come to know that our Candy Saheb has trained a huge number of teachers and sent them to schools across many villages. But what is the result? In all those villages, haven't all the Brahmin folk contrived to ensure that the Malis and Kunbis do not send their children to school by giving them surreptitious advice to the contrary or getting the Kulkarnis to threaten them and so create obstacles in their path of learning?

MISSIONARY: Tch, tch, Patilbua, you speak out of a vengeful attitude. Because now the Brahmin folk have told us straight to our faces that all the rest of the people must have an education and they keep talking about it.

VIDUSHAK: Padreesaheb, if you persevere a little longer, you will see that the roar of all the Kunbis and Malis clamouring together for their rights will reach the steps of the government, since they are now beginning to understand a little, even though they inwardly fear the Brahmins.

HUSBAND: Well, do you think you will be able to guarantee that all Brahmin teachers will pay enough attention to our education, and as declared by their own desire will go to various villages on directions specified by the English officers?

VIDUSHAK: Why! Padreesaheb, even though you English teach your knowledge, do not most English people say about the Brahmins they have taught: 'there is definitely some difference'?

MISSIONARY: Now they say one thing to us openly, and behave in a completely different way with you all; what can we do about this?

VIDUSHAK: This is the track, Saheb, please come on this track; you cannot rely only on the schemes set out by the newly-educated Brahmins and follow the ways specified by them.

HUSBAND: Now how can I alone point out everything?

MISSIONARY: Please tell; why should you not specify things? Nobody can stop you from thinking for yourself.

HUSBAND: I think there should be a policy made by the government's Board of Education, which should estimate the number of Mali and Kunbi inhabitants of each village and the count of their children who must be in school; if this number of children is not admitted, the school must be shut down. Then let us see! These very Brahmins will then start advising the Malis and Kunbis to send their children to school. They may even begin by saying, 'O you Malis and Kunbis, what was written earlier in the shastras that the Shudra cannot write, is all lies.'

VIDUSHAK: Saheb, of course they will say these things. If the Kunbis and Malis do not send their children to be educated, then their own children will have no access to education and will soon have to join the rows of unschooled Mali and Kunbi children and sit down with them. This is what is known as 'Reveal your father, or perform his manes'.[11] But Saheb, will the government pay attention to what this Kunbi is saying? If it does, then it will be for the greater good of the Kunbis, I feel.

MISSIONARY: Patilbua if all Kunbis and Malis have kept their children at home, does it not follow from this that these schools have been shut down?

HUSBAND: How will they shut them down? Some Brahmin children still go to those schools.

VIDUSHAK: Is it ever possible that instead of teaching upper-caste children with a lot of affection and care, they might beat them up?

On the other side, the Brahmins having finished with the ritual of the blessings, Joshi extricated himself from the group and holding in his hand the little vessel and spoon of the sacred water came towards them and standing behind Jogayi's husband, said to him,

JOSHI: Baba, are you ready to go home?

MISSIONARY: Oh Bhatji, please let him talk with me.

VIDUSHAK: What does Joshi know about how the Padreesaheb has worked on the Kunbi all this time, and having taught him like a parrot has now made him capable of being Joshi's teacher!

MISSIONARY: Arrey baba, we have come here to talk to the ignorant, and it is the injunction of our Redeemer to do so.

VIDUSHAK: Praise be to your Saviour that he has, through this English government, devised to come up with several strategies (hidden from the Brahmin's gaze) to save the Malis and Kunbis.

JOSHI: Speak on! Let your Yeshu Christ come. (And turning to the Kunbi said,) All right, baba, scoot and convert if you want. Don't stop yourself; listen to this fellow's advice, and then you can swallow up as many villages as you like! (So saying, he stood fuming to one side).

VIDUSHAK: Little does this Joshi know that Yeshu Christ will not hesitate to purify even his four-faced Brahmadev in a few days' time.

MISSIONARY: Patilbua, the children of the Brahmins have kept up with their education; why is it that the children of your people opted out?

HUSBAND: (taking a look at Joshi's face and appearing a little scared said) Saheb, what can I say now? Why don't you understand?

VIDUSHAK: Isn't it great foolishness on the part of these Kunbis and Malis to hesitate to tell the government or the Sahebs about their many troubles on their own? Since the English government cannot intuit these, how are they ever going to be apprehended or solved? What blindness in broad daylight!

MISSIONARY: Patilbua, please don't be scared of Brahmanbua. Please tell everything truthfully and I will myself, without any let or fear, publish it in *Dnyanodaya*.[12]

VIDUSHAK: Will you make note of my prediction? Soon, in a few days' time, *Dnyanodaya* will sell at such an exorbitant price that the Kunbis will not be able to afford it!

JOSHI: (Softly, so that none should hear, turned his face to Jogayi and said) Jogayi, has your husband lost his senses totally? Now that he is behaving like an equal with the Sahebs, who is going to scour the vessels back home?

VIDUSHAK: Praised be the English; may God be with them always! The English always fraternise with the Malis and Kunbis and treat them as their equals; and the Brahmins wish to have their vessels cleaned by them!

WOMAN: (Kunbi's wife) Maharaj, you are in such a damned hurry about chores! Wait a while. See how the Saheb speaks so much better (about God) than you Brahmins; let me also listen for a bit…

VIDUSHAK: Truthful words are liked by all. This is clearly proven, is it not?

JOSHI: The Kunbi caste is known to be foolish! (He stood there grinding his teeth and chewing upon his lip.)

VIDUSHAK: The Kunbi caste is foolish. No wonder they listened so blindly to the Brahmin all these days, baba! (Before Joshi can say something…)

MISSIONARY: Hush. Hush. Brahmanbua, please do not hurry. Let Patilbua tell the truth about Brahmin children. (He jovially rests the point of his cane on the Kunbi's head and says encouragingly) Speak up, baba, speak! Don't be afraid!

HUSBAND: (stammering and hesitant) Saheb, since the Brahmin kids are of their own caste, they were not beaten up as much as we were. And secondly, suppose one of them did stop going to school and stayed at home, then even the women folk of the village set upon the kid with so much vehemence that it made him go off his food and drink.

MISSIONARY: Well, did your parents appeal if one of the Kunbi Mali kids gave up school and stayed at home? Should they not have counselled you and given you advice?

JOSHI: Wah, Saheb, wah! These are some excellent questions you have asked. That is why I will now tell the Kunbi: become a Padree or spell out the reason why your father and elders did not insist that you to go back to school.

HUSBAND: Joshibua, you won't be angry will you now?

JOSHI: Go on, tell us. What do you care for our anger? What Peshwai do we have now that we might have you punished? Do you people have any fear for Manu's laws now? Do look up, if you want, the Laws of *Manusmriti*, Shlok (Kalam) 205.[13]

VIDUSHAK: (pointing to the audience) Did Manu take permission from the Malis and Kunbis before making his laws?

HUSBAND: Didn't you Brahmin folk always tell our parents that according to the rules of your Manu or Phanu they had no right to learn reading and writing? What could they do then? Could they have gone on strike against your Manu's rules and admitted their children to school? Because you did not allow them access to education, they kept on obeying your orders blindly. But now because of our good fortune in having the English government in Hindustan, there are a few Mali-Kunbis (and God willing, also some Mahars and Mangs) who are capable of proving that your Manu's laws are only worthy of being sold as wrapping paper for snuff. After which, this piece of paper can be crumpled and turned into cowries or pawns for the use of the blind and disabled in charity homes.[14]

VIDUSHAK: (speaking to himself) It is my opinion that someone later may well smoothen the crumpled paper of the snuff packets and sight upon some of the shlokas. Won't they read them then? Therefore, some other means will have to be found to ensure the welfare of the Mali-Kunbis and bring the Brahmins on the right ethical track.

JOSHI: All right then, if our control is threatened when you people go to school and get an education, then how is it that at least till the time the school master started beating you up, your father did send you to school?

HUSBAND: As if you don't know this? Whenever the Superintendent in charge of the schools or any other big Saheb visited and sent orders that children of all castes must be on the rolls of the school, the Bhat Kulkarni used to shove all the Mali and Kunbi children in like so many sheep and fence them in until the important people had finished their visit. Secondly, do you know of any single person from our community who is, at this present time, educated and clever like you people? If there is, let us go to the village where I grew up and you can show me the person.

JOSHI: How is it then that the Sahebs don't know of this?

HUSBAND: How would they come to know of it and who would inform them about it? Who has the gumption to report this to them?

JOSHI: Wasn't your father there?

HUSBAND: My father? Certainly he was there. But does a Patil ever have the guts to report the culpability of the Kulkarni or the Brahmin? (Then he bit his lip and spoke to himself) Will God ever make it possible that all our people can report to the English government the misdoings of the Brahmins without any fear?

VIDUSHAK: (turning his face to the Kunbi) Baba, don't be afraid; all you Malis and Kunbis, as well as the Mahars and Mangs should not be in the least fearful. Ishvar himself has brought the English to your land. And it is he who will free you of all your sorrows.

JOSHI: You are able to speak against us and expose our conniving because this is the Kaliyug in which we live.

VIDUSHAK: (pointing to the audience) The doors of education are open to all castes in this state, yet the Brahmins feel that their cunning tricks should not be exposed even in the Kaliyug.

HUSBAND: Saheb, did you hear? What I said just now, does it in any way smack of trickery or cunning? If you wish, let us go from village to village and, without revealing who we are, question the Brahmins in each village. Then we will know who is deceitful: Joshibua or me. And secondly, all this time their Manu was dancing everywhere and suddenly now it is some Kali or Phali that he is referring to. If now I have begun to reflect upon things and to speak my thoughts, will I not be able to expose their Kali as well? But we can discuss this sometime later, and I will demolish this creature myself since I am now able to perceive the falsity of their thought.

JOSHI: Arrey baba, who said you were cunning? I only said that our Brahmin people are cunning. But you people should not be talking so much. For how long do you think the Sahebs will be here? In the end, you will have to come back to us. Just like the Muslims, sooner or later this English government will also go away, and in a few years the Peshwai will be back. Since Brahmins have been the gurus of all the eighteen varnas from a long time past, it is best that you Shudras should look up to us, for in this alone lies your salvation.

VIDUSHAK: (pointing to the audience) Ishvar himself has sent the English to our country to end the Brahmins' proscription of education for the Shudras and Atishudras and to empower them. Once they are educated, the Shudras and Atishudras will never forget this great obligation to the English and will prefer, by far, the English government to the Peshwai. But if, like the Mughals, the English too ill-treat their subjects, then, like the supreme Shivaji, the newly educated Shudras and Atishudras will establish their own state and, like the Americans, will govern it themselves. But neither the Brahmin's vision nor their hellish Peshwai will ever come back to power in this land. This Joshibua must always remember. Moreover, these Brahmins who have never realised God themselves, how will they ever enable the Shudra to realise the Supreme?

HUSBAND: Ho Bhatji! Your oppressive Peshwai is never going to be able to find a footing again after people have experienced this English government. Don't even remind us of the terrible exploitation of the Shudras, particularly the Atishudras of the Mang and Mahar castes, by the Peshwai. Once our people are educated under the English rule, they will be aware and will never allow the Bhatbrahmans to do what they please.

MISSIONARY: Patil has not said anything that is untrue. Thanks to God's mercy he has now understood the truth and spoken it without fear or favour. Listening to his honest words issuing forth so simply from his mouth, one may hope that God, after first educating the Shudratishudra, will soon establish that the shastras, designed by you Brahmins, are only cunning constructions. Deceived by your words, they worship this stone idol, but He will stop them from worshipping these idols and will declare to them that He is the true, living God. They will recognise him and He will persuade them to live according to his injunctions. You people, on the other hand, say that everyone should bow down only to you. Then how, in what manner, should they bow down to God?

JOSHI: When they bow down to the Brahmin, everything else is subsumed in it.

VIDUSHAK: (pointing to the audience) People bow down to the Brahmins for enlightenment. My message to all Joshis is that now they should no longer hope that the ignorant Kunbis, Malis, Mangs and Mahars will pay obeisance to them. Henceforth, whenever a Brahmin plays his dirty tricks (while officiating at the marriages of Kunbis, Malis), if you send me word, I will immediately reach the place and tick him off. (Saying this, Vidushak said *salaamwalekum* to all the people and went away.)

MISSIONARY: (turning his face to the Kunbi) Baba, my greatest desire is to speak and enlighten people at all such moments when the Brahmin begins to see himself as God's equal. But now it is evening and I must go. However, whenever you have some time on hand please do stop by my bungalow. Then I can explain to you how he has exploited and deceived you in the name of God. I can see clearly now from his words and expression how false and cunning he is. (Saying this, Padreesaheb put on his hat and walked away.)

HUSBAND: (in great hurry tells his wife) I will go to the shop now and settle Joshi's accounts. You go home and make some bhakri and bhaji for us. What we had in the afternoon did not fill my stomach.

Everyone leaves after this. In a little while the Kunbi returns home.

HUSBAND: I am back having settled Joshi's accounts. Is the food ready?

WOMAN: Yes. (She sets a plate of food before him.) Here, please have your meal.

HUSBAND: My dear, you get your plate too. We will eat together today.

WOMAN: Oh, but you finish first.

HUSBAND: My dear, see that you finish your meal quickly. Today we have understood well the importance of education and because of the advice of that helpful Padreesaheb, and all the events that have taken place since morning, the Bhatbrahmans' deceitful exploitation in duping us ignorant Malis, Kunbis and other Shudra castes for generations through their cunning lies about God and religion is now clear as day. We will finish our meal quickly and head out a little beyond to Jotirao Govindrao Phule's house, where his wife Savitribai Phule has started a school for young girls and women. You please start at this school from today itself and I will join the school for adult men which Jotirao Phule has begun right next to it. The couple gives free education in these two schools. We committed a huge mistake by not going to their school when they had urged us to so many times earlier.

WOMAN: (sitting down to her meal) All right. Let us both go every night to the schools run by the Phules and learn to write and read from today. Only then will we be able to understand all the things in the world.

Jogayi and her husband soon finish their meal and, carrying a slate and chalk in their hands, walk towards the night school for adult men and women which Phule has founded to spread literacy and education.

Notes

1. A translation of *Tritiya Ratna*, in *Mahatma Phule Samagra Vangmay* [The Collected Works of Mahatma Phule], eds, Dhananjay Keer, S. G. Malshe, and Y. D. Phadke (Mumbai: Maharashtra Rajya Sahitya Aani Sanskriti Mandal, 1991[1969]), 1–33.

2. A flat, woven receptacle shaped like a tray, used to clean grain.

3. A *baithak* is a *lavani* performance; a gathering of men at a performance of song and music, perhaps erotic in nature, where a tray of betel leaves or the prepared *beeda* (betel leaf stuffed with a variety of ingredients) is passed around.

4. A Marathi proverb: *Looteche gahu ani babache shradh.*

5. *Sandhyavandan*: a ritual performed by Brahmin men twice a day.

6. This injunction by the Vidushak, which also indicates the activity of *reading* the discussion, points to the argument advanced in the introduction (see pp. 35, 53) that *Tritiya Ratna* is a bookish play.

7. This is a significant gesture which Phule makes to the moderate Brahmin reformist group. *Gyan Prakash* or *Dnyan Prakash* was the first Marathi daily begun in 1849 by Gopal Hari Deshmukh, whose pen name was 'Lokahitwadi'. Here Phule is challenging the moderate Brahmin reformer to wake up and note the discrimination and exploitation taking place in plain sight, and publish it.

8. The Kunbi refers to Virgin Mary as 'Mumma Devi'.

9. This specific stage detail seems a deliberate insertion by Phule and reveals the composition of the audience that he would have desired for a staging of his play. He may have expected not only members of the upper caste, who usually frequented theatrical performances, but also English government officials to be present at an enactment of his play. However, this line could also be interpreted in a more generic sense as the government having eyes and ears everywhere.

10. District officer, a government officer responsible for collecting revenues.

11. A Marathi proverb: *Baap daakhiv nahitar pind paad.*

12. *Dnyanodaya* was a Marathi missionary periodical published by the American Marathi mission that contained not only articles expressing overtly Christian beliefs but also a wide range of essays on subjects such as contemporary advances in geography, natural history, medicine, astronomy and philology. It was a very significant publication in western India that exerted considerable influence on the emerging public sphere and print media.

13. The reference to the precise stanza of the *Manusmriti* is not very clear here since Phule does not mention the chapter number.

14. It is interesting to note that this discussion between the Brahmin, the Missionary and the Kunbi takes place in the open space just outside the temple. This space can be construed as a metonym for the public sphere. I am indebted to Christian Lee Novetzke for this insight, as well as the point made in note 6.

Political Uses of Poetry

'Vidyakhatyateel Brahman Pantoji'

The last few years have seen a simmering resistance on Indian university campuses. They came to a boil following the tragic suicide by Rohit Vemula. The repercussions of this cataclysmic event, in combination with resistance to significant policy decisions in the Indian educational system, has created a ferment amongst the youth in university campuses. Several excellent analyses of these have appeared in well-regarded newspapers and periodicals. Many of them position the immediate tragic developments within the larger context of the traditional historical exclusion of the lower castes from learning and education. These analyses form a continuum with other scholarly interventions that have been made since the 1990s in the wake of the recommendations of the Mandal Commission and its implementation, amongst the other significant developments of that tumultuous decade in Indian politics and society.[1] Such examinations of a complex reality attempted by social scientists must be seen together with the several anthologies of Dalit writing in translation published in the last few decades.[2] This body of analytic and creative literature enables an informed debate on the networks of exclusion that operate in formal and informal fashion on Indian campuses and reproduce caste inequalities in the education system of India. This discussion does not, however, intend to address the contemporary or even the post-independence scenario obtained in Indian universities; nor does it attempt to construct an empirical template for such an examination. It proposes only to recuperate and translate a Marathi text, written around the mid-nineteenth century, in order to document one of the earliest modern assertions of caste inequity in the academy, in the hope that this literary intervention may enable us to historicise the continuum of protest against constructions of knowledge and the discriminatory practices in the education system that prevail in India. The literary text under discussion emerges from one of the earliest, and perhaps the most influential, modern movements under the leadership of Jotiba Phule in the Marathi-speaking region of western India during the nineteenth century. Phule's Marathi poem, which is translated into English for the very first time, is titled 'Brahmin Teachers in the Education Department'. It encodes aspiration for education as one of the most important grounds of lower-caste mobilisation.

The next sections will examine the role of the *powada* in Marathi literary tradition, Phule's reinvention of it in 'Brahmin Teachers in the Education Department', followed by its translation in English.

THE POWADA IN MARATHI LITERARY AND PERFORMATIVE TRADITION

An oral and performance-based genre of poetry, the powada marked its beginning during the late seventeenth century, extolling Shivaji's daring exploits, and had established itself by the time the Peshwas consolidated their power. As mentioned above, like the ballad in Western literature, the powada is a commemorative and celebratory form of poetry, with vivid evocations of battles and descriptions of the various victories of the chief or the warlord, as the case may be, meant to inspire valour and affinity with the ruling class. Originally performed by a Dalit community belonging to the Gondhal caste, such itinerant performances knit together the diverse populations of the Marathi-speaking region with their tales of contemporary Maratha history. The first powada according to the gazette of Maharashtra is 'Afzal Khanacha Vadh' performed in 1659 which describes the killing of Afzal Khan by Shivaji as a stirring act of courage and war strategy. Subsequently there were several powadas on Shivaji's heroism commemorating his victories over the Mughal in various battles. The itinerant performances of the powadas commemorating heroes and battles and the circulation of these in the countryside was crucial, as Prachi Deshpande notes, in the creation of a shared historical memory (Deshpande 2007: 56–57). The common folk also identified with this history since the concerns of the foot soldier, who was generally a peasant when not a part of military excursions, and his world of folk religious practices were an integral part of these narrations. The lead singers/composers of the powada are known as *shahirs* in Marathi, and the Peshwa period is known for shahirs such as Ram Joshi, Anant Phandi and Honaji Bala who composed many powadas celebrating the military exploits of the Peshwa rulers (Nadkarni 1921: 172).

As an oral and performative genre, a great deal of improvisation marks the actual performance of the powada which factors in the specific cultural and political features of its immediate surroundings. Traditionally shahirs were known for their ability to compose almost instantaneously as they sang, each performance being a variation on certain set events or well-known historical persons. Even if written versions of powadas are available today (and they were also written down historically: perhaps records of oral performances), a shahir almost never performs from any written text; it is always an extempore performance. Powadas have starkly alternating rhythms and movements to represent the narrator/singer's voice typically addressing different events or persons, known as *chaal*, rendered in my translation as 'movement'.

Within a few decades after the end of the Peshwa rule, marking the change in the ruling dispensation, the early nationalist leaders of Maharashtra began to use the powada as a means of articulating anti-imperialist sentiments, questioning colonial power. However, Phule's preoccupation was with the toiling masses and not with the elite aspiration for freedom. Typically, he employed the powada, as was the case with all his writings, to raise the consciousness of exploitation and oppression amongst the lower-caste masses. Radical as always and original in his invention of new forms or reinvention of existing literary forms, Phule is almost certainly the first person to employ the powada as a satire and an interrogation of Brahmin hegemony. Intriguingly, Phule's reinvention of the powada has set the tradition for its deployment in post-independence India. In the 1950s shahirs such as Amar Sheikh, Annabhau Sathe and others belonging to the Communist Party of India used the powada to expose and interrogate the policies of the government. From the 1980s a new consensus between Ambedkarite forces and the left ideology has marked protests against exploitation. Sambhaji Bhagat is perhaps the most well-known contemporary shahir who sings powadas satirising imperialist globalising forces, communal politics and the age-old caste system.

POLITICAL USES OF THE POWADA

While Phule's powada on Shivaji, titled 'Chhatrapati Shivaji Raje Bosale yancha Powada' where he recuperated the history of Shivaji as a non-Brahmin leader (CWMP 1991[1969]: 34–81), seems to be within the celebratory tradition of the genre, he yet commemorated this beloved Maratha king as a Shudra protector of his people, infusing into his narration the consciousness of caste identity and solidarity. However, in both 'Brahmananche Kasab' ('Priestcraft Exposed' in Phule's English title) that presented the theme of an idyllic pre-Aryan India under the just rule of the folk king Baliraja and the destruction of this by multiple Aryan/Brahmin invasions (ibid.: 91–118) and 'Vidyakhatyateel Brahman Pantoji' (ibid.: 83–90), Phule deploys the form subversively for modern political purposes, interrogating power and hierarchy. It may be noted that in keeping with the traditional features of the powada, Phule does construct in 'Brahmananche Kasab' a historical memory. This memory, however, is not of a recent event but that of the ancient past. It builds on the hypotheses of an Aryan race and invasion, then current in emerging disciplines of comparative philology and Indology. In this powada Phule presents an alternative and subversive counter-historical memory of a harmonious pre-Aryan society destroyed by the cruelty and cunning of the invading Aryan/Brahmins.

In his third ballad, 'Vidyakhatyateel Brahman Pantoji' which he wrote in 1869 (henceforth 'Brahmin Teachers in the Education Department'), Phule jettisons historicity and focuses on contemporary educational institutions and the conditions obtained therein. Structured on two complementing stanzaic forms and rhythms, this powada deftly sketches a realistic portrayal of the rural environment and its intrinsic connection to larger oppressive structures at the macro level. While music and performance are essential for the full appreciation and enjoyment of a powada, we will attempt nevertheless to examine the main issues which Phule dramatises through his presentation of the functioning of a village school.

Phule's 'Vidyakhatyateel Brahman Pantoji'

The powada opens with a moving evocation of hardworking, impoverished, lower-caste parents grieving over their children's lack of access to schools and the sight of their wards at work when they ought to have been getting an education. In sharp satiric couplets, Phule contrasts their situation with the callousness of the Brahmin teacher and the village upper castes who are instrumental in driving the Untouchable Mahar child away, but are eager to 'shake hands with the English'. The alternating longer stanza establishes the larger political background of the times: Brahmins reject the Shudratishudra and curry favour with the English even as they slyly instigate rebellions against the Queen. Like most subaltern leaders, Phule clearly reposes faith in the colonial government to safeguard the interests of the lower castes within the exploitative caste structure. The description of the enslavement of the Shudra and the clever positioning of the reference to the abolitionist movement in North America is meant to show the correspondences between the caste system and slavery. It is also an appeal to the colonial government asking for its understanding and support.

Phule sketches the figure of the Brahmin teacher at work with scathing satire: he favours the Brahmin child and beats up the Shudra children. Phule's stinging derision quickly notes the dozing teacher: the Pantoji in Marathi, a term which superbly captures the hypocrisy of the pompous Brahmin, who is startled awake by the recess bell and rushes home for a leisurely lunch and siesta and who may or may not go back to work. The longer stanza questions the school master's putative virtues since his interests are only in inflating his report for the English inspector and fabricating ideas about the dullness of the Shudra caste.

The alternating rhythms focus on two related spatial and temporal dimensions. The first is the immediate present comprising the village school and its Brahmin teacher doctoring his books so as to please his English superiors. The second is at the macro level caustically critiquing Brahmin duplicity in general: 'Liberal thoughts only to please the English/Back home stone idols are their worship'. The last long stanza is an appeal to the colonial government, pleading that experienced teachers from the lower and Untouchable castes be appointed in order to educate deprived children. It is a petition to the colonial government urging it to reject Brahmin teachers who are more often than not inept, insincere and unconcerned about the education of the lower-caste, underprivileged children. Only then, says the poet, will the English government 'be hailed as great' when it ensures 'schooling for the disadvantaged'.

It is necessary to recuperate, translate and examine this powada in the present context for a number of reasons. I will list only three: First, the conditions of the nineteenth-century academic environment which Phule describes uncannily resemble the contemporary system of public education in rural India. It is crucial to examine its historical evocation if the problem is to be understood comprehensively and if these historical lacunae and the exclusions inherent in the delivery of educational policies are to be addressed with any degree of sincerity. Second, both nationalist and subaltern historiographies have erased the significant contributions of Phule's movement on behalf of the lower castes and his original and radical interventions in the creation of a non-Brahmin identity in the politics and culture of his times. The reasons for the erasure may have been the perception that he is 'soft' and rather uncritical about exploitation resulting from forces of imperialism. However, within the context of his times, modernity in the form of the colonial government and its secular institutions must have seemed a real alternative to Phule, disillusioned as he was by the tenacious hold of the caste structure in the minds and hearts of people. Third, the category known as Dalit literature in the last few decades is perceived, it seems to me, in curiously flattened and unhistorical terms. Phule's literary works form a legacy that helps recuperate this rich past of interrogations and interventions. The translation is an attempt to historicise the significance of a Dalit literary past.

Notes

1. See, for instance, Rege 2010.

2. Note the several anthologies of Dalit writing in English translation published in the last two decades by the Oxford University Press, Orient BlackSwan and Penguin India, among other publishing houses.

'Brahmin Teachers in the Education Department'[1]

Peasants labour, the powerful profit,
Rich kids get an education.

Malis and Kunbis toil to pay taxes,
There is little left to cover their backs.

Tiny hands tend grazing herds,
Small feet wander bare, blister in the sun.

With no time to educate, parents grieve,
Brooding, curse fate and God's will.

Authors of mischief under a sham of learning
Brahmin pundits[2] flourish in little village schools.

The Kulkarni[3] cobbles together a few kids,
Reports excess numbers in the list!

Pollution! they cry, and drive Mahar children out,
But eagerly shake hands with the English.

Movement[4]

We slave for the Brahmins, we do!
Without any grudge or shame
Why do they think we are enemies?
We are eternally slaves:
Even if America repented,
You (the English) will be our lords still.[5]

Other faiths the Brahmins decry; Brahma,
They say, is Supreme.
This is the truth, this the false ethic
Slyly handed down to poor Shudra kids.
The Pundit instills malice against the Queen
And is the abettor of much mischief.[6]
Assured in his rank and station,
Ensures learning only for his ilk.

The Pundit is patient with Brahmin kids,
Repeats lessons and corrects their slips.

A terror when a Shudra child trips,
The Pundit rains blows and slaps his cheeks,

Sends him packing from school,
Keeps full, though, the numbers in his books.

He bows and scrapes when officials visit,
All ready to prate and gossip.

Movement

They say he is virtuous: the school master.
They praise him to the skies, swell his ego.
I know him well and this is what I sing:
An overseer by caste, all he does
Is inspect the muster,
And inflate his report!

The Pundit proclaims falsehoods: he says
The Shudra caste is dull,
Has no love for letters.

The Brahmin is the true seeker they affirm,
Has anyone tested these claims ever?

Selfish fabrications these, so blindly consumed.
The result: no needy child gets an education!

The Pundit is busy with his daily rites,
It's the other kids that mark attendance,

Fool around with the children of the Shudra,
Bully them in his stead.

At eight the Pundit enters with a show of hurry,
Enthroned on his chair, yet restless still

Watchful of the shadows and the clock,
He teaches the Brahmin kids till ten.

Pressing his forehead as if tired,
He mops the sweat off his brow.

Feigning how hard at work he really is,
Slowly rests his head on the table.

Wakes at lunch hour with a start,
In a wink he is off!

Movement

After lunch a blissful slumber,
Then the newspaper;
Perhaps a letter that must be sent,
And to the school only later,
After the midday sun has cooled,
And teach only if it suits his mood.

We speak from our history, we do,
The Pundit turns to dust
All our yearning to learn
And educate.

Brahmins recite the scriptures,
Assert their rights, and dupe
The guileless Shudra.

Extract fees and offerings,
But block their aspiration for learning,

Then hold the Shudra up to ridicule:
These are their wily games and politics.

Liberal thoughts only to please the English,
Back home stone idols are their worship.

Such are the frauds they appoint
And anoint those whom they teach as educated!

They are learned frogs preaching to snakes,
What an end to enlightenment!

Movement

Appoint teachers from other castes, we appeal,
Who are models of true understanding:
They will take over the task of teaching.
Choose some among the Malis and Kunbis;
Others from Mahars and Mangs,
Let's have teachers with experience.

Only then will the tree flower
And hang heavy with ripening fruit.
Only then may the Shudra rejoice
And the English be shamed.

No one cares for the Shudra child, Joti grieves,
Besides a few Christian missionaries.

If you, our lords, are to be hailed as great,
Ensure schooling for the disadvantaged.

Notes

1. A translation of 'Vidyakhatyateel Brahman Pantoji', in *Mahatma Phule Samagra Vangmay* [The Collected Works of Mahatma Phule], eds, Dhananjay Keer, S. G. Malshe, and Y. D. Phadke (Mumbai: Maharashtra Rajya Sahitya Aani Sanskriti Mandal, 1991[1969]), 83–90.

Phule's works addressed two broad sets of public: the first was the subaltern groups that he wished to unite and mobilise politically, and the second was the combine of British administrators and European missionaries whom he wished to enlist in his cause. He wrote in Marathi for the first, but provided some information in English or at least the English translations of the title for the second. The original English title of this poem is 'Our Brahmin-ridden Policy-Educational System'.

2. Phule deploys the word 'Pantoji', then in currency, for the Brahmin school teacher. This word is derived from the root '*pant*' which means a scholar Brahmin, to which the Persian suffix 'ji' is added as a marker of respect. Phule's aim here is to satirise the Brahmin school teacher.

3. Kulkarnis are generally Brahmin and their traditional caste occupation used to be book-keeping and maintaining records in the old rural setting. Village lore depicts the Kulkarni as a person of cunning known for his sharp practices.

4. The *shahir* who sang the powada changed the tempo at intervals known as *chaal*, here translated as 'movement'.

5. Perhaps the first person to see the commonalities between caste oppression in India and slavery in America, Phule's seminal work is the prose polemic titled *Gulamgiri*, which he published in the year 1873 along with a title in English: *Slavery*. Even as Phule believed that the British rule had the potential to unshackle the lower caste and women from Brahmin hegemony, he was engaged in an ongoing struggle to represent this cause to the British administration, which tended on the whole to rely on the elite Brahmin classes.

6. Phule attempts to show the cupidity and cunning of the elite classes to the colonial British government. Phule lived through the events of 1857 but had only contempt for this revolt which he believed was a self-serving attempt to wrest power from the British by Indian elites.

Situating Phule within the History of Education in India

In 1813 the British Parliament introduced a new clause in the charter of the East India Company, directing it to undertake responsibility for the education of Indians and making it incumbent on the Government of India to set apart a sum of not less than one lakh rupees for this purpose. It is important to note that Britain did not yet have in place a formal system of public education that addressed the needs of educating its poor and working-class populations: this would take shape only by 1833. Moreover, it had hardly been the East India Company's original policy to impose a system of education, Western or native, upon its Indian subjects.

These are among several important facts that should be considered in any analysis of the history of education in India. They are helpful in reaching a realistic understanding of an evolving and dynamic situation on the ground during the colonial period, in which events and outcomes in the metropole and the colony were linked in a visceral fashion. As Bernard Cohn has observed, 'metropole and colony have to be seen in a unitary field of analysis' (Cohn 1996: 4). Jotiba Phule's lifelong struggle to enable the marginalised sections of society gain access to education and the several interventions he made in the public sphere of nineteenth-century Maharashtra by means of his activism and writing may be understood better by positioning his attempts against the wider canvas comprising colonial policy, missionary initiatives, and the Indian reciprocation to these. The following discussion will attempt to locate two of Phule's prose writings in English: the 'Preface' to *Gulamgiri* (1873) and his petition submitted to the Indian Education Commission set up in 1882 under the chairmanship of William Hunter against this background. Secondly, how are Phule's interventions to be understood within the framework of the major directions of research in the field of the historiography of education in post-independence India? A brief account of the salient trends and approaches to research in this field is outlined below, followed in the next section by an examination of the background to educational reform in the nineteenth century.

THE CONTEMPORARY FIELD OF STUDY: TRENDS AND DIRECTIONS

Historians who worked on the development of education in India immediately after independence attributed the initiatives behind educational policy to colonial administrative governance. For instance, S. Nurrullah and J. P. Naik examined the role of the colonial government in setting the agenda for educational change and ensuing modernisation, seeing missionary work in education as part of this process (Nurullah and Naik 1943). Some years later, integral to the research trend examining imperialism, the focus was on tracing the connections between developments in education and the growth of Indian nationalism, examining the influence of Western liberal thought in consolidating ideas of an independent Indian nation-state. This direction of research followed two trajectories. The first was the role of the upper-caste Indian elite in the formation and emergence of Indian nationalism; in most cases, these elite sections had been educated in the newly set up government educational institutions in the Bengal, Bombay and Madras Presidencies which offered an 'English' curriculum (McCully 1940; Seal 1971[1968]). The second trajectory of research explored the significance of colonial interest in Oriental studies and the material support and encouragement given to young budding officers in learning languages and studying texts in Sanskrit, Persian and Arabic. Historians examining this phenomenon argued that it succeeded in acquainting Indians with their own culture, thereby setting off a movement towards recovering the idea of a nation conceived in indigenous terms (Kopf 1969).

Connected to these trends, but at a slight remove, is the nationalist reading of the history of education in India. The genesis of this goes back to the early decades of the twentieth century and may also be seen in the public statements made by Mahatma Gandhi and in the philosophy underpinning his experiments in schooling undertaken in the various kinds of community living which he initiated in South Africa and India. These experiments were later concretised in ideas such as *Nai Taleem*. With some variations, these ideas are reflected in Tagore's conceptions and in the founding principles of his initiatives in education as seen in Shantiniketan. In an address given in London in 1931, Gandhi described the widespread system of village-based local schools present in pre-colonial India as a 'beautiful tree' and asserted that after a hundred years of British rule, Indians were more illiterate than before. Philip Hartog, an educationist and the former vice-chancellor of Dacca University, contested these views. He had an extended debate with Gandhi on the veracity of the latter's claims of a system of elementary education in existence before British interventions in India and wrote this up in a book published in 1939 (Hartog 1939). Decades later Dharampal decided to research on Gandhi's assertions and undertook a meticulous examination of the educational surveys initiated in the Bengal, Madras and Bombay Presidencies during the 1820s and 1830s, soon after the clause for the education of Indians was inserted into the Company Charter of 1813. In his book *The Beautiful Tree* Dharampal (2000[1983]), drawing on the data gathered by the British colonial administration, suggested that the British had indeed destroyed the roots of the beautiful tree which had been the indigenous system of village schools. This system of education had once prevailed all over the subcontinent spanning present-day India, Pakistan and Bangladesh, wherein the transmission of basic elementary knowledge, though organised informally, had a continuity through the centuries of Indian history. Dharampal's sources were the reports published by William Adam in the years 1835–38 on the survey of indigenous education conducted in the region of Bengal and Bihar; the survey undertaken during the period 1822–25 in the Madras Presidency ordered by its Governor Sir Thomas Munro, which included the well-known and detailed report by A. D. Campbell, the Collector of Bellary; the survey carried out during the 1820s in the Bombay Presidency; and G. W. Leitner's 1882 survey conducted in the Punjab. Dharampal's book also includes as appendices extracts from a few of these sources. Munro asserted that every village had a school, which was also reiterated in Adam's famous statement that there were around 1,00,000 village schools in Bengal and Bihar when the survey was conducted in the 1830s. G. L. Pendergast and Leitner made similar statements in their reports for the Bombay and Punjab Presidencies. More crucially Adam's reports reveal that elementary education was not exclusive to the upper castes but included Shudra and Untouchable pupils and teachers, though higher education was the sole preserve of the higher castes. The reports from the Bombay Presidency do indicate Shudra presence but not those of Untouchable boys. Except for some reports from the Madras Presidency, none of the surveys note the inclusion of female children in the village schools, and this is an omission which Dharampal does not dwell upon. In his introduction to the book, he puts forward the argument that the indigenous system of schooling had served Indians well and was, in fact, much more advanced in quality and reach than the one obtained in England around the same time. While it is true that there was no free and compulsory education in England till 1870, schooling was becoming widespread in urban areas from the beginning of the nineteenth century in the wake of rapid industrialisation and the efforts of puritans and reformists which will be discussed shortly. Importantly, the curriculum in English schools used printed books which promoted a significant advancement of knowledge, unlike the Indian indigenous system.

In independent India, Gandhi's work on education and his views continue to exert influence on the philosophy underpinning a number of educational initiatives. One of India's most respected academics on education, Krishna Kumar sees in Gandhi's ideas an innate capacity to envision learning as linked to the social and economic needs of the immediate community. He sees them as a critique of the centralised top-down examination-oriented approach promoted by colonial education in order to produce drudges without creative autonomy (Kumar 2005[1991]). In several books and articles, Kumar has argued that India after independence has not been able to shake off the alienating and utilitarian basis of colonial education. However, such views have, in turn, been critiqued as embodying upper-caste Hindu values which patronise the lower castes and deny them their rightful access to intellectual education and restrict their potential to vocational training (Rao, Parimala 2014). Alternative histories of education by Eleanor Zelliot (2002, 2014), Padma Velaskar (2012) and Philip Constable (2000) focus on the struggles of the lower castes and Dalits to power movements that resulted in the creation of educational institutions and/or at least a rightful space within institutions.

From the 1980s, postcolonial historians have worked through the theoretical perspectives offered by Edward Said (distilled in turn from Michel Foucault), and deployed these to understand the colonial exercise of power through its monopoly on knowledge. They question the belief reposed in the colonial power's modernising mission. For instance, in her well-known study, Gauri Viswanathan argues that the liberal ideas of the Enlightenment acted in fact as a mask of conquest, as an instrument of control that in reality worked to strengthen colonial cultural hegemony. The pedagogical construction of English literature thus became a secular mode of inculcating Christian moral principles, thereby molding Indians to colonial purposes (Viswanathan 1989). In recent years such postcolonial positions derived from Said's influential ideas on Orientalism have been questioned. The sharp binary which Said argues existed in the control of Western power over the discourse of non-Western knowledge systems, while perhaps true of the Islamic world, simply does not address 'the seductive and collaborative' way it played out in Indo-European interactions says Braj Ranjan Mani, who discusses the 'collusive role' played by Indian elites in the making of the Oriental stereotype of Indian culture and civilisation (Mani 2005: 195). Not only did the indigenous elite play a substantial role in consolidating the Orientalist body of knowledge, their interests and motives also influenced, to an extent, the framing of colonial policy in India. Emphasising that colonial knowledge was not just a Western superimposition, Sumit Sarkar has drawn attention to the role of privileged groups in enhancing their own autonomous interests and cultural inclinations (Sarkar 1997: 23). In his perceptive work Thomas Trautmann points to substantial ideological differences within British Orientalists and the many shortcomings of the blanket term 'Orientalism' that works more as prejudice in seeing the entire colonised society as a passive victim of colonisation (Trautmann 2004: 17). Parimala Rao asserts that archival evidence does not support the imputations which Viswanathan makes either about colonial interventions or missionary endeavour (Rao, Parimala 2015: 305–307). Robert E. Frykenberg challenges received perceptions surrounding English as a colonial imposition, dismissing it as 'the Myth of Macaulay's Minute', pointing to the initiatives taken by elite Indians to introduce English education in India (Frykenberg 1988: 305). This body of research questioning the general contours of postcolonial theoretical positions shows that the demand for English education was steadily on the rise several years before Thomas B. Macaulay reached the shores of India and dismisses the rather immoderate significance which this theory ascribes to colonial policy, whether seeing it as beneficial or exploitative.

Moreover, though Macaulay's Minute in 1835, Wood's Despatch in 1854 and the Education Commission in 1882 were important statements, these policies were always checked and balanced by the responses to government directives at local levels in small towns and villages, as Constable demonstrates in his incisive paper on Untouchable educational protests in late nineteenth-century western India (Constable 2000). One has to differentiate between this essay which is an example of alternative historiography and the work done by the subaltern studies scholars which is again Foucauldian in its paradigmatic approach and argues that elite transmission of knowledge in colonial India marginalised peasant and tribal forms. Bernard Cohn's celebrated study 'The Command of Language and the Language of Command', for instance, examines the suppression of subaltern knowledge and education (Cohn 1985). Cohn suggests that forms of knowledge that were subterranean in nature and dissented from elite versions began to be systematically marginalised from the colonial times. Contesting this position is the work of historians who examine the agency of women, Dalits, Muslims and working people at large in extending the circumference of educational opportunities for these sections of society. Two volumes edited by Sabyasachi Bhattacharya include excellent studies by several scholars who push against received perspectives and, with a fine eye for archival detail, recover precisely the achievements of pioneering individuals who led crucial movements that resulted in concrete gains for the disprivileged (Bhattacharya 1998; 2002).

More recent research on the historiography of education in India explores the interconnected and entangled histories of colonial rule (Bagchi 2014). It gives prominence to the active investment of Indians in shaping, through the nature of their demands and concerted mobilisation of opinion, not only colonial policy on education but also the actual outcomes on the ground. It also emphasises the less-than-smooth interactions in India between the East India Company, with its arguably rather grubby aims, and the initiatives of Protestant missionaries with the larger set of their evangelical goals; and it underscores the cross-influences of all these on an intrinsically diverse and hierarchical Indian society with its own inherent past of formative encounters with other cultures, such as the Mughal, that had had a structural presence in the indigenous system of schooling already present in the country.

REFORMERS, EVANGELICALS AND THE EAST INDIA COMPANY

It may be significant to note the connections between reformist opinion in Britain, its influence in the British Parliament and the resulting outcomes in the governing schemes of the Company, and locate the unfolding of educational policy in colonial India within the political and social developments taking place in the metropole. Despite popular notions of colonisation and the exclusive duality of the metropole and colony which haunts postcolonial studies, British experiences abroad were not isolated from developments at home.

While a missionary clause had been inserted in the Company's charter as early as 1698, this was mainly to enable the Company to maintain ministers of religion in their factories in India and chaplains aboard ships (Naik and Nurullah 1974[1945]: 33–38). These chaplains were instrumental in starting charity schools for the benefit of Anglo-Indian children as well as initiating in a small way incipient proselytising activities. However, these initiatives came into question after 1765 when the East India Company became a political power. All the energies of the Company were directed to the capture of those kingdoms that were still holding strong. Anxious not to jeopardise its increasingly comprehensive hold over the country even as the Mughal Empire crumbled from within, the Company wished to maintain the appearance of strict religious neutrality and curbed missionary enterprise. However, from the late eighteenth century, information in the form of images and narratives about the colonies was carried back to the metropole by the traffic of adventurers, traders and the few priests stationed in India and started permeating the public discourse in Britain. It is around the same time when the condition of the working class in England and the necessity of addressing its spiritual needs began to impinge upon the consciousness of reformers and evangelicals that they also realised the state of affairs in the non-Christian world. Bourgeois and missionary literature and public lectures presented the British labouring poor and the Empire's heathens as two sides of the same overriding concern (Pennington 2005: 25). Though different creations, yet the British labourer and the pagan in the colony became twinned in the eyes of the evangelical reformer as groups that were spiritually impoverished. We realise today that the source and the process whereby these two groups came to the notice of the reformers and the missionaries were two faces of the same historical phenomenon: the Industrial Revolution and colonisation. The effects of the Industrial Revolution were noted in the breaking up of traditional rural England and the drawing of its inhabitants to an alienating urban landscape without the nurturing ties of religion and kindred. The rapid deterioration of the workers' physical, mental and moral health became the focus of concern, leading to a mobilisation of opinion that legislative protection and Christian compassion were both of urgent necessity in ameliorating the corrosive impact.

By the later decades of the eighteenth century, a host of charitable organisations emerged with the goal of addressing the material and spiritual needs of the illiterate and disprivileged belonging to both British and foreign territories. The anti-slavery movement, the spread of evangelical thought and missionary societies, the proliferation of Sunday schools and the distribution of popular religious tracts are phenomena that marked this period. A few of the men and women who worked with great zeal for the cause were champions of liberal reform. Quite often, however, they were conservatives working to protect the status quo and to consolidate British interests. Yet they were the people heading the winds of change in ideas such as the end to enslavement, universal education and the popular press, the flipside of which was also economic globalisation and religious nationalism (Pennington 2005: 23–24).

The missionary movement was born out of this set of concerns. The Society for Promoting Christian Knowledge was founded as early as 1698, followed in 1701 by the setting up of the Society for the Propagation of the Gospel in Foreign Parts. The 1730s were marked by the charity school movement which led within a few decades to the Sunday school and anti-slavery campaigns. These movements culminated logically in the missionary movement from the late eighteenth century, which concerned itself with the working class and the destitute, extending the scope of its interest to foreigners under British influence. Several major societies and bodies were formed as a part of this groundswell of evangelical thought, and a few of its founders went on to have long careers in India. In 1792 William Carey set up the Baptist Missionary Society, making ardent pleas in his writings for Christian attention to the 'heathen' world seen in the pamphlet 'An Enquiry into the Obligation of Christians to Use Means for the Conversion of the Heathen'. Since Company policy did not permit him entry into British-ruled territories, Carey travelled through other parts of India and finally established one of the first British Missions at Serampore near Calcutta in the Danish-administered part of the region along with William Ward and Joshua Marshman. Confronted by disease, death and immense personal danger, the 'Serampore Trio', as Carey, Ward and Marshman came to be known, set up their missionary press and published many accounts of Hindu practices for consumption back home in addition to printing the Bible and educational material in several Indian languages. Ward went on to publish many voluminous studies of the Hindu religion, becoming the most important source of information for the evangelicals and Utilitarians. Ward's works came to presage a counter-perspective to an impression of Hinduism as a poetic and refined religion in circulation in the metropole as a result of the translations of Sanskrit texts such as the *Shakuntala* and the *Bhagavad Gita* by the Orientalists William Jones and Charles Wilkins, respectively (Potts 1967: 92). In 1795 the London Missionary Society was founded by a group belonging to different Christian denominations. One of the most important British missionary bodies that was to wield immense power in the next two centuries was the Church Missionary Society set up by a group of evangelicals associated with the Anglican Church in 1799. A few years later the Methodist and Scottish churches would follow suit with their own mission outfits. All these missions shared similar concerns about attacking darkness with the light of evangelical knowledge, whether at home or abroad. In his study *Was Hinduism Invented?*, Brian Pennington suggests that the evangelical campaign invigorated and cemented the idea of a national church gluing diverse people such as the Welsh, the Scots and the English in a sense of common national identity (Pennington 2005: 42). This national identity was made possible because it was defining itself against a 'pagan' people such as the Hindus, legitimising the evangelical mission to save the various people under British rule in foreign regions. Visual images of the pagan together with verbal descriptions of Hindu rites were printed and circulated in popular pamphlets in a bid to generate public interest in evangelical activity at home and the pressing need for missions abroad. We will soon examine the influence of missionary literature, including its interpretation of Hinduism, on Phule's formulations of Hindu mythology for political mobilisation.

Protestant Christianity in Britain was beginning to be concerned with its retreat from the lives of the working classes and the poor whose leisure hours had declined due to longer hours demanded by factories. Evangelicals were instrumental in the passage of Sabbath laws and by these means promoting church and Sunday school attendance among the working classes. Sunday schools were the institutions through which the unchurched could be moulded into becoming recognisably Christian: this recognition led to a drive to spread such schools throughout Britain. Though they taught only reading, evangelisation powered a national concern for the reform of the lower classes through education. The spectacle of the French Revolution raging just across the Channel may have no doubt exerted a self-serving prudence amongst the ruling classes to bridge the alienation that the working classes might feel by giving them a stake in the dominant culture of the elites. In times when wealth was pouring into the country thanks to Britain's increasing clout in the colonies, Hannah More preached frugality to both the rich and the poor, seeing it as a necessary virtue in the making of a disciplined Christian character. Her friend and patron, William Wilberforce, Member of Parliament from 1780 to 1825, better known for his fight to abolish the British slave trade, wished to extend the scope of evangelical zeal and bring Christian piety and the Bible to domestic as well as foreign constituencies. Though Wilberforce had nurtured radical leanings in his younger years, with time he was to present two very distinct aspects to his personality: a liberal crusader who led an impassioned battle against slavery, but also a social and political conservative who was instrumental in ruthlessly trampling down assertions of democratic rights and who famously persecuted those who published and sold Thomas Paine's books.[1] This is an important point to note in Phule's context, for in this intrepid Indian subaltern leader one sees influences of both Paine's radical ideas as well as the representations of Hinduism which the British evangelicals propagated in their lectures and writings.

Wilberforce and More were members of the Clapham Sect, an informal association of moderate Anglican evangelicals, which had connections with the ruling forces of government and a concern to bring Christian gospel to all people in Britain and abroad. This group comprised members of Parliament, prominent clergy and government officials with strong connections to India who were able to direct public policy that would extend the reach of Christian institutions and ideas. We must remember that one of its members at the time was the evangelical Charles Grant, who had returned to England after serving several years in India as an employee of the East India Company, rising through its ranks to important positions and was to be elected a Member of Parliament in 1802. Grant joined the Company's Court of Directors in 1804 and was appointed its chairman in 1805. He, along with Wilberforce, was responsible for establishing the spread of missions in India.

In 1792 Grant wrote his highly influential book proposing the evangelisation of the 'heathen' titled *Observations of the State of Society among the Asiatic Subjects of Great Britain* and pressed for 'measures which might be adopted by Great Britain for the improvement in the condition of Asiatic subjects' (Grant, cited in Pennington 2005: 42). Galvanised by the momentum which the missionaries had managed to generate in England, Wilberforce was able to move a resolution for inserting the missionary clause when the Company's charter came up for renewal in 1793. However, the Court of Directors having realised the prudence of being detached in cultural matters and not wanting to have messy religious issues cloud their single-minded pursuit of monopolistic control over trade in India, which meant defeating other European powers such as the French, the Portuguese, the Dutch and the Danes jostling for supremacy in the subcontinent, resisted this pressure from the missionary lobby. This led to considerable hostility in the Company's stance towards the missionaries to which the latter retaliated with criticism of the Company's political and commercial undertakings and the personal conduct of its officers (Naik and Nurullah 1974[1945]: 34–40). We must recall that the impeachment of Warren Hastings, the first Governor General of India, and his long-drawn trial before he was acquitted, took place between 1787 and 1795, and this very public case exemplifies the strong polarisation of opinion that characterised the period. Grant's *Observations* was published in 1797 and was to have considerable influence in stepping up the missionary pressure on the Parliament and the firming up of public opinion on the veracity of its claims. This culminated in the Charter Act of 1813: a milestone as far as developments in the Company's implementation of educational policy in India is concerned.

When the Company's Charter came up in 1813 for its periodic renewal, two issues related to the 'interests and happiness of the native inhabitants of the British dominions in India' were discussed (Naik and Nurullah 1974[1945]: 39). The first of these was the necessity of permitting missionaries to enter and work in the territories of the Company for the education and proselytisation of the Indians. As seen above, the groundwork for this had been carefully prepared, and the missionary lobby had no difficulty in having this approved. However, there was considerable ambivalence on the second question of whether the Company should accept responsibility for the education of the Indian people. Related to this question was also the confusion as to the nature and scope of such educational activities. In times when education was not a state responsibility even in England, the Company resisted the demands which the education clause would impose upon its finances. However, it is surmised that the Company finally acquiesced to the new clause since the opponents of the mission clauses within the organisation felt it was incumbent on them to create a powerful rival agency in Indian education to counteract the results of missionary enterprise. Be that as it may, the Company was directed to set aside a sum of 'not less than one lakh of rupees in each year' and use it for 'the revival and improvement of literature and the encouragement of the learned natives of India and for the introduction and promotion of the knowledge of science among the inhabitants of the British territories in India' (Naik and Nurullah 1974[1945]: 40).

INDIANS, MISSIONARIES AND THE SHAPING OF COLONIAL POLICY

Colonial Policy

From 1765 the East India Company became a political power in India after its resounding victories in Plassey and Buxar had all but reduced the Mughal nawabs to the position of pensioners in the prosperous Bengal and Bihar regions. Soon it was to comprehensively expand its military footprint over territories and rulers in other parts of the country. However, the Company still felt the need to placate the Muslim and Hindu elite it had so summarily displaced and let the cultural aspects of the earlier dispensation continue in order not to affect its territorial expansion and its profitable run of monopoly in trade. Towards this end the Company had to make an investment to understand the land which it had conquered as well as its people and the religious laws that governed their lives. This naturally resulted in an effort to know the religious and legal texts of its Hindu and Muslim populations. Many of its officers in important positions came to nurture a genuine and abiding interest and scholarship in Sanskrit, Persian and Arabic, and believed that the study of classical Indian literature should be encouraged. With the help of native scholars, they were to translate seminal texts from these languages into English. It was this passion that underpinned the earlier volumes of the journal *Asiatic Researches*, which was published by the Asiatic Society founded by William Jones in 1784 'as an advertisement for the beauty and antiquity of Indian civilization' (Pennington 2005: 20). Said's work should alert us, however, to the fact that this passion went along with a strong commitment to Christian theology and the expansion and perpetuation of the colonial state. Guided by these several factors, the Company adopted an Orientalist policy in education between the years 1781–91 that basically encouraged classical learning in Sanskrit and Arabic. It decided to continue with the Indian rulers' support to the madrassas and pathshalas and the grants to pandits and maulvis. The Company founded centres of higher learning during these years, such as the Calcutta Madrassa in 1781 and the Benares Sanskrit College in 1792, reflecting its interest in Orientalist knowledge and learning. Warren Hastings was a Persian scholar and invested his own funds in setting up the Calcutta Madrassa.

It is interesting to note, however, that even with the addition of the new clause in its Charter, the Company was to set up in the next few decades madrassas at Bhagalpur and Jaunpur (1811); the College of Fort St. George which taught Arabic and Persian (1824); Sanskrit Colleges at Calcutta and Poona (1821); the Agra College which taught Arabic and Sanskrit (1824); and the Delhi College for Arabic and Sanskrit (1825) (Rao, Parimala 2020: 2). In 1823 a General Committee of Public Instruction was appointed for the Bengal Presidency with ten members which included people such as H. T. Prinsep, who was to later oppose Macaulay, and the Sanskrit scholar H. H. Wilson, and the grant of one lakh rupees was placed at the disposal of the Committee. In addition to the institutions listed above, between 1823 and 1833 the Committee reorganised the Calcutta Madrassa and the Benares Sanskrit College, undertook the printing and publication of Sanskrit and Arabic books on a large scale and employed native scholars to translate English books containing useful knowledge into the classical Oriental languages (Naik and Nurullah 1974[1945]: 44).

It is important to consider at this point not only the continuities or changes, as they may be, which the East India Company was in the process of implementing, but also take into account the native system of education that was still functional and ongoing, even if the systematic loot of the country's resources by the Company had led to the impoverishment of the land, its people and its systems. In the wake of the insertion of the clause in the 1813 Charter, and in order to decide the educational interventions which the colonial government was expected to make, the governors of the Madras, Bombay and Bengal Presidencies conducted surveys in their respective provinces in the 1820s and 1830s to ascertain and estimate the extent and nature of indigenous education functional in these regions. Though this is often an inescapable feature of postcolonial research, it is paradoxical that contemporary studies on the indigenous educational system of India are premised upon the data gathered by the officers of the East India Company. There is also the possibility of biases and errors which in all likelihood informed the data collated by the different collectors in the provinces depending upon the individual predilections of the concerned officer/s involved in the task. Further, the data gathered in these surveys was by no means uniform in terms of detail and depth. However, these surveys are the only repository we have as a source to understand the institution of indigenous education in the country and since the information it provides is illuminating, a short general discussion based on the reports from different provinces may be in order here.

The indigenous system of education in India had evolved over several centuries and it is possible to see reflected in it the assimilation of different influences which had permeated its composite culture. In reality there were two distinct levels within the system. One strata of institutions was for higher learning in the classical languages; those for Sanskrit were called *tol*s in the Bengal region and *pathshala*s elsewhere: teachers here were always Brahmin, and so too in most cases the students, barring the occasional Kshatriya/Vaishya student. Institutions for higher learning in Persian/Arabic were termed the *madrassas*. Both pathshalas and madrassas were patronised by the rent-receiving leisured elite and were meant for the education of the upper castes/classes. The other system of schools was a basic general education for all classes which included children from the upper-caste and Muslim communities. Scholars see in this partial inclusivity traces of Buddhist influence. However, colonial data reveals that only in schools operating in some provinces were children from Untouchable sections admitted: the Untouchable castes seem to have had access to education in the Bengal Presidency, and while it is difficult to ascertain this in the data collected from the Madras Presidency, quite clearly schools in the Bombay Presidency do not show records of Untouchable children. Muslim children could also find religious training in *maktabs* or elementary religious schools generally attached to village mosques (Acharya 1978: 1983). None of these institutions was open to female children; the girl child, it appears from the data, was simply not sent to school. Elite Muslim families generally had private arrangements for the education of the females within the domestic sphere. This may have been the practice in some wealthy/royal Hindu families as well. The vernacular system of schooling was not maintained by any revenue or land endowments: it was sustained by the scholars and their parents by way of small fees and/or gifts to the teachers who could be of any caste or religion. Data from the Bengal Presidency shows Muslim teachers in a predominantly Hindu district and vice versa; it also shows teachers from the lower castes. There was no dependence or connection between the vernacular and Sanskrit/Persian schools of higher learning. These vernacular schools were a single-teacher informal arrangement between the parents in a village and the teacher with no external authority or examination system; neither were there formally allocated buildings or textbooks. Though schools in some districts did indicate a definite curriculum, this was not a uniform feature. These schools were secular in nature and taught the three R's with emphasis on writing and arithmetic in which boys were generally enrolled for a period of five years. Reports returned by A. D. Campbell from the Bellary district, Thomas Jervis from the

Konkan district and William Adam's three reports on the state of education in Bengal in the 1830s are a unique record of the Indian educational system before colonial influence began to percolate into the countryside, and they offer a wealth of information and detail. Though completely informal and decentralised the indigenous education system did seem to be well-established even as it closed its doors to the female and Untouchable populations.

The question that needs to be asked is this: what were the effects of colonial educational policies on the indigenous system and how are these to be mapped? From 1813 to 1835 the Company, as seen above, put its energies in supporting higher education in the classical languages of India. The policy of the General Committee of Public Instruction appeared in these years to be guided by one of the stipulations of the clause quoted earlier: 'the revival and improvement of literature and the encouragement of the learned natives of India'. The impetus behind this understanding was certainly a belief in the famous *downward filtration theory*: that the Company need only educate the upper classes of society and be assured that this class would take it upon itself to spread education amongst the masses (Naik and Nurullah 1974[1945]: 42); it was also coupled with the intrinsic admiration that some of the Committee's members and Company officers felt, as seen above, for the classical languages and literatures of India. Secondly, the Company was reluctant to take up the second stipulation of the clause: the introduction and promotion of the knowledge of science among Indians: it is necessary to repeat the point that no formal instruction of the sciences was in practice in England during these times. Related to this part of the clause was also the question of the language that should form the medium for this new curriculum in India if and when it was systematised into formal education. It was Charles Grant who had forcefully emphasised that English should be the means to educate and thereby save Indians from the backwardness of their cultural and religious practices. Though they belonged to different generations and ideological persuasions, Grant's views in his *Observations* undoubtedly looked forward to Macaulay's in/famous Minute of 1835, upon which was based Lord William Bentinck's Resolution in the same year. The well-known differences between the Anglicists and the Orientalists unfolded in the decades between these two personalities and in the wake of the work of the Committee, which garnered considerable criticism from several quarters.

The most surprising opposition came from elite Indians led by Raja Ram Mohan Roy in the Bengal Presidency who submitted a memorial to the Governor-General Lord Amherst in 1823, urging the government to abort the plans of establishing a Sanskrit College at Calcutta and made a plea to instead 'promote a more liberal and enlightened system of instruction, embracing mathematics, natural philosophy, chemistry, anatomy, with other useful sciences' among other demands (Cutts 1953: 828). We will examine the mobilisation of Indian opinion on the question of education shortly. However, in 1824 the General Committee of Public Instruction received a sharp reprimand from the Court of Directors dismissing 'mere Hindoo or mere Mahomedan literature' as frivolous learning and reminding it that its primary duty lay in utilising funds for 'useful learning' (Naik and Nurullah 1974[1945]: 44). Though the Committee gave a spirited reply justifying its actions, in time the pressure of public opinion grew in favour of English education wherein the work of the missionaries in popularising the study of English played, without doubt, a significant role. The result of the polarisation was that the Committee was split into two contending groups: the Anglicists and the Orientalists, and though this ideological conflict was sought to be resolved with Macaulay's forceful Minute of 1835, we see that even after nearly 200 years, the debate on the medium of instruction in India is an issue, the meaningful and amicable resolution of which is nowhere in sight.

Although much ink has been spilt on Macaulay's caustic and illiberal words on Indian literature, one direction of recent research argues that postcolonial research may have been quite off the mark after all on both its assessment of Macaulay and the actual outcomes of the Minute on the ground. Macaulay made recommendations that educational policy in India should be structured with the aim to spread Western learning in the medium of English and that the existing institutions of Oriental higher learning should be used towards that purpose. Like Charles E. Trevelyan, Macaulay was not opposed to the teaching of Sanskrit along with modern science in schools and colleges that were open to all; they were both not in favour of exclusive Sanskrit colleges that were open only to Brahmins. Influenced as he was by English radicalism, Thomas Paine in particular, Macaulay had little sympathy for either elite Orientalists or devout evangelicals. He was part of a like-minded group belonging to the new generation of which Trevelyan was also a part, who believed in intellectual modernisation and technological progress and the power of education to effect the uplift of India (Prior, et al. 2001: 106). He was appalled by the inequities of Indian social practices and truly desired to end these by means of education, and so within days of his famous Minute on education, Macaulay took up William Adam's proposal to survey indigenous schools in the Bengal Presidency with the aim of formulating a policy on vernacular schools. In the many Anglo-Vernacular schools that he helped found in the region of Bengal and Bihar, the curriculum consisted of vernacular education with the addition of English, modern geography and science. Contrary to received perceptions about Macaulay's intentions, Parimala Rao asserts that his other Minutes on education stress secular education in the vernacular languages, the necessity of such schools in the rural hinterlands and also the imperative of erasing social hierarchy in the classroom (Rao, Parimala 2020: 167–169). In his tribute to Macaulay, Surendranath Bannerjea claimed in a lecture delivered in 1878 that Macaulay had framed a section in the Charter of 1833 (even before he had touched the shores of India) to the effect that 'no native of India shall by reason only of his religion, place of birth, descent, colour… be disabled from holding any place, office or employment under the said company' thereby holding an assurance that Indians would not face discrimination (ibid.: 173).

Trevelyan and Macaulay had hoped that 'the artificial institution of caste' would not survive when the youth of India were trained to disregard it through modern education: 'the process of enlightening our subjects will proceed simultaneously with that of uniting them among themselves' (Rao, Parimala 2020: 180). Realising the threat that modern schools and the ideas of equality for which Macaulay had worked hard posed for its own survival, Rao argues that 'the government of India began to systematically dismantle his educational ideas' (ibid.: 181). Adam's scheme of working through the available system of village schools and linking these to modern institutions of higher education was struck down, and the government went back to its support of madrassas and Sanskrit schools (ibid.). Macaulay's efforts and influence in Indian education, Rao suggests, were far too short-lived.

It is puzzling, however, that Rao does not account for the fact that after Bentinck, Governor General Auckland and Macaulay worked together to ensure that English replaced Persian as the official and court language in 1837, which was the natural precursor to Lord Hardinge's 1844 resolution that prescribed English as a preferred qualification for government service. It was English, and not the vernaculars, that was promoted in all domains of power, including the judiciary, after the resolution was passed. In effect, it reinforced the position of the elites in Indian society, since it was they who had the benefit of modern education in the medium of English, and government funds were in reality dedicated to the education of a small, privileged group. Not surprisingly English was also the language favoured by prominent Indian intellectuals and reformers in the hope that it would 'help to diffuse the light and knowledge of the West and be conducive to the amelioration of the intellectual and moral condition of the British subject' (Majumdar 1947: 131).

Moreover it is necessary to examine the role played by administrators in directing and effecting policies in the different presidencies. While the ire of Indian nationalists is focused on Macaulay, the more expedient role played by British administrators such as Mountstuart Elphinstone, Thomas Munro and John Malcolm in the actual framing of policy at the regional level and the delivery of concrete decisions in the provinces has been elided. In comparison with Macaulay, who lived in India for barely four years, administrators in the provinces had extended careers in India and perforce chose to engage with the dynamics of pre-existing structures of administration in order not to antagonise existing social hierarchy. Reciprocity and mutual accommodation with the traditional elite who had manned these structures was a self-serving option, considering their willingness to function as the local allies of the colonial power. Quite clearly this class was expedient as the interface between the British and the people, and not unsurprisingly therefore, the appeasement of the Brahminical elite was enforced at the level of policy.

The foregoing discussion has looked at the developments leading to the insertion of the clause of education in the Charter of 1813 as well as the formulation of Macaulay's Minute in 1835. Two other milestones in colonial policy will be briefly touched upon before examining the interventions of the missionaries. Prodded by the urgency to show some advancement in education for the review of their Charter in 1854, the Company sent a despatch to the Governor-General of India. Known as Wood's Despatch, it has been hailed as the magna carta of Indian education since it made three important recommendations. The first of these was the creation of a Department of Education in each of the five provinces into which British territory of India was divided, which would be headed by a Director of Public Instruction (DIP); it also specified uniform terms of designation for all the other officers working in the department. The DIP was expected to submit to the government an annual report on the progress of education in the province. The second recommendation was the establishment of universities at Calcutta, Bombay and Madras for awarding degrees in arts, medicine, law and engineering. The third, and perhaps the most important recommendation, related to the establishment of a network of graded schools all over the country. This network envisaged the universities and affiliated colleges at the top, below which were placed the high schools that gave instruction either in the medium of English or any one of the vernacular languages, and at the lowest tier were the indigenous primary schools. Wood's Despatch articulated the realisation that hitherto the focus had been geared towards the support of institutions of higher education and thereby the expenditure of public funds on 'very small numbers of natives drawn from the higher classes' and proposed to remedy this by adopting a grant-in-aid system to encourage indigenous schools (Naik and Nurullah 1974[1945]: 80). Effectively, this meant government withdrawal from education and the promotion of other agencies including missionary initiatives and private Indian effort. While the first two recommendations were promptly executed by the government, the last proposal to encourage mass education predictably ran into trouble in different provinces, even as the political situation became turbulent with the onset of the Revolt of 1857. The Despatch also suggested that educated Indians must be encouraged through opportunities in government positions, linking education to government employment, and importantly it pointed out the necessity of educating women. These recommendations acquire a great deal of significance in the context of Phule's interventions on these subjects, and his critique of the Brahminical social structure.

The Indian Education Commission was set up in 1882 under the chairmanship of William Hunter in order to review the progress made on the recommendations of Wood's Despatch. The Revolt of 1857 resulted in the abolition of the East India Company, and the Crown took over the administration of India. The periodical reviews at the time of the renewal of the Charter were now abandoned, and the Education Commission was appointed in its stead. The appointment of the Commission was also partly an attempt to address the concerns of the missionaries who were on an agitation in England questioning the government's inaction in executing the recommendation of Wood's Despatch. Phule submitted his Memorial to this Commission: it is an impassioned plea to the colonial government to build the foundations of primary education and promote the access of the marginalised castes to such government-funded schooling.

Missionary Initiatives

Catholic missionaries in the Portuguese ruled settlements at Goa, Daman, Diu, Cochin and on the Hooghly were the first to establish modern schools in India (Heredia 1995: 2). These schools were in the vernacular, but as a means of strengthening Portugal's hold on Goa, Konkani was banned and school masters were instructed to teach only in Portuguese. As far back as 1543, the Jesuits opened a college named after St. Paul in Goa; though it was meant initially to train priests, it soon expanded its scope, as in most Jesuit institutions, to other students as well. Elementary schools were begun by Catholic missionaries in the settlements ruled by the French such as

Pondicherry, Mahe, Chandernagore and Yaman (Heredia 1995: 3). The indigenous schools in these regions were soon replaced by parish schools. Before Bombay was given away by the Portuguese, Catholic education thrived under the Franciscans in this city who 'were not only the first missionaries, but also the first school masters' (ibid.). In early eighteenth century, the British expelled the Franciscans, and for more than a century till the founding of St. Xavier's College by the Jesuits, Catholic mission activity was in a decline in Bombay. Catholic missionaries in India, says Rudolf Heredia, can be distinguished by the four distinct kinds of institutions which they founded: elementary schools attached to churches, orphanages where vocational training was provided over and above elementary education, seminaries for theological instruction for priesthood and Jesuit and other colleges for higher studies.

Though both Catholic and Protestant missionaries denounced Hindu idolatry, polytheism and superstition, the Protestant groups in India carried British anti-Catholicism to this distant land and expressed their inherent suspicion of Catholic religious practices which they argued became an accommodation to Hindu paganism with the purpose of proselytisation. The similarity between Roman and Hindu idolatry was an oft-repeated theme in Protestant discourse (Teltscher 1995: 90–98). The first to start schools amongst the Protestant missions were the Danes working in the Madras Presidency, where by 1725 they had started four schools for Christians and 17 schools for non-Christians (Heredia 1995: 2333). It was again to the Madras Presidency that the first Protestant English Missions came in 1727 and started schools in different cities of this province. From 1793 missions of the Baptist and London Missionary Society groups started work in Bengal; other English Protestant missions had settlements in Surat, Meerut, Agra, Calcutta and the south. The beginnings of the Protestant mission to India in the eighteenth century were modest: we have traced above the reluctance of the Company to open their territories to the missionaries. However, this changed rapidly in the first decades of the nineteenth century once the Charter of 1813 was renewed.

Earlier sections of this chapter have referred to the work of the Serampore Mission under Danish protection and in the face of opposition from the East India Company. Protestant missionaries on the whole came from humbler backgrounds, and seldom had the means to access higher education in the universities; this was a privilege generally open to both the Company officers as well as the evangelicals affiliated to the Anglican Church. There was an inherent difference of class between the two groups, which can also be perceived in the empathy for the lower castes and Untouchables which the Protestant missionaries instinctively brought into their mission activities. The Serampore Trio, Carey, Marshman and Ward, formed a group that concerned itself with education right from 1800 when they first got together, all the more remarkable considering that each of them had been brought up in humble circumstances and educated at village elementary schools in England. Their later education was by and large self-taught. They started schools initially in Serampore and nearby areas, incrementally expanding their footprint in the entire region of the Bengal province. By 1818 they had established over 100 elementary schools and also Serampore College for higher education. The object of these institutions was not directly evangelical; it was more of a '*preparatio evangelica*' where education would be the means to, in Marshman's words 'enable people to see things just as they are when their understanding matured' (Laird 1972: 87). In the early years their pupils were mainly Europeans and Eurasians; as the Mission's presence stabilised in the region, their schools and the College admitted native Christians, Brahmins, Muslims as well as the lower castes, including those of no caste, i.e. Untouchables. These initiatives must be mapped together with the Trio's enormous output in philology, translation, printing and discursive writing. Ward's books on Hinduism have been indicated above; Carey produced dictionaries and grammars of Bengali and other Indian languages including Marathi and over 30 Bible translations in different Indian languages. Carey's contribution to the development of Bengali prose is acknowledged (Laird 1968: 93). In charge of teaching Marathi at Fort William College from 1804, William Carey compiled and printed at his mission in Serampore a book on Marathi grammar and the Marathi translation of the Bible. Marshman worked on Chinese. Significantly their work in education, their publications and the missionary work in general facilitated connections with all sections of native society including intellectuals, reformers and ordinary Indians who would later petition the government for similar educational opportunities.

Unlike the English Baptist missionaries who were by and large self-educated, Scottish missionaries were generally products of the universities in Scotland who not only taught English and modern sciences from the beginning in their schools but were also instrumental in introducing reformist thought. Alexander Duff, who came to India in 1830, belonged to the Scottish Protestant Presbyterian missionary, and with the help of Kamal Bose, an affluent Hindu who offered him a building, began a school in Kolkata which later expanded into an immensely popular missionary college (Rao, Parimala 2020: 90). Duff also headed a school in rural Bengal later, specially invited to do so by the descendant of a local raja impressed by his achievements in Kolkata. Duff's work in Bengal exercised a formative influence on missionary efforts that followed his interventions during these decades.

The missionaries of the Free Church of Scotland who came to western India were informed by a similar zeal to proselytise through a 'massive educational effort' in which instruction in Western arts and sciences was introduced together with the scriptures (O'Hanlon 2010[1985]: 64). The Scottish and American missionaries who established missions in western India shared the understanding that the Hindus were, in Duff's words, 'infatuated victims of hellish superstitions' and that it was the duty of Christians to slay the demons of idolatry and other superstitious evils by holding these up to rational questioning (cited in Pennington 2005: 101). Like him they also believed the best strategy to do this was to convert the leaders of society and in this way set an example for the people to follow. The way to achieve this, it was felt, was through an intellectual interrogation of Hindu practices, its religious authority and theology through organising public debate, printing pamphlets and periodicals, in addition to the popular evangelical strategy of the wayside pulpit. All these missionary strategies for dissemination of evangelical thought can be seen in *Tritiya Ratna*, though Phule's missionary stops short of any attempt to proselytise, contenting himself only with opening the peasant's worldview on idolatry, religion and the reality of divinity.

These beliefs and strategies are also reflected in the work of a few prominent missionaries who were based in the western region and with some of whom Phule was undoubtedly in touch. The earliest Scottish missionary to arrive in the western region was Donald Mitchell in 1823 who focused on setting up small vernacular schools and on direct evangelism.[2] John Wilson who came to Bombay in 1828 bent his energies to interrogating Hindu beliefs, refuting its doctrines in public debates that were later published in the form of pamphlets. James and Murray Mitchell divided their time between Pune and Bombay, while Robert Nesbit worked in Nasik and Ahmednagar, and Stephen Hislop was based in Nagpur. As pioneers of vernacular print culture in India, missionary intervention in general was hugely significant in the precipitation of a broad-based public discourse. Missionary discourse also had an important role in developing prose in different Indian vernacular languages. In western India the circulation of tracts was an important aspect of evangelism. The Bombay Tract and Book Society which had been founded in 1827 was reorganised in 1848 under Murray Mitchell, and in 1855 it was reported in *Dnyanodaya* that the Society had published a total of 55,207 books and tracts of various kinds.

Starting from 1842, *Dnyanodaya*, the most significant Marathi missionary periodical of western India, was printed from Bombay as a bi-monthly by the American Marathi Mission. Similar to the worldview of the Scottish missionaries, the journal combined essays espousing Christian beliefs with articles on a wide array of secular subjects such as recent advances in astronomy, medical science and aspects of world geography and natural history. The underlying theme of the articles was to show the capacity of Western science to harness the natural world for human benefit; through these it attempted to link progress in the material world with the idea of a benevolent Creator who presided over all human beings, created equally in his image. The *Dnyanodaya* contrasted these Christian ideas of divinity with the often contradictory Hindu notions of divine nature which could be pantheistic or polytheistic and indeed, at times, described as without any attribute. Hindu gods could commit harmful, even sinful, acts; they could be cruel and unjust, and it was necessary to propitiate them through the intermediation of exploitative Brahmins. Hindu doctrines lacked a universally valid ethic, and its practices were often brutal and senseless. The journal stressed the idea of a basic spiritual equality which sometimes also found reflection in the preoccupations articulated by its readers in the correspondence section. Discrimination based on caste and the social condition of women were other concerns that informed the journal's polemical questioning of the Hindu religion. Amongst its readers the *Dnyanodaya* listed a wide range of subscribers including Hindu reformers such as Phule and Baba Padmanji, Christians, British administrators and missionaries, which gives an idea of its reach and influence in nineteenth-century Maharashtra. It is revealing that in Phule's very first literary work written in 1855, *Tritiya Ratna*, the Vidushak, who ventriloquises the young author, makes a reference to this journal thereby indicating the audience which Phule must have had in mind while writing the play.

Like Baptist and other missionary groups in Bengal, Scottish missionaries based in western India made the learning of Sanskrit and the vernacular language of the region a priority 'the better to understand and refute Hindu religious texts' (O'Hanlon 2010[1985]: 66). Robert Nesbit published a critique of the *Bhagavad Gita* and John Stevenson a translation of the *Rgveda*. John Wilson's writings were serialised in missionary periodicals, and therefore his interrogations of Hindu doctrines and practices had a wide and popular reach. In his book *India Three Thousand Years Ago* published in 1858, he combined his reading of Hindu religious texts, building on the interpretations of these by Sanskrit scholars such as H. H. Wilson and John Muir, and the contemporary preoccupation with the theory of Aryan invasions to question the legitimacy of Hindu religion and traditions. John Wilson drew upon theories current in Orientalist discourse in this book and attempted to locate Sanskrit texts within a quasi-historical description of the origins of the Aryan races, their invasion of the Indian sub-continent resulting in the overpowering of the people originally living there and the beginnings of the Vedic/Aryan culture in India. He went on to offer a detailed interpretation of the historical significance of different entities such as the *dasyas*, *rakshas*, *ugras*, *pishchas*, *asuras*, *yakshas*, *shigravas*, and *kikatas*, asserting that they clearly referred to the indigenous tribes who resisted the presence of the alien Aryans. John Wilson linked this interpretation to an argument that caste had no place in the social system that prevailed in ancient India; the term Kshatriya, he said, referred in the Vedas only to a person possessing landed property, and the Brahmins were only a profession and not a caste; the hierarchies of caste and notions of ritual purity are not to be found in the Vedas. The sacred texts of the Hindus, the missionaries argued, contained largely descriptions of the worship of the natural elements. However, by means of jealously guarding these texts, the Brahmins arrogated to themselves influence and power. Like other missionary writers, John Wilson pointed out the discrepancies between the Vedas and contemporary nineteenth-century Hindu practices that severely oppressed the lower castes and women. He argued that the majority of Hindus do not understand Sanskrit and live in continued ignorance of their religion and 'are thus, in a great degree, prevented from thinking for themselves' precisely because the sacred texts are rendered hidden and inaccessible by the Brahmins (cited in O'Hanlon 2010[1985]: 79).

India Three Thousand Years Ago in particular had enormous influence on the construction of a subaltern ideological stand mobilised by Phule against Brahminical hegemony and caste hierarchy. While 'The Significance of *Tritiya Ratna*' in this volume attempts an analysis of the role of the character of the Missionary in this construction, Phule's other writings also deploy missionary discourse on the subject of Brahminical privilege to underscore his own arguments, as we shall soon see.

The Role of Indians in Shaping Educational Policy

The Charter of 1813 not only opened the doors to missionaries, it also became a rallying point for British and Indian liberal reformers to write petitions to the colonial government and demand the introduction of modern education in India. We have discussed above the reluctance of the East India Company to use the money mandated by British Parliament for the education of Indians for at least two decades after the Charter was renewed. Leading Indian intellectuals found in the work of the missionaries support and legitimation for their own interventions in the reform of Indian society in areas such as the uplift of women's position and education. By the second decade of the nineteenth century, wealthy Indians were making endowments to establish schools and colleges that taught European curriculum in the medium of English (Cutts 1953: 826–827). While examples of such agency can be seen all over the country, we could examine one of the most well-known interventions made in Calcutta.

As early as 1816, Raja Ram Mohan Roy and David Hare (Scottish watchmaker and philanthropist) worked on a proposal to establish a school with modern curricula. This proposal had the support of liberal British officials and non-officials, Indian reformers and influential public figures of Bengal, including conservatives such as Radhakant Deb who was a defender of the *sati*. It is clear that there was unity amongst the Indian elite on the question of secular modern education in the medium of English; they contributed towards a permanent endowment and pooled a fund of Rs 113,179 to establish the Vidyalaya in 1817. The first institution for modern secular education in India, it would be named Presidency College several decades later and was elevated to Presidency University in 2010, just a decade ago. The Vidyalaya, also referred to as the Hindu College by the British, comprised a school (pathasala) and an academy/college (mahapathasala) and it taught modern sciences, Classical and English literature and philosophy (Rao, Parimala 2020: 77–78). In 1822 Roy established the Anglo-Hindu school with the support of Indian and European friends, where instruction was free, for the benefit of poor students who could not pay their fees. In 1830 he was to help Alexander Duff found the Scottish Church College, again an institution for modern education in the medium of English. Ram Mohan Roy's open letter to the Governor-General Lord Amherst in 1823 (cited earlier) attacked the policy of the General Committee of Public Instruction and requested the government to 'provide a college furnished with the necessary books, instruments and other apparatus' so that Indians would have the benefit of a 'more liberal and enlightened system of instruction' and not continue to remain in ignorance. A scholar of Sanskrit himself, Roy questioned the usefulness of Sanskrit studies. Though this letter was placed before the Court of Directors, it was rejected by the Committee, dominated by Orientalists, on the grounds that the government had to 'go with the tide of popular prejudice' against modern education (Rao, Parimala 2020: 82–83). This assertion clearly ran contrary to the actual demand for modern education as evidenced in the number of independent schools established by students who had passed out of the Vidyalaya, which H. H. Wilson himself admitted. Ram Mohan Roy's petition was taken up later by Trevelyan, Macaulay and Bentinck: historians suggest the possibility that Macaulay drew from the contents of Roy's letter in the declaration: 'What we spend on the Arabic and Sanscrit Colleges is not merely a dead loss to the cause of truth. It is bounty money paid to raise up champions of error' (cited in Cutts 1953: 828).

It is undeniable that Ram Mohan Roy pioneered the movement for women's reform and modern education which is also reflected in the rationalism and the spirit of enquiry in his writings. It is also true, however, that practices such as sati, enforced widowhood and the purdah system, which he strove to change, obtained amongst the elite and upper castes. Women from less privileged sections had comparatively more freedom, and their sexuality was not as obsessively controlled: widow-remarriage, for instance, was quite common as was their visibility outside the four walls of domesticity. Roy's interventions in education were also intended for the elite sections of his society. Roy readily acknowledged his debt to Western education and thought; yet the worldview he inherited was constructed by the Brahminical milieu, which he never questioned. David Kopf suggests that early Indian upper-caste reformers 'used the idea of the West as a means for modernizing their own traditions…for pouring the new wine of modern functions into the old bottles of Indian culture' (Kopf 1969: 205). Oriental scholarship and the praise it showered on ancient Indian texts and culture had an undoubted influence in shaping Roy's understanding of Vedic society as utopian and contemporary practices as degenerative. It is no surprise therefore that Roy's campaign against sati was founded upon the rationale that it had no scriptural sanction and that the reforms he was pursuing were in consonance with the ancient texts. As Lata Mani argues,

> Tradition was not the ground on which the status of women was being contested. Rather the reverse was true: women

> in fact became the site on which tradition was debated and reformulated. What was at stake was not women but tradition. (Mani, Lata 1989: 118)

Braj Ranjan Mani asserts that Orientalist ideas of the Brahminical glories of ancient India were integral to the agenda of reform. Since both the reformers and the reactionaries opposing reforms, such as abolishing the sati, dipped into the same sacerdotal texts to prove their respective points, the scriptures continued to acquire legitimacy; the reformers seldom campaigned on liberal ideals of equality or reason. These reformists neither fully adopted the ideals of Western enlightenment: humanism and rationalism; nor did they campaign to create public opinion on the inhumanity and absurdity of retrograde gender and caste practices. Further, the demand for English education and better representation in the colonial administration were also oriented to modernise a tiny and privileged section of Bengali society. While they did decry contemporary caste practices, they did so on the grounds that these practices had deviated from the 'genuine Brahmanical religion taught by the Vedas, as interpreted by the inspired Manu'. No attempt was made to secure equal access to education and political institutions for the lower castes; instead Roy declared that he would wish the doors be shut for 'persons of lower classes' and include only the 'respectable and intelligible classes' (Mani, Braj Ranjan 2005: 199–205).

Ram Mohan Roy's championing of the English language, his camaraderie with the Anglicists and the pioneering of what is often termed the Bengal Renaissance produced a new class of prosperous Bengalis educated in modern institutions, the *bhadralok*, who would have an enormous influence on the culture of the region. Historians argue that even a generation later, this elite class played a significant role in influencing colonial policy on education. The recommendations made by Wood's Despatch in 1854 favoured a shift in government policy and the dedication of funds to the basic education of the masses in the vernacular medium. However, little change could be made in this direction in the Bengal region because of 'the vocal resistance put forward by the Bengali bhadralok, including stalwarts of reform such as Ishwarchandra Vidyasagar, against changing the course of educational development paved by their guru Macaulay' (Acharya 1995: 670).

The record of the voices of the less privileged sections petitioning for schools in the early part of the nineteenth century can be seen in the correspondence of the missionary Richard Mardon, associated with the Serampore Mission. His letters written during the years 1810–12 make repeated references to the requests for schools made by the locals in the region of Malda. Once they had lost the fear of losing caste if they attended the mission school, the villagers realised that their anxieties about the imposition of an alien religion were unfounded (Laird 1968: 96). The popularity of the Serampore Mission can be gauged from the large number of schools which the Serampore Trio opened in response to the requests made by the natives of villages in the Bengal province, as well as the comprehensive secular curriculum in the vernacular devised by Marshman.

Bombay Presidency came under the control of the British in 1818, much later than the Bengal region, and developments in education here unfolded differently. Perhaps the most influential officer of the East India Company in western India, Mountstuart Elphinstone, was resident during the Peshwa regime and played a significant role in the transfer of power to the British after the Anglo-Maratha War in 1818. A social conservative loath to change caste equations which might impact British power by provoking the elite Brahmins, Elphinstone avoided any encouragement or support to missionary activity since the missionaries worked amongst the lower castes and Untouchables. Reforms in administrative structure were made cautiously, treading a fine balance between change and tradition. Not wishing to risk conflict, he was not in favour of educating the lower castes and decided to devote the Dakshina Fund (see p. 7, this volume) traditionally kept aside by the Peshwas for the support of learned Brahmins, to establish the Poona Sanskrit College in 1821. Scholarships were instituted for the study of the Dharmashastras and the Vedas. It is pointed out that Elphinstone's educational policy was designed principally for the upper castes. In accordance with the traditional divisions of caste, his government came up with a dual education system where the indigenous vernacular schools were to be functional for the basic 'education of the lower order', and Sanskrit and English were to be offered in higher education as a conciliatory gesture to the elite in the western region (Chavan 2013: 125–127). The result was a dual-language, hierarchised education policy. Elphinstone's discriminatory stance, leading to selective access to English favouring the elite at the cost of the lower castes, was continued by John Malcolm who took over as the Governor of Bombay Presidency in 1827. As Anil Seal has pointed out, Elphinstone's policies might have possibly saved British dominion in western India; at any rate, they certainly postponed the decline of Brahminical preeminence in the Bombay province (cited in Chavan 2013: 133).

Archival research in colonial official documents reveals that a large number of petitions were received around this time from different districts such as Panvel, Thane, Vashi, Konkan, Ahmedabad and a host of smaller towns, urging the government to establish English schools and support the existing indigenous network of schools and integrate these within the modern curricula (Rao, Parimala 2020: 96–99). Records of schools established during the period are also available. We must remember that missionary initiatives in education had already begun in this period, thereby shaping the people's aspirations towards modern education. In 1823 an institution to teach engineering to European and native boys was established in Bombay. Though initially the policy was to teach European students in the medium of English and deploy Marathi and Gujarati for the Indian students, in a couple of years English became the de facto medium and it was discovered that native boys had performed much better than the European students (ibid.: 106).

Just like Presidency College which served as a model, Elphinstone College, established in 1835, was the result of an initiative taken by a group of the leading elite of Bombay. Representing the diversity of cosmopolitan Bombay, the group included Hindus, Muslims and Parsis; its leading figure was the educationist and philanthropist Jagannath Shankarseth. Together they raised a sum of more than two lakh rupees for the purpose of establishing a modern institution 'to teach English language and the arts and sciences of Europe' (cited in Rao, Parimala 2020: 109). Though an elite initiative with the intention of catering to students from the upper sections of society, many of the founders were sympathetic to reformist ideas. Unlike reformist Indian opinion in the Bengal Presidency, which by and large restricted itself to interventions on behalf of upper-caste women, a great many Brahmin reformers in the Bombay Presidency *advocated* caste reform, though many of them may have fallen short in actual praxis in their personal lives (Keer 2000[1964]: 136–137). Shankarseth, for instance, believed that while English education must of necessity be restricted to the elite, the masses must receive an education, even if in the vernacular. The point to be noted is that such views were part of an established discourse on social reforms addressing both women and the lower castes including Untouchables.

During the early decades of the nineteenth century the colonial appeasement of the Brahmins took place alongside the questioning of Brahminical privilege by the missionaries. We must remember that English reformist thought was also in circulation amongst the educated Indian elite. Perhaps these cross-currents provided a fertile space to produce ideas of reform amongst some discerning Brahmins. It is possible to see in the Bombay Presidency the earliest liberal interrogation of the caste system and a concerted effort towards caste and gender reform together with the advocacy of education for the lower castes. One of the first Indian teachers at Elphinstone College was Bal Shastri Jambhekar who was appointed assistant professor in mathematics and head of the College School when it was established in 1838. In 1840 he was promoted as educational inspector and a full professor in Elphinstone College. In 1832 Jambhekar had already started western India's first Anglo-vernacular weekly, the *Darpan*, which reflected the concerns of the class of the first generation of upper-caste, Western-educated males and its aspiration to open Indian society to the advantages of Western literary and scientific knowledge as well as attempt a 'revaluation of her (India) traditional social and religious beliefs'. In 1840 Jambhekar began the Marathi periodical *Digdarshan*, replacing the *Darpan*. *Digdarshan* ran for four years, and the articles published here attempted to expose the readers to geography, history and natural sciences, besides essays in which caste privileges of the Brahmins and the practice of child marriage were attacked. The *Prabhakar*, edited jointly by Jambhekar and the reformer Bhau Mahajan, began its circulation in 1845, and for more than a decade it was the main vehicle for reformist opinion in the Bombay Presidency. It spoke out strongly against caste hierarchy, the privileges of Brahmins and the necessity of reforming the position of women and the lower castes. Education and the importance of focusing on moral and material benefits were stressed. We must remember that the missionary bi-monthly *Dnyanodaya* was contemporaneous to the *Prabhakar*, and in fact the early issues of the former carried extracts of essays and letters from the latter in order to buttress its own slant on the need for reform of Hindu practices. Well-known reformer Gopal Hari Deshmukh, the 'Lokahitavadi', lent the *Prabhakar* much of its intellectual character, and his letters on the decadence of the Brahmins and the abject state of the Hindu social order were often republished in the missionary magazine (O'Hanlon 2010[1985]: 90–94).

Elphinstone College offered the intellectual trigger for the founding of reformist organisations such as the Marathi Dnyan Prasarak Sabha, founded in 1848 by a group of reformers and students of the college, which set itself the task of bringing to light the 'faults and shortcomings of the people of this country' (cited in O'Hanlon 2010[1985]: 95). Dadoba Pandurang Tarkhadkar, a teacher at the college, was its first president. It published a newspaper which reflected its statement of intention, questioning caste privileges, the observance of empty rites and rituals, the importance of true knowledge and spirituality. Dadoba Tarkhadkar, who was known for educational work in the Surat region, was also a leading figure in the founding of a radical secret society around the same time in Bombay called the Paramahansa Mandali (The Society of the Supreme Being); students of Elphinstone College were recruited as members to both these societies. The Paramahansa Mandali professed the dismantling of idolatry, caste hierarchy and practices of exclusion, and promoted widow remarriage and the education of women and the lower castes. Its list of members was kept a secret; however, they were involved in radical acts that included the eating of bread and milk from common vessels and the desecration of the images of gods (O'Hanlon 2010[1985]: 98–101). While it is not clear if Phule was a member of any of the Mandali's branches in Pune, Satara, Ahmadnagar, Belgaum and Ratnagiri, there was an intrinsic connection between this society and Phule's own Satyashodhak Samaj begun in 1873. A definitive text laying out the Mandali's beliefs and expounding its central propositions, perhaps authored by Dadoba Tarkhadkar himself, was published in 1868 with the title: *A Discussion on Religion*. This same book was used by Phule as a manifesto of the Satyashodhak Samaj, and copies of it were distributed as a part of its propaganda campaign (O'Hanlon 2010[1985]: 99–100).

Amongst Indian reformers, Phule's place in the articulation, on behalf of the marginalised lower castes and women, of the right of access to education and its implementation in concrete terms is definitive, substantial and unprecedented. In the repertoire of Indian voices leading the cause of education in colonial India, Phule expresses a radical and original vision of his historical understanding of contemporary society. The analysis of his experiments with two different literary genres included in this volume reflects this vision. Before moving on, however, to examine Phule's prose writings in English included in the present volume: the 'Preface' to *Gulamgiri* and 'Memorial Addressed to the Education Commission' in 1882, we must also take note of the many instances of petitions written by the lower and Untouchable castes in the Bombay Presidency, urging the government to make provisions to admit their wards into schools, to which recent research has drawn attention.

Recent archival research in the historiography of education has facilitated a shift away from the primacy of the role of either the colonial government or the missionaries in promoting education for Untouchables. Though supportive to the cause of lower-caste education, missionary effort too was circumscribed by the limitations imposed upon it by the Indian social context as more recent studies recognise.[3] In his incisive paper titled 'Sitting on the school verandah: the ideology and practice of untouchable educational protest in late 19th century western India', Constable argues that 'low-caste Hindus sought to use missionary education (and conversion) to develop indigenous ideologies/protests which aimed at freedom from caste structures, disabilities and untouchable discrimination' (Constable 2000: 385). Based on three meticulously researched case studies, Constable shows the agency of lower-caste/Untouchable parents and activists militating against educational discrimination meted out by caste Hindu parents in a general environment marked by the ambivalence of the colonial government administrators in favour of the downward filtration theory. He suggests that 'while missionaries provided educational institutions for untouchable students, the demand for these was driven by the untouchable communities' and that 'the social protest that emerged from such education, though often supported by missionaries...was largely initiated by the untouchables themselves' (Constable 2000: 386). In her poignant study, Eleanor Zelliot shows a Dalit student sitting outside on the verandah and leaning in through the window of the schoolroom with the rain falling on him. The yearning of the lower castes for education and the hostility of caste Hindus is encapsulated in this image. Her paper is a tribute to the early reformers in admitting Untouchable children into schools despite insurmountable difficulties, and in particular to the efforts of Phule and his associates who opened schools to save the Untouchable children from such a plight (Zelliot 2014). Lahuji Salve, a valued associate of Phule from the Untouchable Mang community, was one such hero who helped recruit many Dalit students to Phule's schools.[4]

The discussion above has attempted to explore the agency of Indians, whether elite or subaltern, in shaping educational change during the colonial period; clearly Indians played an integral role in these developments, at times they indeed proved to be catalytic.

PHULE'S MANIFESTO FOR EDUCATION IN *GULAMGIRI* (1873)

Phule's substantial and wide gamut of interventions in the field of subaltern education have been discussed in the short biographical note (see pp. 4–12, this volume). They include actual educational work on the ground; the formation of a cohesive ideological front against upper-caste hegemony in traditional and modern institutions; the substantiation of this in polemical tracts and experiments in literary writing; the establishment of societies that disseminated the ideology in an organised and structured fashion and through this the attempt to mobilise the several categories of the disenfranchised: the Shudratishudra; and the framing of petitions and memorials on contemporary policy changes that held the possibility of educational opportunities for the constituency he represented.

Phule includes in the text of 'Memorial Addressed to the Education Commission' a part of his 'Preface' to *Gulamgiri*, the prose polemic written in 1873 and perhaps the best known of his works. As such it may be of relevance to discuss this earlier text and Phule's preface to it in English as a prelude to discussing the later petition. The theory of the Aryan invasion had become the focus of Orientalist and nationalist engagement from the early decades of the nineteenth century as earlier discussed. The discourse concerning the Aryan race can be seen as a 'shared myth' as Romila Thapar suggests, seen equally in the preoccupation with origins amongst nineteenth-century European Indologists and in the urgency shown by elite Indian national leaders in the wake of this research, to reclaim the glory of Vedic culture (Thapar 1992: 71). The quest for these early societies, which would help locate the historical trajectory of different Indo-European language-cultures, appears to have marked both the metropole and colony. However, taking a cue from missionary writing, Phule and later Ambedkar, subverted this nationalist historical quest and by means of a 'counter-hegemonic/ taxonomic inversion' proposed an alternative historical model in which the subaltern class could find itself an identity and centrality (Figueira 2002: 5).

Gulamgiri embodies Phule's passionate indictment of Brahmanism: it is the articulation of a revolt against the cruelty and hypocrisy of Hindu caste society, in which Phule calls upon his readers to discard all caste feeling and practice. Completely realistic, Phule is only too aware that caste cannot be uprooted so easily: 'We know perfectly well that the Brahman will not descend from this self-raised pedestal and meet his kunbi and low-caste brethren on an equal footing without a struggle' (CWMP 1991[1969]: 134). Unsurprisingly the book created a furore, and several newspapers refused to publicise it because of its hard-hitting manifesto. This polemical work is a radical deconstruction of caste ideology. In contrast to upper-caste nationalist historiography which saw India as the victim of both Muslim invasions and British colonisation, Phule presents the Aryan Brahmin as the original coloniser of the indigenous people: the Kshatriyas.

G. P. Deshpande argues that Phule was the first reformer to think of Indian society as divided into two classes: he saw 'caste both as a category in the productive process, and as something that facilitated the dominance of the brahmans in the ideological sphere'. Even if Marxist terminology was not available to him, Phule conceived of caste as both the base and the superstructure of Indian society (Deshpande 2002: 8–9). He brought together all productive castes who are engaged in the production labour in one category, the Shudratishudra, in which he included women of all castes oppressed as they were by male domination. Against this class he pitted the non-productive and exploitative male Brahmins who lived off the back-breaking labour of the Kunbis, Malis, Dhangars, Muslims, Bhils, Kolis, Mahars and Mangs who had been, so ran his counter-historical narrative, fragmented into different exclusive castes by the wily invader, the Aryan Brahmin. By enabling an understanding of the reality of their oppression and their oppressor, Phule hoped to unite the peasant castes with the Untouchables and Muslims, and so create what would be known today as the Bahujan Samaj. In order to forge this potential unity Phule, says Deshpande, rejected both 'the endlessly regressing hierarchy' of the caste system which structures society into different levels as well as the 'centrality of the pollution principle' which is the basis of the hierarchy and exclusivity of caste communities (ibid.: 8). He focused on 'production conditions rather than production relations' and took an 'undifferentiated view of the peasantry' which may not have been the reality of caste relations in rural areas (Deshpande 2002: 14). However, this united front was the only way the oppressed had of subduing exploitative Brahmins. The underlying theme of Phule's book emphasises that this unity is only possible when Shudratishudra have the benefit of true historical knowledge based on reason. It is a point to be noted that Vithal Ramji Shinde, the Maratha reformer who took forward Phule's mission of educating the lower caste, conceived of the term 'Bahujan Samaj' as the solidarity of the oppressed. In an article titled 'Bahujan Paksh', which has come to be seen as an important document in the history of anti-caste movements in Maharashtra, Shinde spelt out the common interests of the Bahujan society oppressed by upper-caste patriarchy.

Gulamgiri is structured in the form of a dialogue between the author Jotirao and a younger colleague Dhondiba which is reminiscent of dialogic discussions from classical Europe as well as Upanishadic and Buddhist literature (Deshpande 2002: 17). Drawing substantial inspiration from John Wilson's book *India Three Thousand Years Ago* (discussed earlier), Phule presents a conceptual framework that historicises the Brahminical oppression of the lower castes. In a deliberate strategy Phule reads the mythological puranic story of the ten avatars of Vishnu historically, providing his interlocutor a rational grid of explanation through which to understand the fantastic as the history of unethical and violent appropriation. By means of deconstructing mythology through the lens of rationality Phule's performative reading can be seen as an attempt to raise consciousness. Phule's aim is to show the objectification of consciousness which the dominant deploy in the process of enslavement, and stress the necessity of empirical and historical knowledge to unmake and raise consciousness (Devare 2011: 74; Vendell 2014: 55). It has been acknowledged that in emphasising the subjugation of consciousness by the Brahminical class and its monopoly on textual knowledge, Phule clearly anticipates Gramsci's notion of hegemony by almost a century (Chavan 2013: 20).

Phule's ideological position quite evidently was in complete contrast to that of the upper-caste social reformers. Not only did he believe that radical ideology must be underpinned by a praxis that complemented it, he re-interpreted Brahminical mythology from a rational, historical perspective. This was his strategy to debunk the myth of the golden Vedic past subscribed to with equal fervour by Indologists and upper-caste nationalists. In his reading, 'the ancient wonder that was India' was nothing but exploitative self-interest masquerading as religion. By the same token, the contemporary display of elitist nationalism was nothing but a renewed bid to build a nation on the foundations of caste oppression and slavery. Only education would enable the downtrodden to realise the historical lies on which the privilege of Brahminical order was based. Only education would cut away the chains of enslavement binding the

Shudratishudra in coils of ignorance. Unlike upper-caste reformers, Phule had no intention of seeing the present as the corrupted version of a glorious past, nor to push reforms by citing the correct interpretation of Brahminical texts. He completely rejected these texts and strove to construct an alternative society which he termed Balistan: it would be a society founded on reason, equality and brotherhood. In these egalitarian ideals one may see reflected Phule's admiration for the figure of Jesus (whom he called Yashwant, a champion of equality and love), who became a kind of alter-ego of Bali Raja, the mythical Indian king, who represented for Phule justice and benevolence. Phule also hailed Mohammad as a prophet of brotherhood in one of his poems, though he had made it clear that he had no faith in revealed religions.

Gulamgiri is divided into 16 parts; the first and the seventh are devoted to a caustic and ribald exposé of Brahma, the creator. The second to the sixth parts as well as the eighth part each examine a specific incarnation of Vishnu. Phule makes a selection of these incarnations departing partially from the chronology of the different avatars given in the puranic narration.[5] The first six incarnations: Matsya, the fish; Kurma, the tortoise; Varah, the boar; Narsimha, half-lion half-man; Vaman, the dwarf; and Parshuram, the axe-wielding Brahmin are seen as real historical figures heading different phases of Aryan invasions. But having deconstructed puranic mythology in rational and secular terms, though it must be said, without attempting to search for historical evidence to back his claims, Phule proceeds to narrate an alternative set of stories in which he portrays the brave Shudratishudra as the original undivided Kshatriya class. In his narration these indigenous inhabitants of India had fiercely battled the invading Aryans/Brahmins; however, the enemy had not only killed them in large numbers but by its duplicity had caused grievous destruction by means of fragmenting them into different hierarchical castes thereby fracturing their unity. The wily Brahmins had then hidden this exploitative history through capture and appropriation of all textual knowledge. Phule's interrogation of Brahminical mythology is established by means of narrating a 'mytho-history of strategy, encounter and domination' underlining the tactics of coercion and consent by which the invading Aryans/

Brahmins had established their dominance over the lower caste to indoctrinate and thereby enslave them (Vendell 2014: 55). In the ninth and the tenth part, Jotirao and Dhondiba discuss the origin of the Vedas and the Brahmins' suppression, through Shankaracharya's intervention, of Buddhist ascendency in India. The last six parts of *Gulamgiri* shift focus to contemporary times and the continued control of Brahmins over all aspects of nineteenth-century society in Maharashtra, including religion, education, work, economy and general quotidian living. Briefly put, Phule's intention is to locate the contemporary marginalisation of the lower castes within the larger historical context, and to see this marginalisation primarily as the result of a deliberate ideological ploy of the Brahmins to perpetuate the ignorance of the Shudratishudra.

It is natural therefore that Phule's most enduring and keenly felt protestation is in the field of education, and the charge most vehemently made is that Brahmins, not content with their hegemonic control of traditional textual knowledge, also corner all the benefits of modern education, continuing to leave Shudratishudra ignorant and unschooled. In the Marathi text of *Gulamgiri*, Jotirao minces no words in telling Dhondiba bluntly that the British too have continued the policy of appeasing the Brahmins. However, deeply concerned that his appeal should reach the colonial administration and Protestant missionaries, Phule not only wrote his preface to the book in English, but also added a translated title in English, *Slavery*, to his Marathi work. We have seen above that the colonial educational policy in the Bombay Presidency implemented Marathi as the medium at primary and lower secondary levels of schooling and English at all subsequent levels of higher education. This bilingual policy had an enormous impact on the emergent print culture which in turn led to the creation of a bilingual modern Marathi public sphere. As a subaltern leader Phule made use of remarkable linguistic diversity in his writings. He affixed English titles to many of his Marathi works, also introducing them in English. He imported the spoken language of the subaltern into his Marathi with a large number of Urdu/Dakhani words, in the process subverting Sanskritised upper-caste Marathi and Brahminical worldviews (Mokashi-Punekar 2017: 152). Phule's works show an acute awareness of the politics of language and the 'dynamics of representation in the colonial public sphere', his own political position and the overwhelming necessity to publicise and mobilise support for his cause (Naregal 2002[2001]: 98).

A careful analysis of the 'Preface' to *Gulamgiri* reveals Phule's canny and astute understanding of the hierarchical position of the languages constituting the bilingual public sphere.[6] The title page of the book has the rather arresting title, in English, 'Slavery: In this civilised British Government under the cloak of Brahmanism exposed by Jotirao Govindrao Fule', followed by the Marathi title *Gulamgiri*, underneath which Phule states in Marathi that the objective of his book is to aid and educate the people. The dedication in English precedes its translation in Marathi on the subsequent page:

> To/ The Good People of the United States/ As a Token of Admiration for their/ Sublime Disinterested and/ Selfsacrificing Devotion/ in the cause of Negro Slavery; and with an earnest desire, that my countrymen/may take their noble example as their guide in the emancipation of their Sudra Brethren/from the trammels of Brahmin thraldom./ The Author. (CWMP 1991[1969]: 124)

Through his dedication Phule not only pays a tribute to the movement against slavery in the United States but also places his narrative about the oppression of the Shudratishudra within the global discourse on racial oppression. Moreover, by invoking the question of race in the context of the emancipation of the African-Americans, Phule was able to make connections to the preoccupations of comparative philology and its hypothesis of the Aryan race. In this sense the very title and contents of this text are the earliest and perhaps the most important precursors to the efforts of the contemporary Dalit movement today to embody its struggle within the larger global assertion of racial oppression.

Hoping to bring to the notice of colonial power the historic marginalisation of the Shudratishudra, and the systematic blocking of their aspirations by Brahmins ensconced in positions of power in contemporary institutions, the 'Preface' to *Gulamgiri* contains a concise but forceful summary of the main theme of the book, namely the exploitation of the Shudratishudra from very ancient times as well as an analysis of the contemporary situation. The three epigraphs Phule attaches at the beginning of the 'Preface' show not only his familiarity with ancient Greek classical writers such as Homer, but also with current Orientalist historiography and philology, which last, he uses strategically to score points and build his arguments in the ensuing discussion. In a sense, through the epigraphs Phule astutely locates the arguments of his own book within European literary and analytic traditions. He begins on an incisive note, drawing substantially, as noted earlier, from Orientalist and missionary accounts of India:

> Recent researches have demonstrated beyond a shadow of doubt that the Brahmins were not the aborigines of India. At some remote period of antiquity, probably more than 3000 years ago, the Aryan progenitors of the present Brahmin Race descended upon the plains of Hindoostan from regions lying beyond the Indus, the Hindoo Koosh, and other adjoining tracts. (CWMP 1991[1969]: 127; pp. 179–180, this volume)

Listing the unchallenged privileges enjoyed by the Brahmins and the thraldom under which the Shudra and Atishudra, like the American slave, are subject, Phule goes on to analyse the monopoly of the Brahmins in all contemporary spatial locations: the field, the village, the temple, the court, the administrative office and the school. Pleading that the European officers 'generally view men and things through Brahmin spectacles and hence the deplorable ignorance they often exhibit in forming a correct estimate of them', Phule appeals to the British government on behalf of 'my poor, illiterate and ignorant Sudra brethren' on at least two counts. First that it should check the monopoly of the Brahmins and allow at least 'a sprinkling of the other castes to get into public service' (CWMP 1991[1969]: 134–137). Phule argues that if this is not feasible in the present state of education, given the fact that the Brahmins employed in the education department and in schools have never contributed to the advancement and education of their less fortunate fellow men, the government should reconsider its allocation to higher education that benefits only the Brahmins, and expend some financial outlay to the education of the masses, since in fact much of the revenue of the state is generated from the blood and sinew of the labouring classes.

These arguments were carried forward in the 'Memorial' submitted to the Indian Education Commission about a decade later, where Phule connected them in a comprehensive and meticulous conceptual framework to indicate the glaring lacunae in the system of education in the country, the yawning abyss between the elite and the subaltern and a possible roadmap to ensure that all marginalised sections including the lower castes, women and minorities have access to learning. We could now examine Phule's petition to the Indian Education Commission.

MEMORIAL ADDRESSED TO THE INDIAN EDUCATION COMMISSION (1882)

The English preface to *Gulamgiri* gathered renewed significance some years later when Lord Ripon, the Viceroy, appointed an Education Commission for India in 1881. Chaired by Sir William Hunter, it was the first in a series of Commissions in modern India appointed to look into the situation of contemporary education and recommend changes. We have discussed above that this was the first body to be set up after India was taken over by the Crown, and its brief was also to gauge the extent to which the recommendations of Wood's Despatch had been implemented. We must recall that this Despatch of 1854 had urged the implementation of basic education for the masses and suggested the means to achieve this end. As a public figure who had contributed immensely to the education of women and the lower castes, Phule was requested to make a deposition to the Hunter Commission. Phule alluded to his earlier work *Gulamgiri* in his Memorial Address to the Commission on 19 October 1882. Phule's testimony was in English and it emphasised the utmost necessity of primary education for the Shudratishudra up to the age of twelve. His deposition used excerpts from his 'Preface' to *Gulamgiri*, portions of which are reproduced below:

> I wrote some years ago a Marathi pamphlet exposing the religious practices of the Brahmins, and…the present system of education, which by providing ampler funds for higher

> education, tended to educate Brahmins and the higher classes only, and to leave the masses wallowing in ignorance and poverty.
>
> ...the greater portion of the revenues of the Indian Empire are derived from the ryot's labour—from the sweat of his brow. ...
>
> That Government should expend profusely a large portion of revenue thus raised on the education of the higher classes, for it is these only who take advantage of it, is anything but just or equitable. (CWMP 1991[1969]: 134; p. 192, this volume)

In these forceful passages from *Gulamgiri* focusing on the necessity of state funding of universal primary education, Phule urges the colonial government to assume responsibility for the education of the masses. He is critical of British educational policy for ignoring the need of basic primary education for the lower castes and has sharp words for the government's ingenuous belief in the downward filtration theory. It is a travesty of faith that the Brahmins would ever concern themselves with the education of the Shudratishudra. He clearly articulates the unfairness of the system wherein the government spends the revenue amassed from the produce created by the labouring castes on the education of the upper castes who have contributed nothing to the production of wealth. The children of the rich who benefit from government policy go on to become successful and care nothing for poor children who have had to give up their rights to primary education. Not only is higher education ensured for the upper caste, they also monopolise all government posts. The petition is a succinct account of the unfairness of government policy, exacerbating the already unjust system of caste hierarchy. Phule is acutely conscious of the influence that Brahmins in government posts have on shaping the perceptions of British officers. In all the works included for analysis in this volume: *Tritiya Ratna*, 'Vidyakhatyateel Brahman Pantoji' and the 'Preface' to *Gulamgiri*, Phule is concerned about the Brahmin's manipulative tactics in reporting to British officers that the lower castes have neither any love nor aptitude for learning. His fear is that long-standing traditional exclusions from learning that at last had a chance of redressal in the modern liberal ethos ushered in by the British 'were being confirmed and reinforced by the colonial power structure' (Mani, Braj Ranjan 2005: 274).

Phule makes a number of significant connections which reflect his canny understanding of the political economy underpinning the traditional society ordered on the basis of the caste structure. He is undoubtedly the first Indian revolutionary thinker to connect caste hegemony to economic status. During pre-British days, in times of enforced orthodoxy under the Peshwas, caste-based rules prevailed as the everyday norm. Each of the three texts that has been examined so far: *Tritiya Ratna*, 'Vidyakhatyateel Brahman Pantoji' and *Gulamgiri* points to the hegemonic role of the Brahmins and their control of the scriptures as the root of all exploitation. They also indicate that exclusive rights over textual knowledge is an intrinsic and unalienable aspect of economic exploitation and that the lower castes were forced to function in this oppressive structure. He is perhaps the first thinker to understand that Brahmins functioned not only as 'religious-social castes but also as economic occupational classes' (Joshi and Raman 1991: 1325). Phule was convinced that poverty and economic want was the main cause of the social backwardness of the lower castes.

Mahesh Gavaskar writes that the political economy of pre-British days granted many vested parties the right to agricultural produce. These extended from service providers at the village level and beyond the village level in an interlinked two-tier structure. Within the village the practice of the hereditary *balutedari*[7] system determined the share allotted to the tiller and all other castes which functioned in a state of reciprocal, yet hierarchical, interdependencies. Beyond the village was an entire hierarchy going up to the Mughal emperor or in the western region of India, the Peshwa.[8] During the long span leading to the first half of the nineteenth century, the British got rid of the top half of this two-tier structure and institutionalised in its place either the zamindari system to collect land revenue (as in other parts of India) or the ryotwari system, as in the Deccan region. In the ryotwari system the cultivator paid revenue directly to the colonial state, thereby cancelling the role of several intermediaries. The ryotwari system changed the system of land-ownership and introduced a new legal system in the village. Hitherto land was owned by the village community as a whole, but in this new system it could be owned by individual *mirasdars*.[9] These individuals quite obviously began to perceive the balutedari system as exploitative and parasitical upon agricultural produce (Gavaskar 2007[1999]: 92–93). Gail Omvedt suggests that the introduction of the new legal system eroded the role of the *patil* (the village headman generally from a dominant non-Brahmin caste) and bolstered the role of the Brahmin *kulkarni* (the village accountant). While Brahmin lawyers and clerks dominated the courts in urban areas, the kulkarni, who as the accountant was the keeper of land records in the village, came to have a pivotal role in rural Maharashtra (Omvedt 2011[1976]: 73–74). One can only estimate how this potential coil of upper-caste relations must have affected the poor Kunbi cultivator which Phule indicates graphically in his later text *Shetkaryacha Asud*: *The Cultivator's Whipcord.* Connected to these changes was the slow attrition of the balutedari system and the evolving penetration of a monetary economy which may have made the Brahmin *joshi* (village priest and astrologer) more prominent in rural areas even as the educated Brahmin had a monopoly in the new avenues opening up in the cities (Gavaskar 2007[1999]: 93).

Gail Omvedt discusses various modern initiatives undertaken by the administration such as the building of roads, bridges, railroads and buildings that linked agriculture in the western region to the world economy. These initiatives also required contractors to supply resources and labour. The business of contracting was an important source of wealth after the 1850s, and the processes of contracting and subcontracting that proliferated frequently involved a great deal of corruption. At the top of this money-making enterprise were British officers who, says Omvedt, were often engaged in extracting their share of the government monies, despite the image of incorruptibility built by the civil service. Elite Indians, including Brahmins and merchant classes, formed the next level. To the many non-Brahmins at the lower levels of the contracting process, who were often the aspiring poor, contractual business offered a novel opportunity of making their way up in the economic scale. If a particular kind of product was needed it was often the leading member of that artisan caste who contracted to supply it. Phule, we must remember was also a successful sub-contractor in some of these public works (Omvedt

2011[1976]: 67–68). This mobility in turn engendered the need to acquire literacy skills to make their way in the new world of incipient opportunities.

The colonial institutions of administration together with a surge in the technology of print communication opened up novel avenues of employment which facilitated migration from rural areas into urban centres. We have already noted that the Brahmins had made a smooth transition from their elite positions connected to textual knowledge systems in the traditional order to consolidate employment opportunities in colonial bureaucracy and related institutions. Under Elphinstone, a politically conservative administrator, the old Peshwa traditions such as the system of *dakshina* was continued in newer forms such as scholarships to Brahmins in Sanskrit studies and the setting up of a Sanskrit College in Pune, as noted earlier. Even though some of these institutions were gradually modified to open them up to modern subjects as well as to students of other castes, it was the Brahmins who were able to monopolise both Western education and the resulting opportunities of employment. Phule's acute understanding of the way the dice were loaded in favour of the Brahmins may be seen in the paragraph which Phule reproduces from his 'Preface' to *Gulamgiri*:

> One of the most glaring tendencies of Government system of high-class education has been the virtual monopoly of all the higher offices under them by Brahmins. ...if Government looks a little less after higher education which is able to take care of itself and more towards the education of the masses there would be no difficulty in training up a body of men every way qualified and perhaps far better in morals and manners. (CWMP 1991[1969]: 245; pp. 193–194, this volume)

Having sketched a social and economic framework as a background to his fervent appeal to the Indian Education Commission, Phule goes on to offer a short and succinct roadmap to achieve his goal: education for the lower castes and women. This blueprint for universal basic education discussed under three broad heads: primary education, indigenous schools and higher education, is based on an insider's lived experience of the social and economic realities confronting the lower caste. It comes as a shock to anyone reading Phule's petition today to see how closely these realities match with what is obtained on the ground in many parts of contemporary India. When he speaks of the special cess collected by government which 'does not appear to be spent for the purpose for which it is collected', or the 'deplorable state of education among the peasantry' and their 'entire dependence upon the learned and intelligent classes', Phule's words echo the truth of a more or less similar condition which continues to prevail amidst state apathy and societal callousness. It must be noted that Phule does not argue that the government withdraw its aid from higher educations since the 'withdrawal of State aid from higher education cannot but be injurious to the spread of education in general.' His only appeal is 'that as one class of the body politic has been neglected, its advancement should form as anxious a concern as that of the other' since 'Education in India is still in its infancy' (CWMP 1991[1969]: 251).

Undoubtedly it was Phule who pioneered the cause of subaltern education in India, including in his definition of the Shudratishudra, not only lower castes but also women of all castes. Though other reformers before him perceived the urgent necessity of modern education and started initiatives towards this end, none of them addressed the concerns of the lower castes or of the necessity for women (of all castes) to receive an education. Quite clearly, Phule was the first to combine initiatives in founding schools for lower-caste girls, girls of all castes, lower-caste boys and night schools for poor working adults with polemical and literary writing demonstrating the utmost significance of education for the emancipation of oppressed classes. He was also the first to plead for universal, compulsory and free primary education (Joshi and Raman 1991: 1327). He included the Muslim community within the fold of the masses comprising the working-class populations, stating that 'Primary education of the masses should be made compulsory up to a certain age, say at least 12 years. Muhammadans also hold aloof from these (government) schools, as they some-how evince no liking for Marathi or English. There are a few Muhammadan primary schools where their own language is taught' (CWMP 1991[1969]: 247). He urged the Commission to recommend the allocation of government funds for setting up primary schools for the lower castes and Muslims in mofussil towns and villages, since the few schools for the lower castes that were available were located in cities such as Pune or Bombay. The Brahmin teachers of other schools refused to admit children of the lower castes on grounds of caste norms asserting that the upper-caste students would not sit beside them.

It was Phule's wish that the Commission meet the poor and illiterate populations to gain a first-hand understanding of their abject conditions which would guide them in framing a policy guaranteeing universal primary education. The Commission, however, did not accede to his request, and bitterly disappointed, Phule could only remark: 'The Hunter Commission did not interview farmers. It relied solely on the discussions it had with Parsis, Christians and Brahmins and accepted their word as final. Hence, the report of this Commission will not benefit the illiterate and the poor' (cited in Mani, Braj Ranjan 2005: 273). Predictably the Hunter Commission did not accept Phule's demand that primary education must be made universal and compulsory for lower-caste children up to the age of twelve. A few years later in 1891, Phule accused Sir William Hunter of complete ignorance of the state of Shudras and Atishudras. He is reported to have stated, 'Huntersaheb is indulging in meaningless and idle loquaciousness' (cited in Deshpande 2002: 101). The deposition is also testimony to Phule's increasing rancour and disillusionment with the upper-caste reformist project even as he continued to regard Western education as the most important medium of emancipation for marginalised groups, waging a hard and lonely battle to towards implementing this goal.

Phule's vision of education had a number of interrelated aims, each of which may be seen in the texts analysed in this volume. The central purpose was intellectual emancipation from the thrall of Brahminical Hinduism: to raise consciousness by means of educating the lower castes and thereby unmask 'relations of domination and subordination hinged upon the knowledge of a dominant class' (Vendell 2014: 53). Modern education, Phule was convinced, was the tool to transform the consciousness of the oppressed collective which in turn would result in a transformed social order. Education would help cultivate the faculty of rational discernment: his idea of a *satyashodhok* was precisely the conscious practice of discernment which, he argued, would facilitate the process of reform from below. The Satyashodhak Samaj sought to achieve a transformed society based on the clear light of reason and the desire for democratic public good. In order to deliver public good, it was imperative that the lower castes share equally in the employment opportunities emerging in the rapidly modernising times. Only education would help them acquire gainful employment, and employment would put an end to the endemic and grinding poverty of the masses.

Phule's Memorial to the Education Commission also makes recommendations about the components of a curriculum suitable for common people. It is in fact a proposal to do away with elitism in primary education, seeking to connect the classroom curriculum with the day-to-day life of the labouring classes. While Phule perceived education as an emancipatory force, in the hands of the upper castes, education had become neo-Brahminical and non-egalitarian (Joshi and Raman 1991: 1327). Somewhat like Gandhi's formulations in *Nai Taleem*, Phule proposed to inject production-based knowledge in the form of vocational training in primary education. Consider for instance, the following passage in his petition:

> The course of instruction should consist of reading, writing Modi and Balbodh and accounts, and a rudimentary knowledge of general history, general geography, and grammar, also an elementary knowledge of agriculture and a few lessons on moral duties and sanitation. …In connection with lessons in agriculture, a small model farm, where practical instruction to the pupils can be given, would be…productive of the greatest good to the country. (CWMP 1991[1969]: 241; p. 197, this volume)

There is however a positional difference between Phule on the one hand, and Gandhi/Tagore on the other. All three stressed the necessity of productive manual training, or, as in the case of Tagore: artistic activities, performed together by the teacher and the students in a spirit of cooperative fellow-feeling. Yet for Gandhi this was a crucial step to stress the significance of manual labour in the reform of the prevailing paradigm of colonial education which catered largely to the upper castes; for Phule it was a way of linking the curriculum with the workaday lives of poor, lower-caste children, so as to direct the curriculum to lived experience. He also proposed special concessions and incentives to the students of backward castes in the form of scholarships and prizes as a way of inducing such children into the portals of the school. It would also be a way to encourage their parents to keep the children in school and not take them off the rolls in order to enlist them in menial chores to contribute to the family's productive labour and add to its meagre earnings.

Phule proposed that the government should start more schools exclusively for the children of the backward castes since they were not allowed to sit along with the other children. We may recall here studies by Constable and Zelliot, amongst others, discussed in earlier sections and the struggles of lower-caste parents to admit their wards into government schools. More importantly Phule had a rather radical proposition, as seen in the excerpt quoted below, to ensure that lower-caste children did not face discrimination from Brahmin teachers. We must remember that the *powada* 'Brahmin Teachers in the Education Department' included in this volume presents precisely this same point.

> I think teachers for primary schools should be trained, as far as possible, out of the cultivating classes, who will be able to mix freely with them and understand their wants and wishes much better than a Brahmin teacher, who generally holds himself aloof under religious prejudices. These would, moreover, exercise a more beneficial influence over the masses…will not feel ashamed to hold the handle of a plough or the carpenter's adze when required, and who will be able to mix themselves readily with the lower orders of society. …To secure a better class of teachers and to improve their position, better salaries should be given. (CWMP 1991[1969]: 248–249; p. 196, this volume)

Phule in fact argued for affirmative action and positive discrimination so that the sections historically denied learning and kept out of schools were able to function as equal members in the modern world. His critique of Brahmins was not only on the basis of ideology but stemmed from a nuanced understanding that colonial policy had enhanced the sacerdotal primacy of the class by making available for it the secular position of the educated elite (Anupama Rao 2010[2009]:

13). Conceptualising caste hierarchy in modern terms of exclusion and inequality, Phule was the earliest radical thinker and activist, as we can see in his petition, to frame historical injustice within the language of rights. This impetus was carried forward by Ambedkar from the 1920s who translated caste exclusion and inequality into 'secularized terms with expanded political range' so as to 'extend the range and signification of a "right" to include forms of life without prior political visibility' (Anupama Rao 2010[2009]: 14). A negative identity thus became the basis of the assertion of collective political rights. Anupama Rao suggests that the history of Indian democracy is inseparable from the interventions of 'anticaste radicals' who fought to represent caste as the practice of inequality, which explains why caste has only deepened in significance as democracy takes root in the country, producing a unique form of political assertion. Unlike Western democracies, democratic politics in India has meant the assertion of collective rights and the emancipation of communities rather than a struggle for individual autonomy. Undoubtedly Phule's long career devoted to the emancipation of the Shudratishudra laid the foundations of India's own version of democratic liberalism. His several literary and polemical writings and a lifetime of incredibly significant interventions enabled later torchbearers like Ambedkar to carry the movement forward. Ambedkar's fiery intellect and his enormous commitment to the cause ensured that the rights of the lower castes as equal citizens of the country and the laws for their inclusion and positive affirmative action are enshrined in the Indian constitution. The Constitution of India, which secures India's dream of democratic polity, is Ambedkar's resounding answer to the *Manusmriti*. Phule's legacy of questioning Brahminical texts culminates in this most significant document of modern India, which has been seen in recent studies as a people's constitution. Contrary to elite opinion which sees the Constitution of India as having had little influence on the teeming masses of the nation, scholars of law and social movements assert that not only did the Indian constitution enfranchise the largest population in the world, it came alive in the popular imagination so that ordinary people were empowered by it to lead movements that produced through litigation, alternative ethical models of citizenships (De 2018). As a pioneer and leader of the earliest subaltern movement in India who focused on emancipation through reason and equality, Phule continues to be an inspiring force.

Notes

1. This paragraph and the next summarises the excellent analysis put forward by Pennington 2005: 30–40.
2. The next couple of paragraphs are based on Rosalind O'Hanlon's excellent discussion in O'Hanlon 2010[1985]: 64–65.
3. For instance, see studies by Susan Bayly (1989), and Henriette Bugge (1994). Also cited by Philip Constable (2000).
4. See Zelliot 1996; Constable 1997 and 2001; and Anupama Rao (2010[2009]) for details on lower caste and Dalit leadership, and the mobilisation on the issue of education during the 1890s and the early decades of the 20th century, i.e. between the two remarkable periods led by Jotiba Phule and Dr B. R. Ambedkar.
5. See O'Hanlon 2010[1985]: 135–140; and Devare 2011: 37–71 for a detailed analysis.
6. This part of the discussion is based on Mokashi-Punekar 2017: 149–171.
7. *Balutedari* was a hereditary system of twelve trades/castes who were paid in kind with village produce for services they rendered to the village in a complex barter system.
8. Much of the credit for bringing about the land revenue settlement in the Deccan region, which formed the basis for subsequent revenue arrangements, is given to the 17th-century Habshi military leader Malik Ambar, who has also been seen as the founder of Maratha nationalism. See Shyam 1968; and Eaton 2005.
9. *Mirasdars* were landowners who had to pay annual taxes under the ryotwari system.

'Preface' to *Gulamgiri*

'The day that reduces a man to slavery takes from him the half of his virtue.'

Homer

'Our system of Government in India is not calculated to raise the character of those subject to it, nor is the present system of education one to do more than *over-educate the few*, leaving the mass of the people as ignorant as ever and still mere[1] [sic] at the mercy of the few learned; in fact, it is an extension of the demoralizing Brahmin-ridden policy, which, perhaps, has more retarded the progress of civilization and improvement in India generally than anything else.'

Col. G. J. Haly, *On Fisheries in India*

'Many ages have elapsed since peculiar resources were afforded to the Brahmins; but the most considerate cosmopolite would hesitate to enroll them amongst the benefactors of the world. They boast of vast stores of ancient learning. They have amassed great riches, and been invested with unbounded power, but to what good end? They have cherished the most degrading superstitions and practised the most shameless impostures. They have arrogated to themselves the possession and enjoyment of the rarest gifts of fortune and perpetuated the most revolting system known to the world. It is only from a diminution of their abused power that we can hope to accomplish the great work of national regeneration.'

[Herbert] Mead, *Sepoy Revolt*[2]

Recent researches have demonstrated beyond a shadow of doubt that the Brahmins were not the aborigines of India. At some remote period of antiquity, probably more than 3000 years ago, the Aryan progenitors of the present Brahmin Race descended upon the plains of Hindoostan from regions lying beyond the Indus, the Hindoo Koosh, and other adjoining tracts. According to Dr Pritchard, the Ethnologist, they were an off-shoot of the Great Indo-European race, from whom the Persians, Medes, and other Iranian nations in Asia and the principal nations in Europe like-wise are descended. The affinity existing between the Zend, the Persian and the Sanskrit languages, as also between all the European languages, unmistakably points to a common source or origin. It appears also more than probable that the original cradle of this race being an arid, sandy and mountainous region, and one ill calculated to afford them the sustenance which their growing wants required, they branched off into colonies, East and West. The extreme fertility of the soil in India, its rich productions, the proverbial wealth of its people, and the other innumerable gifts which this favoured land enjoys, and which have more recently tempted the cupidity of the Western nations, no doubt, attracted the Aryans, who came to India, not as simple emigrants with peaceful intentions of colonisation, but as conquerors. They appear to have been a race imbued with very high notions of self, extremely cunning, arrogant and bigoted. Such self-gratulatory, pride-flattering epithets as आर्य, भूदेव etc., with which they designated themselves, confirm us in our opinion of their primitive character, which they have preserved up to the present time, with, perhaps, little change for the better. The aborigines whom the Aryans subjugated, or displaced, appear to have been a hardy and brave people from the determined front which they offered to these interlopers. Such opprobrious terms as (शूद्र) Sudra, 'insignificant,' महारी 'the great foe,' अंत्यज, चांडाळ etc. with which they designated them, undoubtedly show that originally they offered the greatest resistance in their power to their [the Aryans] establishing themselves in the country, and hence the great aversion and hatred in which they are held. From many customs[3] traditionally handed down to us, as well as from the mythological legends contained in the sacred books of the Brahmins, it is evident that there had been a hard struggle for ascendancy between the two races. The wars of Devas and Daityas or the Rakshasas, about which so many fictions are found scattered over the sacred books of the Brahmins, have certainly a reference to this primeval struggle. The original inhabitants with whom these earthborn Gods, the Brahmins, fought, were not inappropriately termed Rakshas,[4] that is the protectors of the land. The incredible and foolish legends regarding their form and shape are no doubt mere chimeras, the fact being that these people were of superior stature and hardy make. Under such leaders as Brahma, Purshram[5] and others, the Brahmins waged very protracted wars against the original inhabitants. They eventually succeeded in establishing their supremacy and subjugating the aborigines to their entire control. Accounts of these conquests, enveloped with a mass of incredible fiction, are found in the books of the Brahmins. In some instances they were compelled to emigrate, and in others wholesale extermination was resorted to. The cruelties which the European settlers practised on the American Indians on their first settlement in the New World, had certainly their parallel in India on the advent of the Aryans and their subjugation of the aborigines. The cruelties and inhuman atrocities which Purshram committed on the Kshetrias,[6] the people of this land, if we are to believe even one-tenth of what the legends say regarding him, surpass our belief and show that he was more a fiend than a God. Perhaps in the whole range of history it is scarcely possible to meet with such another character as that of Purshram, so selfish, infamous, cruel and inhuman. The deeds of Nero, Alaric or Machiavelli sink into insignificance before the ferocity of Purshram. The myriads of men and defenceless children whom he butchered, simply with a view to the establishment of his coreligionists on a secure and permanent basis in this land, is a fact for which generations ought to execrate his name, rather than deify it.

This, in short, is the history of Brahmin domination in India. They originally settled on the banks of the Ganges whence they gradually spread over the whole of India. In order, however, to keep a better hold on the people they devised that weird system of mythology, the ordination of caste, and the code of cruel and inhuman laws, to which we can find no parallel amongst other nations. They founded a system of priestcraft so galling in its tendency and operation, the like of which we can hardly find anywhere since the times of the Druids. The institution of Caste, which has been the main object of their laws, had no existence among them originally. That it was an after-creation of their deep cunning is evident from their own writings. The highest rights, the highest privileges and gifts, and everything that would make the life of a Brahmin easy, smooth-going and happy—everything that would conserve or flatter their self-pride—were specially inculcated, and enjoined, whereas the Sudras and Atisudras were regarded with supreme hatred and contempt, and the commonest rights of humanity were denied them. Their touch, nay, even their shadow, is deemed a pollution. They are considered as mere chattels, and their life of no more value than that of [the] meanest reptile; for it is enjoined that if a Brahmin, 'kill a cat or an ichneumon, the bird Chasha, or a frog or a dog, a lizard, an owl, a crow or a Sudra' he is absolved of his sin by performing the चांद्रायण प्रायश्चित, a fasting penance, perhaps for a few hours or a day and requiring not much labour or trouble. While for a Sudra to kill a Brahmin is considered the most heinous offence he could commit, and the forfeiture of his life is the only punishment his crime is considered to merit. Happily for our Sudra brethren of the present day our enlightened British Rulers have not recognised these preposterous, inhuman and unjust penal enactments of the Brahmin legislators. They no doubt regard them more as ridiculous fooleries than as equitable laws. Indeed, no man possessing even a grain of common sense would regard them as otherwise. Anyone, who feels disposed to look a little more into the laws and ordinances as embodied in the *Manava Dharma Shastra* and other works of the same class, would undoubtedly be impressed with the deep cunning underlying them all. It may not, perhaps, be out of place to cite here a few more instances in which the superiority or excellence of the Brahmins is held and enjoined on pain of Divine displeasure.

> The Brahmin is styled the Lord of the Universe, even equal to the God himself. He is to be worshipped, served and respected by all.
>
> A Brahmin can do no wrong.
>
> Never shall the King slay a Brahmin, though he has committed all possible crimes.
>
> To save the life of a Brahmin any falsehood may be told. There is no sin in it.

No one is to take away anything belonging to a Brahmin.

A king, though dying with want, must not receive any tax from a Brahmin, nor suffer him to be afflicted with hunger or the whole kingdom will be afflicted with famine.

The feet of a Brahmin are holy. In his left foot reside all the तीर्थ (holy waters at places of pilgrimage) and by dipping it into water he makes it as holy as the waters at the holiest of shrines.

A Brahmin may compel a man of the servile class to perform servile duty, because such a man was created by the almighty only for the purpose of serving Brahmins.

A Sudra, though emancipated by his master, is not released from [a] state of servitude; for, being born in a state which is natural to him, by whom can he be divested of his natural attributes?

Let a Brahmin not give temporal advice nor spiritual counsel to a Sudra.

No superfluous accumulation of wealth shall be made by a Sudra, even though he has the power to make it, since a servile man who has amassed riches becomes proud, and by his insolence or neglect he gives pain even to Brahmins.

If a Sudra cohabit with a Brahminee adulteress, his life is to be taken. But if a Brahmin goes even unto the lawful wife of a Sudra he is exempted from all corporal punishment.

It would be needless to go on multiplying instances such as these. Hundreds of similar ordinances including many more of a worse character than these can be found scattered over their books. But what can have been the motives and objects of such cruel and inhuman Laws? They are, I believe, apparent to all but to the infatuated, the blind and the self-interested. Anyone who runs may read them. Their main object in fabricating these falsehoods was to dupe the minds of the ignorant and to rivet firmly on them the chains of perpetual bondage and slavery which their selfishness and cunning had forged. The severity of the laws as affecting the Sudras, and the intense hatred with which they were regarded by the Brahmins can be explained on no other supposition but that there was, originally between the two, a deadly feud, arising as we have shown above, from the advent of the latter into this land. It is surprising to think what a mass of specious fiction these interlopers invented with a view to hold the original occupiers of the soil fast in their clutches, and working on their credulity, rule securely for ages yet to come. Anyone who will consider well the whole history of Brahmin domination in India, and the thraldom under which it has retained the people even up to the present day, will agree with us in thinking that no language could be too harsh by which to characterise the selfish heartlessness and the consummate cunning of the Brahmin tyranny by which India has been so long governed. How far the Brahmins have succeeded in their endeavours to enslave the minds of the Sudras and Atisudras, those of them who have come to know the true state of matters know well to their cost. For generations past they have borne these chains of slavery and bondage. Innumerable Bhut writers, with the selfsame objects as those of Menu[7] [sic] and others of his class, added from time to time to the existing mass of legends, the idle phantasies of their own brains and palmed them off upon the ignorant masses as of Divine inspiration, or as the acts of the Deity himself. The most immoral, inhuman, unjust actions and deeds have been attributed to that Being who is our Creator, Governor and Protector, and who is all Holiness himself. These blasphemous writings, the products of the distempered brains of these interlopers, were received as gospel truths, for to doubt them was considered as the most unpardonable of sins. This system of slavery, to which the Brahmins reduced the lower classes, is in no respects inferior to that which obtained a few years ago in America. In the days of rigid Brahmin dominancy, so lately as that of the time of the Peshwa, my Sudra brethren had even greater hardships and oppression practised upon them than what even the slaves in America had to suffer. To this system of selfish superstition and bigotry, we are to attribute the stagnation and all the evils under which India has been groaning for many centuries past. It will, indeed, be difficult to name a single advantage which accrued to the aborigines from the advent of this intensely selfish and tyrannical sect. The Indian Ryot (the Sudra and Atisudra) has been in fact a proverbial Milch Cow. He has passed from hand to hand. Those who successively held sway over him cared only to fatten themselves on the sweat of his brow, without caring for his welfare or condition.

It was sufficient for their purposes that they held him safe in their clutches for squeezing out of him as much as they possibly could. The Brahmin had at last so contrived to entwine himself round the Sudra in every large or small undertaking, in every domestic or public business, that the latter is by custom quite unable to transact any concern of moment without his aid.

This is even true at the present time. While the Sudra on the other hand is so far reconciled to the Brahmin yoke, that like the American slave he would resist any attempt that may be made for his deliverance and fight even against his benefactor. Under the guise of religion the Brahmin has his finger in everything, big or small, which the Sudra undertakes. Go to his house, to his field or to the court to which business may invite him, the Brahmin is there under some specious pretext or other, trying to squeeze out of him as much as his cunning and wily brain can manage. The Brahmin despoils the Sudra not only in his capacity of a priest, but does so in a variety of other ways. Having by his superior education and cunning monopolised all the higher places of emolument, the ingenuity of his ways is past finding out, as the reader will find on an attentive perusal of this book. In the most insignificant village as in the largest town, the Brahmin is the all in all; the be all and the end all of the Ryot. He is the master, the ruler. The Patell of a village, the headman, is in fact a nonentity. The Koolkurnee, the hereditary Brahmin village accountant, the notorious quarrel-monger, moulds the Patell according to his wishes. He is the temporal and spiritual adviser of the ryots, the Soucar in his necessities and the general referee in all matters. In most instances he plans active mischief by advising opposite parties differently, so that he may feather his own nest well. If we go up higher, to the Court of a Mamlutdar, we find the same thing. The first anxiety of a Mamlutdar is to get round him, if not his own relatives, his castemen to fill the various offices under him. These actively foment quarrels and are the media of all corrupt practices prevailing generally round about these Courts. If a Sudra or Atisudra repairs to his Court, the treatment which he receives is akin to what the meanest reptile gets. Instead of his case receiving a patient and careful hearing, a choice lot of abuse is showered on his devoted head, and his prayer is set aside on some pretext or other.

Whereas if one of his own castemen were to repair to the Court on the self-same business, he is received with all courtesy and there is hardly any time lost in getting the matter right. If we go up still higher to the Collector's and Revenue Commissioner's Courts and to the other Department of the Public Services, the Engineering, Educational etc., the same system is carried out on a smaller or greater scale. The higher European officers generally view men and things through Brahmin spectacles, and hence the deplorable ignorance they often exhibit in forming a correct estimate of them. I have tried to place before my readers in the concluding portions of this book what expedients are employed by these Brahmin officials for fleecing the Coonbee in the various departments to which business or his necessities induce him to resort. Any one knowing intimately the working of the different departments, and the secret springs which are in motion, will unhesitatingly concur with me in saying that what I have described in the following pages is not one-hundredth part of the rogueries that are generally practised on my poor, illiterate and ignorant Sudra brethren. Though the Brahmin of the old Peshwa school is not quite the same as the Brahmin of the present day, though the march of Western ideas and civilisation is undoubtedly telling on his superstition and bigotry, he has not as yet abandoned his time-cherished notions of superiority or the dishonesty of his ways. The Beef, the Mutton, the intoxicating beverages stronger and more fiery than the famed *Somarasa*, which their ancestors once relished, as the veriest dainties are fast finding innumerable votaries among them.

The Brahmin of the present time finds to some extent, like Othello, that his occupation is gone. But knowing full well this state of affairs, is the Brahmin inclined to make atonement for his past selfishness? Perhaps, it would have been useless to repine over what has been suffered and what has passed away, had the present state been all that is desirable. We know perfectly well that the Brahmin will not descend from his self-raised high pedestal and meet his Coonbee and low-caste brethren on an equal footing without a struggle. Even the educated Brahmin who knows his exact position and how he has come by it, will not condescend to acknowledge the errors of his forefathers and willingly forego the long cherished false notions of his own superiority. At present not one has the moral courage to do what only duty demands, and as long as this continues, one sect distrusting and degrading another sect, the condition of the Sudras will remain unaltered, and India will never advance in greatness or prosperity.

Perhaps a part of the blame in bringing matters to this crisis may be justly laid to the credit of the Government. Whatever may have been their motives in providing ampler funds and greater facilities for higher education and neglecting that of the masses, it will be acknowledged by all that in justice to the latter this is not as it should be. It is an admitted fact that the greater portion of the revenues of the Indian Empire are derived from the Ryot's labour—from the sweat of his brow. The higher and richer classes contribute little or nothing to the state's exchequer. A well-informed English writer states that,

> 'Our income is derived, not from surplus profits, but from capital; not from luxuries but from the poorest necessaries. It is the product of sin and tears.'

That Government should expend profusely a large portion of revenue thus raised on the education of the higher classes, for it is these only who take advantage of it, is anything but just or equitable. Their object in patronising this virtual high-class education appears to be to prepare scholars, 'Who, it is thought, would in time vend learning without money and without price.' 'If we can inspire,' say they 'the love of knowledge in the minds of the superior classes, the result will be a higher standard of morals in the cases of the individuals, a large amount of affection for the British Government, and an unconquerable desire to spread among their own countrymen the intellectual blessings which they have received.'

Regarding these objects of Government the writer, above alluded to, states that:—

> 'We have never heard of philosophy more benevolent and more utopian. It is proposed by men who witness the wondrous changes brought about in the Western world, purely by the agency of popular knowledge, to redress the defects of the two hundred millions of India, by giving superior education to the superior classes and to them only.' ... 'We ask the friends of Indian Universities to favour us with a single example of the

> truth of their theory from the instances which have already fallen within the scope of their experience. They have educated many children of wealthy men, and have been the means of advancing very materially the worldly prospects of some of their pupils. But what contribution have these made to the great work of regenerating their fellowmen? How have they begun to act upon the masses? Have any of them formed classes, at their own homes or elsewhere, for the instruction of their less fortunate or less wise countrymen? Or have they kept their knowledge to themselves, as a personal gift, not to be soiled by contact with the ignorant vulgar? Have they in any way shown themselves anxious to advance the general interests and repay philanthropy with patriotism? Upon what grounds is it asserted that the best way to advance the moral and intellectual welfare of the people is to raise the standard of instruction among the higher classes? A glorious argument this for aristocracy, were it only tenable. To show the growth of the national happiness, it would only be necessary to refer to the number of pupils at the colleges and the lists of academic degrees. Each wrangler would be accounted a national benefactor; and the existence of Deans and Proctors would be associated, like the game laws and the ten-pound franchise, with the best interests of the Constitution.'

Perhaps the most glaring tendency of the Government system of high-class education has been the virtual monopoly of all the higher offices under them by the Brahmins. If the welfare of the Ryot is at heart, if it is the duty of Government to check a host of abuses, it behoves them to narrow this monopoly, day by day, so as to allow a sprinkling of the other castes to get into the public service. Perhaps some might be inclined to say that it is not feasible in the present state of education. Our only reply is that if Government look a little less after higher education and more towards the education of the masses, the former being able to take care of itself, there would be no difficulty in training up a body of men every way qualified and perhaps far better in morals and manners.

My object in writing the present volume is not only to tell my Sudra brethren how they have been duped by the Brahmins, but also to open the eyes of Government to that pernicious system of high-class education which has hitherto been so persistently followed and which statesmen like Sir George Campbell, the present Lieutenant Governor of Bengal, with broad and universal sympathies, are finding to be highly mischievous and pernicious to the interests of Government. I sincerely hope that Government will ere long see the error of their ways, trust less to writers or men who look through high-class spectacles and take the glory into their own hands of emancipating my Sudra brethren from the trammels of bondage which the Brahmins have woven round them like the coils of a serpent. It is no less the duty of such of my Sudra brethren as have received any education to place before Government the true state of their fellowmen and endeavour to the best of their power to emancipate themselves from Brahmin thraldom. Let there be schools for the Sudras in every village; but away with all Brahmin school-masters! The Sudras are the life and sinews of the country, and it is to them alone and not to the Brahmins that the Government must ever look to tide them over their difficulties, financial as well as political. If the hearts and minds of the Sudras are made happy and contented, the British Government need have no fear for their loyalty in the future.

1st June, 1873 **Joteerao Phooley**

Notes

1. This is probably a typographical error; perhaps the word is 'more'. But both 1969 and 1991 editions of the *Collected Works* have 'mere'.

[2. Herbert Mead, *The Sepoy Revolt: Its Causes and its Consequences* (London: John Murray, 1857), 293.]

3. A most remarkable and striking corroboration of these views is to be found in the religious rites observed on some of the grand festivals which have a reference to Bali Raja, the great king who appears to have reigned once in the hearts and affections of the Sudras and whom the Brahmin rulers displaced. On the day of *Dushara*, the wife and sisters of a Sudra, when he returns from his worship of the *Shumi Tree* and after the distribution of its leaves, which are regarded on that day as equivalent to gold, amongst his

friends, relations and acquaintances, he is greeted at home with a welcome इडा पिडा जावो आणि बळीचें राज्य येवो 'Let all troubles and misery go, and the kingdom of Bali come.' Whereas the wife and sisters of a Brahmin place on that day in the foreground of the house an image of Bali, made generally of wheaten or other flour, and when the Brahmin returns from his worship of the *Shumi Tree* he takes the stalk of it, pokes with it the belly of the image and then passes into the house. This contrariety, in the religious customs and usages obtaining amongst the Sudras and the Brahmins and of which many more examples might be adduced, can be explained on no supposition but that which I have tried to confirm and elucidate in these pages.

[4. Transliterated from the Marathi and a play on the word '*raksha*', which means to protect.]

[5. Phule's spelling of Parashuram in this 'Preface'.]

[6. It is suggested that the term 'Kshatriya' is etymologically derived from *kshetra*: region, land; and *kshetrias*: the people of this land.]

[7. Manu.]

Memorial Addressed to the Education Commission[1]

A Statement for the Information of the Education Commission

My experience in educational matters is principally confined to Poona and the surrounding villages. About 25 years ago, the missionaries had established a female school at Poona but no indigenous school for girls existed at the time. I, therefore, was induced, about the year 1854,[2] to establish such a school, and in which I and my wife worked together for many years. After some time I placed this school under the management of a committee of educated natives. Under their auspices two more schools were opened in different parts of the town. A year after the institution of the female schools, I also established an indigenous mixed school for the lower classes, especially the Mahars and Mangs. Two more schools for these classes were subsequently added. Sir Erskine Perry, the president of the late Educational Board, and Mr. Lumsdain, the then Secretary to Government, visited the female schools and were much pleased with the movement set on foot, and presented me with a pair of shawls. I continued to work in them for nearly 9 to 10 years, but owing to circumstances, which it is needless here to detail, I seceded from the work. These female schools still exist, having been made over by the committee to the Educational Department under the management of Mrs. Mitchell. A school for the lower classes, Mahars and Mangs, also exists at the present day, but not in a satisfactory condition. I have also been a teacher for some years in a mission female boarding school. My principal experience was gained in connection with these schools. I devoted some attention also to the primary education available in this Presidency and have had some opportunities of forming an opinion as to the system and *personnel* employed in the lower schools of the Educational Department. I wrote some years ago a Marathi pamphlet exposing the religious practices of the Brahmins, and, incidentally among other matters, adverted therein to the present system of education, which, by providing ampler funds for higher education, tended to educate Brahmins and the higher classes only, and to leave the masses wallowing in ignorance and poverty. I summarised the views expressed in the book in an English preface attached thereto, portions of which I reproduce here so far as they relate to the present enquiry:—

> 'Perhaps a part of the blame in bringing matters to this crisis may be justly laid to the credit of the Government. Whatever may have been their motives in providing ampler funds and greater facilities for higher education, and neglecting that of the masses, it will be acknowledged by all that in justice to the latter, this is not as it should be. It is an admitted fact that the greater portion of the revenues of the Indian Empire are derived from the ryot's labour—from the sweat of his brow. The higher and richer classes contribute little or nothing to the state exchequer. A well-informed English writer states that our income is derived, not from surplus profits, but from capital; not from luxuries, but from the poorest necessaries. It is the product of sin and tears.
>
> 'That Government should expend profusely a large portion of revenue thus raised on the education of the higher classes, for it is these only who take advantage of it, is anything but just or equitable. Their object in patronising this actual high-class education appears to be to prepare scholars who, it is thought, would in time vend learning without money and without price. If we can inspire, say they, the love of knowledge in the minds of the superior classes, the result will be a higher standard, of morals in the cases of the individuals, a large amount of affection for the British Government, and unconquerable desire to spread among their own countrymen the intellectual blessings which they have received.
>
> 'Regarding these objects of Government the writer above alluded to, states that we have never heard of philosophy more

benevolent and more utopian. It is proposed by men who witness the wondrous changes brought about in the Western world, purely by the agency of popular knowledge, to redress the defects of the two hundred millions of India, by giving superior education to the superior classes and to them only. We ask the friends of Indian Universities to favour us with a single example of the truth of their theory from, the instances which have already fallen within the scope of their experience. They have educated many children of wealthy men and have been the means of advancing very materially the worldly prospects of some of their pupils. But what contribution have these made to [the] great work of regenerating their fellowmen? How have they begun to act upon the masses? Have any of them formed classes at their own homes or elsewhere, for the instruction of their less fortunate or less wise countrymen? Or have they kept their knowledge to themselves, as a personal gift, not to be soiled by contact with the ignorant vulgar? Have they in any way shown themselves anxious to advance the general interests and repay the philanthropy with patriotism? Upon what grounds is it asserted that the best way to advance the moral and intellectual welfare of the people is to raise the standard of instruction among the higher classes? A glorious argument this for aristocracy, were it only tenable. To show the growth of the national happiness, it would only be necessary to refer to the number of pupils at the colleges and the lists of academic degrees. Each wrangler would be accounted a national benefactor; and the existence of Deans and Proctors would be associated, like the game laws and the ten-pound franchise, with the best interests of the Constitution.

'One of the most glaring tendencies of Government system of high-class education has been the virtual monopoly of all the higher offices under them by Brahmins. If the welfare of the Ryot is at heart, if it is the duty of Government to check a host of abuses, it behoves them to narrow this monopoly day by day so as to allow a sprinkling of the other castes, to get into the public services. Perhaps some might be inclined to say that it is not feasible in the present state of education. Our only reply is that if Government looks a little less after higher education which is able to take care of itself and more towards the education of the masses there would be no difficulty in training up a body of men every way qualified and perhaps far better in morals and manners.

'My object in writing the present volume is not only to tell my Shudra brethren how they have been duped by the Brahmins, but also to open the eyes of Government to that pernicious system of high-class education, which has hitherto been so persistently followed, and which statesmen like Sir George Campbell, the present Lieutenant Governor of Bengal, with broad universal sympathies, are finding to be highly mischievous and pernicious to the interests of Government. I sincerely hope that Government will ere long see the error of their ways, trust less to writers or men who look through high-class spectacles, and take the glory into their own hands of emancipating my Shudra brethren from the trammels of bondage which the Brahmins have woven around them like the coils of a serpent. It is no less the duty of each of my Shudra brethren as have received any education to place before Government the true state of their fellowmen and endeavour to the best of their power to emancipate themselves from Brahmin thraldom. Let there be schools for the Shudras in every village; but away with all Brahmin school-masters! The Shudras are the life and sinews of the country, and it is to them alone, and not to the Brahmins, that Government must ever look to tide over their difficulties, financial as well as political. If the hearts and minds of the Shudras are made happy and contented, the British Government need have no fear for their loyalty in the future.'

PRIMARY EDUCATION

There is little doubt that primary education among the masses in this Presidency has been very much neglected. Although the number of primary schools now in existence is greater than those existing a few years ago, yet they are not commensurate to the requirements of the community. Government collects a special cess for educational purposes, and it is to be regretted that this fund is not spent for the purposes for which it is collected. Nearly nine-tenths of the villages in this Presidency, or nearly 10 lakhs of children, it is said, are without any provision, whatever, for primary instruction. A good deal of their poverty, their want of self-reliance, their entire dependence upon the learned and intelligent classes, is attributable to this deplorable state of education among the peasantry.

Even in *towns* the Brahmins, the Purbhoos, the hereditary classes, who generally live by the occupation of pen, and the trading classes seek primary instruction. The cultivating and the other classes, as a rule, do not generally avail themselves of the same. A few of the latter class are found in primary and secondary schools, but owing to their poverty and other causes they do not continue long at school. As there are no special inducements for these to continue at school, they naturally leave off as soon as they find menial or other occupation. In *villages* also most of the cultivating classes hold aloof owing to extreme poverty, and also because they require their children to tend cattle and look after their fields. Besides an increase in the number of schools, special inducements in the shape of scholarships and half-yearly or annual prizes to encourage them to send their children to school and thus create in them a taste for learning, is most essential. I think primary education of the masses should be made compulsory up to a certain age, say at least 12 years. Muhammadans also hold aloof from these schools, as they somehow evince no liking for Marathi or English. There are a few Muhammadan primary schools where their own language is taught. The *Mahars*, *Mangs*, and other lower classes are practically excluded from all schools owing to caste prejudices, as they are not allowed to sit by the children of higher castes. Consequently special schools for these have been opened by Government. But these exist only in large towns. In the whole of Poona and for a population exceeding over 5,000 people, there is only one school and in which the attendance is under 30 boys. This state of matters is not at all creditable to the educational authorities. Under the promise of the Queen's Proclamation I beg to urge that Mahars, Mangs, and other lower classes, where their number is large enough, should have separate schools for them, as they are not allowed to attend the other schools owing to caste prejudices.

In the present state of education, payment by results is not at all suitable for the promotion of education amongst a poor and ignorant people, as no taste has yet been created among them for education. I do not think any teacher would undertake to open schools on his own account among these people, as he would not be able to make a living by it. Government schools and special inducements, as noted above, are essential until such a taste is created among them.

With regard to the few Government primary schools that exist in the Presidency, I beg to observe that the primary education imparted in them is not at all placed on a satisfactory or sound basis. The system is imperfect in so far as it does not prove practical and useful in the future career of the pupils. The system is capable of being developed up to the requirement of the community, if improvements that will result in its future usefulness be effected in it. Both the teaching machinery employed and the course in instruction now followed, require a thorough remodelling.

(a) The teachers now employed in the primary schools are almost all Brahmins; a few of them are from the normal, training college, the rest being all untrained men. Their salaries are very low, seldom exceeding Rs. 10, and their attainments also very meagre. But as a rule they are all unpractical men, and the boys who learn under them generally imbibe inactive habits and try to obtain service, to the avoidance of their hereditary or other hardy or independent professions. I think teachers for primary schools should be trained, as far as possible, out of the cultivating classes, who will be able to mix freely with them and understand their wants and wishes much better than a Brahmin teacher, who generally holds himself aloof under religious prejudices. These would, moreover, exercise a more beneficial influence over the masses than teachers of other classes, and who will not feel ashamed to hold the handle of a plough or the carpenter's adze when required, and who will be able to mix themselves readily with the lower orders of society. The course of training for them ought to include, besides the ordinary subjects, an elementary knowledge of agriculture and sanitation. The untrained teachers should, except when thoroughly efficient, be replaced by efficient trained teachers. To secure a better class of teachers and to improve their position, better salaries should be given. Their salaries should not be less than Rs. 12 and in larger villages should be at least Rs. 15 or 20. Associating them in the village polity as auditors of village accounts or registrars of deeds, or village postmasters or stamp vendors, would improve their status, and thus exert a beneficial influence over the people among whom they live. The schoolmasters of village schools who pass a large number of boys should also get some special allowance other than their pay, as an encouragement to them.

(b) The course of instruction should consist of reading, writing Modi and Balbodh[3] and accounts, and a rudimentary knowledge of general history, general geography, and grammar, also an elementary knowledge of agriculture and a few lessons on moral duties and sanitation. The studies in the village schools might be fewer than those in larger villages and towns, but not the less practical. In connection with lessons in agriculture, a small model farm, where practical instruction to the pupils can be given, would be a decided advantage and, if really efficiently managed, would be productive of the greatest good to the country. The text-books in use, both in the primary and Anglo-vernacular schools, require revision and recasting as much as they are not practical or progressive in their scope. Lessons on technical education and morality, sanitation and agriculture, and some useful arts, should be interspersed among them in progressive series. The fees in the primary schools should be as 1 to 2 from the children of cess-payers and non-cess payers.

(c) The supervising agency over these primary schools is also very defective and insufficient. The Deputy Inspector's visit once a year can hardly be of any appreciable benefit. All these schools ought at least to be inspected quarterly if not oftener. I would also suggest the advisability of visiting these schools at other times and without any intimation being given. No reliance can be placed on the district or village officers owing to the multifarious duties devolving on them, as they seldom find time to visit them, and when they do, their examination is necessarily very superficial and imperfect. [A] European Inspector's supervision is also occasionally very desirable, as it will tend to exercise a very efficient control over the teachers generally.

(d) The number of primary schools should be increased—
   (1) By utilising such of the indigenous schools as shall be or are conducted by trained and certificated teachers, by giving them liberal grants-in-aid.
   (2) By making over one half of the local cess fund for primary education alone.
   (3) By compelling, under a statutory enactment, municipalities to maintain all the primary schools within their respective limits.
   (4) By an adequate grant from the provincial or imperial funds.

Prizes and scholarships to pupils, and capitation or other allowances to the teachers, as an encouragement, will tend to render these schools more efficient.

The Municipalities in large towns should be asked to contribute whole share of the expenses incurred on primary schools within the municipal area. But in no case ought the management of the same to be entirely made over to them. They should be under the supervision of the Educational Department.

The municipalities should also give grants-in-aid to such secondary and private English schools as shall be conducted according to the rules of the Educational Department, where their funds permit, such grants-in-aid being regulated by the number of boys passed every year. These contributions from municipal funds may be made compulsory by statutory enactment.

The administration of the funds for primary education should ordinarily be in the hands of the Director of Public Instruction.

But if educated and intelligent men are appointed on the local or district committees, these funds may be safely entrusted to them, under the guidance of the Collector, or the Director of Public Instruction. At present, the local boards consist of ignorant and uneducated men, such as Patels, Inamdars, Surdars, &c. who would not be capable of exercising any intelligent control over the funds.

INDIGENOUS SCHOOLS

Indigenous schools exist a good deal in cities, towns and some large villages, especially where there is a Brahmin population. From the latest reports of Public Instruction in this Presidency, it is found that there are 1,049 indigenous schools with about 27,694 pupils in them. They are conducted on the old village system. The boys are generally taught the multiplication table by heart, a little Modi writing and reading, and to recite a few religious pieces. The teachers, as a rule, are not capable of effecting any improvements, as they are not initiated in the art of teaching. The fees charged in these schools range from 2 to 8 annas. The teachers generally come from the dregs of Brahminical society. Their qualifications hardly go beyond reading and writing Marathi very indifferently, and casting accounts up to the rule of three or so. They set up as teachers as the last resource of getting a livelihood. Their failure or unfitness in other callings of life obliges them to open schools. No arrangements exist in the country to train up teachers for indigenous schools. The indigenous schools could not be turned to any good account, unless the present teachers are replaced by men from the training colleges and by those who pass the 6th standard in the vernaculars. The present teachers will willingly accept State aid, but money thus spent will be thrown away. I do not know any instance in which a grant-in-aid is paid to such a school. If it is being paid anywhere, it must be in very rare cases. In my opinion no grants-in-aid should be paid to such schools unless the master is a certificated one. But if certificated or competent teachers be found, grant-in-aid should be given and will be productive of great good.

HIGHER EDUCATION

The cry over the whole country has been for some time past that Government have amply provided for higher education, whereas that of the masses has been neglected. To some extent this cry is justified, although the classes directly benefitted by the higher education may not readily admit it. But for all this no well-wisher of his country would desire that Government should, at the present time, withdraw its aid from higher education. All that they would wish is, that as one class of the body politic has been neglected, its advancement should form as anxious a concern as that of the other. Education in India is still in its infancy. Any withdrawal of State aid from higher education cannot but be injurious to the spread of education generally.

A taste for education among the higher and wealthy classes, such as the Brahmins and Purbhoos, especially those classes who live by the pen, has been created, and a gradual withdrawal of State aid may be possible so far as these classes are concerned; but in the middle and lower classes, among whom higher education has made no perceptible progress, such a withdrawal would be a great hardship. In the event of such withdrawal, boys will be obliged to have recourse to inefficient and sectarian schools much against their wish, and the cause of education cannot but suffer. Nor could any part of such education be entrusted to private agency. For a long time to come the entire educational machinery, both ministerial and executive, must be in the hands of Government. Both the higher and primary education require all the fostering care and attention which Government can bestow on it.

The withdrawal of Government from schools or colleges would not only tend to check the spread of education, but would seriously endanger that spirit of neutrality which has all along been the aim of Government to foster, owing to the different nationalities and religious creeds prevalent in India. This withdrawal may, to a certain extent, create a spirit of self-reliance for local purposes in the higher and wealthy classes, but the cause of education would be so far injured that the spirit of self-reliance would take years to remedy that evil. Educated men of ability, who do not succeed in getting into public service, may be induced to open schools for higher education on being assured of liberal grants-in-aid. But no one would be ready to do so on his own account as a means of gaining a livelihood, and it is doubtful whether such private efforts could be permanent or stable, nor would they succeed half so well in their results. Private schools such as those of Mr. Vishnu Shastree Chiploonkar and Mr. Bhavey, exist in Poona, and with adequate grants-in-aid may be rendered very efficient, but they can never supersede the necessity of the high school.

The missionary schools, although some of them are very efficiently conducted, do not succeed half so well in their results, nor do they attract half the number of students which the high school attracts. The superiority of Government schools is mainly owing to the richly paid staff of teachers and professors which it is not possible for a private school to maintain.

The character of instruction given in the Government higher schools, is not at all practical, or such as is required for the necessities of ordinary life. It is only good to turn out so many clerks and schoolmasters. The Matriculation examination unduly engrosses the attention of the teachers and pupils, and the course of studies prescribed has no practical element in it, so as to fit the pupil for his future career in independent life. Although the number of students presenting for the Entrance examination is not at all large when the diffusion of knowledge in the country is taken into consideration, it looks large when the requirements of Government service are concerned. Were the education universal and within easy reach of all, the number would have been larger still, and it should be so, and I hope it will be so hereafter. The higher education should be so arranged as to be within easy reach of all, and the books on the subjects for the Matriculation examination should be published in the Government Gazette, as is done in Madras and Bengal. Such a course will encourage private studies and secure larger diffusion of knowledge in the country. It is a boon to the people that the Bombay University recognises private studies in the case of those presenting for the entrance examination. I hope, the University authorities will be pleased to extend the same boon to higher examinations. If private studies were recognised by the University in granting the degrees of B.A., M.A. &c., many young men will devote their time to private studies. Their doing so will still further tend to the diffusion of knowledge. It is found in many instances quite impossible to prosecute studies at the colleges for various reasons. If private studies be recognised by the University, much good will be effected to the country at large, and a good deal of the drain on the public purse on account of higher education will be lessened.

The system of Government scholarships, at present followed in the Government schools, is also defective, as much as it gives undue encouragement to those classes only, who have already acquired a taste for education to the detriment of the other classes. The system might be so arranged that some of these scholarships should be awarded to such classes amongst whom education has made no progress.

The system of awarding them by competition, although abstractedly equitable, does not tend to the spread of education among other classes.

With regard to the question as to educated natives finding remunerative employments, it will be remembered that the educated natives who mostly belong to the Brahminical and other higher classes are mostly fond of service. But as the public service can afford no field for all the educated natives who come out from schools and colleges, and moreover the course of training they receive being not of a technical or practical nature, they find great difficulty in betaking themselves to other manual or remunerative employment. Hence the cry that the market is overstocked with educated natives who do not find any remunerative employment. It may, to a certain extent, be true that some of the professions are overstocked, but this does not show that there is no other remunerative employment to which they can betake themselves. The present number of educated men is very small in relation to the country at large, and we trust that the day may not be far distant when we shall have the present number multiplied a hundred-fold, and all betaking themselves to useful and remunerative occupations and not be looking after service.

In conclusion, I beg to request the Education Commission to be kind enough to sanction measures for the spread of female primary education on a more liberal scale.

Poona,
19th October 1882

Joteerao Govindrao Phooley,
Merchant and Cultivator and
Municipal Commissioner,
Peth Joona Ganja.

Notes

1. Education Commission, Bombay, Vol. II (Calcutta, 1884), 140–145.
2. This is a typographical error; the correct date should be 1851.
3. Modi: a running script in which most Marathi correspondence and account-writing used to take place. It was taught in schools till well into the 1940s. Balbodh: elementary reading.

Works Cited and Referred

Acharya, Poromesh. 1978. 'Indigenous Vernacular Education in Pre-British Era: Traditions and Problems'. *Economic and Political Weekly* 13(48): 1981–1988.

———. 1995. 'Bengali "Bhadralok" and Educational Development in 19th Century Bengal'. *Economic and Political Weekly* 30(13): 670–673.

Bagchi, Barnita. 2014. 'Connected and Entangled Histories: Writing Histories of Education in the Indian Context'. *Paedagogica Historica* 50(6): 813–821.

Banahatti, S. N. 1957. *Marathi Rangabhumicha Itihas*, Volumes 1 and 2. Pune: Venus Prakashan.

Bayly, Susan. 1989. *Saints, Goddesses and Kings: Muslims and Christians in South Indian Society, 1700–1900*. Cambridge: Cambridge University Press.

Bhagat, Datta, ed. 2001. *Jotirao Phule Likhit Trutiya Ratna: Marathi Bhaashetla Pahile Aadhunik Natak*. Srirampur: Shabdalaya Prakashan.

Bhat, G. K. 1982. 'The Vidushaka in Sanskrit Drama'. *Sahapedia* 11(2), January. National Centre for the Performing Arts, Mumbai. Available at: https://www.sahapedia.org/the-vidushaka-sanskrit-drama-gk-bhat (accessed 20 January 2023).

Bhatia, Nandi. 2004. *Acts of Authority/Acts of Resistance: Theatre and Politics in Colonial and Postcolonial India*. Ann Arbor: University of Michigan Press.

———, ed. 2009. *Modern Indian Theatre: A Reader*. New Delhi: Oxford University Press.

Bhattacharya, Sabyasachi, ed. 1998. *The Contested Terrain: Perspectives on Education in India*. New Delhi: Orient BlackSwan.

———, ed. 2002. *Education and the Disprivileged: Nineteenth and Twentieth Century India*. New Delhi: Orient BlackSwan.

Bhave, Vasudev Krishna. 1976[1936]. *Peshwekalin Maharashtra*. New Delhi: Indian Council for Historical Research.

Brueck, Laura. 2006. 'Dalit Chetna in Dalit Literary Criticism'. *Seminar Web Edition* 558. Available at: https://www.india-seminar.com/2006/558/558%20laura%20r.%20brueck.htm (accessed 20 January 2023).

Bugge, Henriette. 1994. *Mission and Tamil Society: Social and Religious Change in South India, 1840–1900*. Richmond, Surrey: Curzon Press.

Chakravarti, Uma. 1998. *Rewriting History: The Life and Times of Pandita Ramabai*. New Delhi: Kali for Women.

Chatterjee, Minoti. 2004. *Theatre Beyond the Threshold: Colonialism, Nationalism, and the Bengali Stage, 1905–1947*. New Delhi: Indialog.

Chatterjee, Partha. 1993. *The Nation and its Fragments: Colonial and Post-colonial Histories*. Princeton: Princeton University Press.

Chatterjee, Sudipto. 2009. 'The Nation Staged: Nationalist Discourse in Late 19th Century Bengali Theatre'. In *Modern Indian Theatre: A Reader*, ed. Nandi Bhatia. New Delhi: Oxford University Press.

Chausalkar, Ashok. 1990. *Mahatma Phule ani Shetkari Chalwal*. Mumbai: Lok Vangmaya Griha.

Chavan, Dilip. 2013. *Language Politics under Colonialism: Caste, Class and Language Pedagogy in Western India*. Newcastle upon Tyne: Cambridge Scholars Publishing.

Chitale, M. B. 1877[1871]. 'Preface' in *Manorama Natak*. Pune: Dnyanachakshu Chhapkhana.

Cohn, Bernard. 1985. 'The Command of Language and the Language of Command'. In *Subaltern Studies IV: Writings on South Asian History and Society*, ed. Ranajit Guha. New Delhi: Oxford University Press.

_____. 1996. *Colonialism and Its Forms of Knowledge: The British in India*. Princeton, N.J.: Princeton University Press.

Constable, Philip. 1997. 'Early Dalit Literature and Culture in Late Nineteenth- and Early Twentieth-Century Western India'. *Modern Asian Studies* 31(2): 317–338.

_____. 2000. 'Sitting on the School Verandah: The Ideology and Practice of 'Untouchable' Educational Protest in Late Nineteenth-century Western India'. *The Indian Economic and Social History Review* 37(4): 383–422.

_____. 2001. 'The Marginalization of a Dalit Martial Race in Late Nineteenth-and Early Twentieth-Century Western India'. *The Journal of Asian Studies* 60(2): 439–478.

Cutts, Elmer H. 1953. 'The Background of Macaulay's Minute'. *The American Historical Review* 58(4): 824–853.

Dalmia, Vasudha. 2006. *Poetics, Plays, and Performances: The Politics of Modern Indian Theatre*. New Delhi: Oxford University Press.

Dalrymple, William. 2019. *The Anarchy: The Relentless Rise of the East India Company*. London and Oxford: Bloomsbury Publishing.

Dandekar, Vishwnath Pandurang. 1941. *Marathi Natya-srishti,* Khanda 1: *Pauranik Natake*. Badode: V. P. Dandekar.

——. 1945. *Marathi Natya-srishti*, Khanda 2: *Samajik Natake*. Badode: V. P. Dandekar.

De, Rohit. 2018. *A People's Constitution: The Everyday Life of Law in the Indian Republic*. Princeton and Oxford: Princeton University Press.

Deshpande, G. P. 1999a. 'History, Politics and the Modern Playwright'. In *Theatre India*, Volume 1. New Delhi: National School of Drama.

——. 1999b. *Nataki Nibandha: Rahimatpurkaranchi Nibandhamala*. Mumbai: Lokvangmaya Griha.

——. 2002. 'Introduction'. In *Selected Writings of Jotirao Phule*, ed. G. P. Deshpande, 1–22. New Delhi: LeftWord Books.

——. 2004[2000]. *Modern Indian Drama: An Anthology*. New Delhi: Sahitya Akademi.

Deshpande, Prachi. 2007. *Creative Pasts: Historical Memory and Identity in Western India 1700-1960*. New Delhi: Permanent Black.

Devare, Aparna. 2011. *History and the Making of a Modern Hindu Self*. New Delhi: Routledge.

Dharampal. 2000[1983]. *The Beautiful Tree: Indigenous Indian Education in the Eighteenth Century*. Mapusa: Other India Press.

Eaton, Richard M. 2005. *A Social History of the Deccan, 1300–1761: Eight Indian Lives*. Cambridge and New York: Cambridge University Press.

Figueira, Dorothy M. 2002. *Aryans, Jews, Brahmins: Theorizing Authority through Myths of Identity*. Albany: State University of New York Press.

Frykenberg, Robert E. 1988. 'The Myth of English as a 'Colonialist' Imposition upon India: A Reappraisal with Special Reference to South India'. *Journal of the Royal Asiatic Society of Great Britain and Ireland* 2: 305–315.

Gajarwala, Toral Jatin. 2013. *Untouchable Fictions: Literary Realism and the Crisis of Caste*. New York: Fordham University Press.

Gandhi M. K. 1989[1909]. *Hind Swaraj: Or, Indian Home Rule*. Ahmedabad: Navajivan Publishing House.

Gavaskar, Mahesh. 2007[1999]. 'Colonialism within Colonialism: Phule's Critique of Brahmin Power'. In *Dalits in Modern India: Vision and Values* (second edition), ed. S. M. Michael. New Delhi: Sage Publications.

Gokhale, Shanta. 2000. *Playwright at the Centre: Marathi Drama from 1843 to the Present*. Calcutta: Seagull Books.

Guha, Ranajit. 1974. 'Neel-Darpan: The Image of Peasant Revolt in a Liberal Mirror'. *The Journal of Peasant Studies* 2(1):1–46.

Hartog, Philip. 1939. *Some Aspects of Indian Education Past and Present*. Oxford: Oxford University Press.

Heredia, Rudolf C. 1995. 'Education and Mission: School as Agent of Evangelisation'. *Economic and Political Weekly* 30(37): 2332–2340.

Jog, R. S. 1973. *Marathi Vangmayacha Itihas*, Khanda 3. Pune: Maharashtra Sahitya Parishad.

Joshi, Satyakam and K. S. Raman. 1991. 'Jotirao Phule: An Incomplete Renaissance'. *Economic and Political Weekly* 26(21): 1325–1327.

Keer, Dhananjay. 2000[1964]. *Mahatma Jotirao Phule: Father of the Indian Social Revolution*. Bombay: Popular Prakashan.

Keer, Dhananjay, S. G. Malshe and Y. D. Phadke, eds. 1991[1969]. *Mahatma Phule Samagra Vangmay* [The Collected Works of Mahatma Phule, fifth edition]. Mumbai: Maharashtra Rajya Sahitya Aani Sanskriti Mandal.

Kopf, David. 1969. *British Orientalism and Bengal Renaissance: The Dynamics of Indian Modernization 1773–1835*. Berkeley: University of California Press.

Kosambi, Meera. 2015. *Gender, Culture and Performance: Marathi Theatre and Cinema before Independence*. New Delhi: Routledge.

Kulkarni, A. V. 1961[1903]. *Marathi Rangbhoomi*. Pune: Venus Books.

Kulkarni, V. D. 1974. *Sangit Saubhadra: Ghatana ani Swarup*. Pune: Vinas Prakashan.

Kumar, Krishna. 2005[1991]. *Political Agenda of Education: A Study of Colonialist and Nationalist Ideas*. New Delhi: Sage.

Kumbhojkar, Shraddha. 2018. 'Marathi Theatre in Transition'. In *Re-searching Transitions in Indian History*, eds. Radhika Seshan and Shraddha Kumbhojkar. New York: Routledge.

Laird, M. A. 1968. 'The Contribution of the Serampore Missionaries to Education in Bengal, 1793–1837'. *Bulletin of the School of Oriental and African Studies, University of London* 31(1): 92–112.

_____. 1972. *Missionaries and Education in Bengal, 1793–1837*. Oxford: Clarendon Press.

Lal, Anand. 2009. 'A Historiography of Modern Indian Theatre'. In *Modern Indian Theatre: A Reader*, ed. Nandi Bhatia. New Delhi: Oxford University Press.

Majumdar, J. K. 1947. 'The Abolition of Persian as Court Language in British India'. *Bombay University Journal* XVI: 131.

Majumdar, S. B. 1913. 'Shakespearechi Natake va Tyanche Bhashantar'. *Rangbhumi*, 1–3, August.

Mani, Braj Ranjan. 2005. *Debrahmanizing History: Dominance and Resistance in Indian Society*. New Delhi: Manohar Publishers.

Mani, Lata. 1989. 'Contentious Traditions: The Debate on Sati in Colonial India'. In *Recasting Women: Essays in Colonial History*, eds K. Sangari and S. Vaid, 88–126. New Delhi: Kali for Women.

Marathe, K. B. 1979. *Marathi Rangabhoomicha Poorvaranga*. Pune: Shrividya Prakashan.

McCully, B. T. 1940. *English Education and the Origins of Indian Nationalism*. New York: Columbia University Press.

Mokashi-Punekar, Rohini. 2012. 'The Bharuds of Eknath: Performance, Humour and Satire'. In *Indian Satire in the Period of First Modernity*, eds. Monika Horstmann and Heidi Pauwels. Wiesbaden: Harrassowitz Verlag.

_____. 2016. 'Education and its Contestatory Histories: Jotiba Phule's Interventions in Nineteenth Century Maharashtra'. *dialog* 29: 46–64, Spring.

_____. 2017. 'Language as Contestation: Phule's Interventions in Education in Nineteenth-Century Maharashtra'. In *A Multilingual Nation: Translation and Language Dynamic in India*, ed. Rita Kothari, 149–171. New Delhi: Oxford University Press.

More, Sadanand. 2007. *Lokmanya Te Mahatma*, Vol. I. Pune: Rajhans Prakashan.

Mukherjee, Tutun, ed. 2005. *Staging Resistance: Plays by Women in Translation*. New Delhi: OUP India.

Nadkarni, M. K. 1921. *A Short History of Marathi Literature*. Baroda: Luhana Press.

Naik, J. P. and Syed Nurullah. 1974[1945]. *A Students' History of Education in India (1800–1973): Revised Sixth Edition*. New Delhi: Macmillan India.

Naregal, Veena. 2002[2001]. *Language Politics, Elites and the Public Sphere: Western India under Colonialism*. Glasgow: Anthem Press.

Nemade, Bhalchandra. 1982. 'Jotirao Phule yanchi Gadyashaili'. In *Mahatma Phule Gaurav Granth*, ed. Hari Narke, 698–706. Mumbai: Maharashtra State Government Publication.

Nurullah, Syed and J. P. Naik. 1943. *History of Education in India during the British Period*. Macmillan India.

O'Hanlon, Rosalind. 1994. *A Comparison between Women and Men: Tarabai Shinde and the Critique of Gender Relations in Colonial India*. Madras: Oxford University Press.

_____. 2010[1985]. *Caste, Conflict, and Ideology: Mahatma Jotirao Phule and Low Caste Protest in Nineteenth-Century Western India*. New Delhi: Permanent Black.

Omvedt, Gail. 2011[1976]. *Cultural Revolt in a Colonial Society: The Non-Brahman Movement in Western India*. New Delhi: Manohar.

Patil, Sharad. 1987. *Das Shudranchi Gulamgiri*. Wari: Prajna Press.

Pennington, Brian K. 2005. *Was Hinduism Invented? Britons, Indians, and the Colonial Construction of Religion*. Oxford and New York: Oxford University Press.

Phule, Jotiba. 1991[1969]. *Mahatma Phule Samagra Vangmay* [The Collected Works of Mahatma Phule, fifth edition], eds Dhananjay Keer, S. G. Malshe and Y. D. Phadke. Mumbai: Maharashtra Rajya Sahitya Aani Sanskriti Mandal.

Potts, Daniel E. 1967. *British Baptist Missionaries in India, 1793–1837: The History of Serampore and Its Missions*. Cambridge: Cambridge University Press.

Prior Katherine, Lance Brennan and Robin Haines. 2001. 'The Role of English, Persian and Other Esoteric Tongues in the Dismissal of Sir Edward Colebrooke as Resident of Delhi in 1829'. *Modern Asian Studies* 35(1): 75–112.

Radhakrishnan, P. 1990. 'Indigenous Education in British India: A Profile'. *Contributions to Indian Sociology* 24(1): 1–27.

Raikar, Sitaram. 1979. '"Introduction" to Phule's *Trutiya Ratna*.' *Purogami Satyashodhak* 5(2), April–June.

_____, ed. 1981. *Amhi Pahilele Phule*. Poona.

Rao, Anupama. 2010[2009]. *The Caste Question: Dalits and the Politics of Modern India*. New Delhi: Permanent Black.

Rao, Parimala V. 2010. *Foundations of Tilak's Nationalism: Discrimination, Education and Hindutva*. New Delhi: Orient BlackSwan.

_____. 2014. 'Compulsory Education and the Political Leadership in Colonial India, 1840–1947'. In *New Perspectives in the History of Indian Education*, ed. Parimala V. Rao, 151–175. New Delhi: Orient BlackSwan.

_____. 2015. 'Trends in the Historiography of Indian Education: A Critical Review'. *Jahrbuch fuer historische Bildungsforschung* 21: 293–313.

Rao, Parimala V. 2020. *Beyond Macaulay: Education in India, 1780–1860.* London and New York: Routledge.

Rege, Sharmila. 2010. 'Education as *Trutiya Ratna*: Towards Phule-Ambedkarite Feminist Pedagogy'. *Economic and Political Weekly* 45(44).

Sarkar, Sumit. 1997. *Writing Social History*. New Delhi: Oxford University Press.

Sathe, Makarand. 2015. *A Socio-Political History of Marathi Theatre: Thirty Nights*, Volume 1. Translated from the Marathi original by Makarand Sathe, Irawati Karnik and Shanta Gokhale. New Delhi: Oxford University Press.

Seal, Anil. 1971[1968]. *The Emergence of Indian Nationalism: Competition and Collaboration in the Later Nineteenth Century*. London and New York: Cambridge University Press.

Shyam, Radhey. 1968. *Life and Times of Malik Ambar*. New Delhi: Munshiram Manoharlal Publishers.

Solomon, Rakesh. 2009. 'Towards a Genealogy of Indian Theatre Historiography'. In *Modern Indian Theatre: A Reader*, ed. Nandi Bhatia. New Delhi: Oxford University Press.

Teltscher, Kate. 1995. *India Inscribed: European and British Writing on India, 1600–1800.* Delhi: Oxford University Press.

Thapar, Romila. 1992. *Interpreting Early India*. New Delhi: Oxford University Press.

Tharu, Susie and K. Lalitha, eds. 1993[1991]. *Women Writing in India: 600 B.C. to the Early Twentieth Century*. Volume 1. New Delhi: Oxford University Press.

Trautmann, Thomas R. 2004. *Aryans and British India*. New Delhi: Yoda Press.

Velaskar, Padma. 2012. 'Education for Liberation: Ambedkar's Thought and Dalit Women's Perspectives'. *Contemporary Education Dialogue* 9(2): 245–271.

Vendell, Dominic. 2014. 'Jotirao Phule's *Satyashodh* and the Problem of Subaltern Consciousness'. *Comparative Studies of South Asia, Africa and the Middle East* 34(1): 52–66.

Viswanathan, Gauri. 1989. *Masks of Conquest: Literary Study and British Rule in India*. New York: Columbia University Press.

Zelliot, Eleanor. 1996[1992]. *From Untouchable to Dalit: Essays on the Ambedkar Movement*. New Delhi: Manohar.

——. 2002. 'Experiments in Dalit Education: Maharashtra, 1850–1947'. In *Education and the Disprivileged: Nineteenth and Twentieth Century India*, ed. Sabyasachi Bhattacharya, 35–49. Delhi: Orient BlackSwan.

Zelliot, Eleanor. 2003[1982]. 'A Medieval Encounter between Hindu and Muslim: Eknath's Drama-Poem *Hindu-Turk Samvad*'. In *India's Islamic Traditions, 711-1750*, ed. Richard Eaton. New Delhi: Oxford University Press.

——. 2014. 'Dalit Initiatives in Education, 1880–1892'. In *New Perspectives in the History of Indian Education*, ed. Parimala V. Rao, 45–67. New Delhi: Orient BlackSwan.

Index

Abhyankar, R. S. 36
  Swaira-sakesha 36
affirmative action 41, 176, 177
'Afzal Khanacha Vadh' 113
agriculture 1, 11, 171, 175, 196–97
Akhyan 25, 30
Alam Ara 20
allegory 20, 25
Ambedkar, Babasaheb 66, 161, 177
American Marathi Mission 149
'An Enquiry into the Obligation of Christians to Use Means for the Conversion of the Heathen' 132
Anglican Church 133, 147
Anglicists 140–41, 154
Aryans 151, 164, 165, 180–81
  Aryan Brahmin 72, 162
Asiatic Researches 137
Asiatic Society 137
Atishudra/Atisudra 107–08, 167, 174, 182, 184, 185
atrocity(ies) 51, 181
audiences 17, 20, 24–26, 31–38, 42, 44, 46, 49–57, 59, 61, 67, 71, 73, 78, 105, 107–08, 150
autonomy 127, 177

backwardness 4, 140, 170
'Bahujan Paksh' 163
Bahujan Samaj 162–63
Balistan 73, 164
ballad 1, 10–11, 25, 113, 115
balutedari system 170–71
Banerjea, Krishna Mohan 17
  The Persecuted, or Dramatic Scenes Illustrative of the Present State of Hindoo Society 17
Baptist Missionary Society 132
Barua, Gunabhiram 18
  Ram Navami 18
Barua, Hemchandra 18
  Kania Kirtan 18
Bengal Presidency 137–39, 141–42, 157
Bengal Renaissance 154
bhadralok 154–55
Bhagavad Gita 133, 150
Bhagwata Purana 24
Bhagwat, N. H. 36
  Mor L.L.B Prahasan 36
Bhave, Vishnudas 17, 21, 23, 27–33, 37, 46, 60, 62
  dramatic efforts 32
  Raja Gopichand 17, 31
  Sita Swayamwara 17, 27–30
Bible 132, 134, 147
bigotry 184, 186
Board of Education to the Bombay Government 5
Bombay Presidency 23, 28, 127, 138–39, 155–59, 165
Bombay Tract and Book Society 149

Brahmananche Kasab 10–11, 115
Brahmanism 11, 24, 161, 166
Brahmin 2, 5–11, 22–25, 28–30, 32, 36, 38, 42–45, 48–54, 56–57, 61, 64–68, 70–74, 76–86, 89–96, 98–108, 113–17, 119–21, 138, 142, 147, 149, 151, 155, 157–58, 162, 164–72, 174, 176, 179–86, 188–89, 192–96, 199–200
  Aryan 72, 162
  exploitative 149, 162
  monopoly of 42, 167
  priests 11, 22
  reformist 7, 9
  teachers 8, 10, 73, 102, 117, 174, 176
Brahminical order 69, 164
Brahmin-ridden policy 179
Britain 124, 130–31, 133–35
British India 18
British Missions 132
British Parliament 12, 124, 130, 151
British Political Agents 23
British rule 45, 73–74, 126, 133

Calcutta Madrassa 137
caste(s) 1–11, 14, 17–18, 21–23, 28–29, 36–44, 46–51, 53–54, 57, 60, 63–74, 77, 85, 90, 103, 105–09, 112–17, 120, 122, 125, 127–28, 139, 142, 145, 147, 150–51, 153–77, 181, 186, 188, 193, 195
  communities 5, 21, 23, 162
  hegemony 3, 10, 44, 160, 170
  hierarchy 3, 14, 49, 51, 65, 68–71, 151, 158, 169, 177
  Kunbi 22, 77, 85, 105
  lower 1–2, 4–6, 8, 10–11, 14, 39–40, 43, 65, 68–69, 112, 116–17, 128, 139, 147, 151, 154–60, 163, 165, 168–70, 172–75, 177
  Mahar 2, 77, 108, 116, 119
  Mang 2, 6, 70, 108, 160
  marginalised 70, 145
  practices 154, 161
  privileges 157–58
  relations 74, 162, 171
  Shudra 2, 116, 120
  structures 68–69, 116–17, 170
  Untouchable 4, 41, 117, 139, 159
  upper 2–5, 7, 9–11, 18, 21, 23, 28–29, 36–38, 40, 51, 53, 57, 64, 67, 70, 72, 103, 116, 125, 127–28, 139, 153, 155, 157, 160, 162–64, 166, 169, 171, 174–75
Censorship Act of 1876 18–19
character(s) 3, 6, 19, 24–25, 27, 37, 39, 42, 44–45, 47–48, 50–63, 66–67, 71, 73, 151, 179, 181
  babu 19
  Christian 134
  entry and exit of 27, 59
  Muslim 62
  peasant 19
  secular 24
charity school movement 132
Charters of the East India Company 12
Chhatrapati Shivaji Raje Bhosale Yancha Powada 10, 115
child/children 2, 17–18, 36, 41, 43, 64, 78, 81, 83, 94, 101–06, 116–17, 119–22, 127, 131, 139, 157, 160, 169, 174, 176, 181, 188, 193, 195, 197
  female 127, 139
  girl 139
  lower-caste 41, 174, 176
  Mahar 116, 119
  marriage 18, 36, 158
  Untouchable 139, 160
Chitale, M. B. 36
  Manorama Natak 36
Chitnis, M. B. 21
  Yugyatra 21

Christianity 3–4, 9, 45, 133
conversion to 3–4, 9
Christian missionary(ies) 3, 6, 42–43, 45, 62, 73, 96, 122
Christians 132, 146–48, 150, 174
Church Missionary Society 19, 133
civilisation 128, 137, 179, 186
class
Brahminical 14, 50, 53, 73, 163
dominant 67, 174
elite 35, 51–53, 154
lower 134, 154, 184, 191, 195, 200
middle 19, 28–29, 70, 200
ruling 7, 31, 113, 134
subaltern 67, 161
working 46, 68, 124, 131–34, 173
Cohn, Bernard 124, 129
'The Command of Language and the Language of Command' 129
colleges 142, 144, 146, 152, 188, 193, 199–202
Sanskrit 137–38, 141–42, 155, 172
colonial
administration 126, 154, 165
government 7, 23, 28, 42, 53, 73, 116–17, 125, 138, 145, 151, 159–60, 169
policy 12, 65, 124, 128–30, 136, 144, 154, 176
power 66, 114, 128, 143, 166, 170
rule 7, 42, 50, 130
colonialism 16, 73
colonisation 129–31, 162, 180
comedy 34, 52, 62
Company Charter of 1813 126, 130, 135, 138, 144, 146, 151
Company Charter of 1833 142
Company Charter of 1854 144
Company's Court of Directors 134
conflict 44–46, 50–51, 57, 64, 66, 141, 155
consciousness 39, 42, 45–46, 48, 63, 67–68, 71, 114–15, 131, 163, 174
Constitution of India 177
Court of Directors 134–35, 141, 153
cruelty 51, 64, 115, 161, 181
culture 10, 15, 21–22, 28, 32–33, 117, 125, 128, 130, 134, 138, 149–50, 153–54, 161, 165
Indian 128, 153
language 15, 21–22, 33
print 32, 149, 165
Vedic 150, 161
cunning 8, 43, 51, 56, 63, 91–92, 107–09, 115, 180, 182–85
curriculum 125, 127, 139–40, 142, 152, 155–56, 175–76

dakshina 7–8, 49, 56, 58, 61, 64, 89, 94, 155, 172
Dakshina Prize Committee 5–8, 17, 28, 32, 53, 66, 74, 155
Dalits 14, 21, 40, 64, 66–69, 112–13, 117, 128–29, 160, 166
chetna 68
consciousness 68
identity 68
literature 14, 66–69, 117
movement 166
narratives 64
Shahirs of Maharashtra 25, 114–15
students 160
writers 14, 68–69
writing in translation 112
Darpan 18–19, 20, 65–66, 157
Dashavtara 24
Dave, Ranchhodbhai 18
Lalita Dukhdarshak 18
Deshpande, G. P. 6, 9, 12, 15–16, 28, 45, 71, 73, 114, 162–63, 174
Nataki Nibandha 28

Dharampal 126–27
  Beautiful Tree, The 126
Dhondiba 6, 163, 165
dialogue(s) 10, 25, 30–31, 34, 37, 44, 48–50, 54–56, 59, 6–66, 163
  between a Brahmin and a Maulana 25
  in *Tritiya Ratna* 64–65
  Plato's 44
  Socratic 42, 45
  Vidushak's 45, 53, 65
Digdarshan 157
Din Bandhu 11
discrimination 54, 142, 150, 159–60, 176
divinity 45, 47, 148–49
Dnyanodaya 30, 104, 149–50, 158
dogma 3, 45
domination 44, 67, 162, 165, 174, 181, 184
  Brahmin 181, 184
downward filtration theory 140, 160, 169
drama 8, 15–22, 24–36, 38, 42, 46–47, 51–52, 54–55, 57–59, 62–63, 66–67, 69, 74
  companies 17, 27, 32
  European 16, 46, 63
  folk 55, 57
  Indian 15, 29
  Marathi 18, 21, 24, 28, 31, 36, 38, 47, 52, 54, 66, 69, 74
  modern 8, 15, 24, 58–59
  nationalist 19, 35
  prose 26, 33–34
  Sanskrit 15–16, 32, 35, 42, 51–52, 55, 58, 62
  social 18, 20, 34, 38
  Western 16, 59, 63
dramatic
  action 44, 59
  composition 27, 66
  conventions 17, 35, 37, 46, 55–58, 61–63, 67
  forms and practices 14–16, 22, 24, 32, 56, 58, 62
  poems 30
  presentation 24, 30, 32
Dutt, Michael Madhusudan 17
  Buro Shaliker Ghare Ron 18
  Ekei ki Bale Sabhyata 18

East India Company 12, 23, 35, 124, 126, 130–32, 134–38, 140, 144–47, 151, 155
  policy 124, 132
economy 165, 170–71
education 1, 3, 5–7, 12, 14, 28, 32, 39–40, 42–45, 69–70, 72–73, 82, 101–07, 109, 112–13, 116–17, 119–20, 124–30, 132, 134–47, 151–60, 164–65, 167–69, 172–75, 179, 185, 187–89, 191–202
  access to 1, 39, 45, 103, 105, 124, 139, 154, 159
  basic 154, 168, 172
  colonial 127–28, 175
  colonial policy on 12, 130, 154
  developments in 125, 155
  elementary 126–27, 146
  English 39, 129, 141, 154, 157
  formal 124, 140
  high-class 187–89, 192–94
  higher 127, 140, 143–44, 147, 156, 165, 167, 169, 172–73, 187–88, 192–93, 199–201
  indigenous 126, 138, 140
  initiatives in 126, 156
  interventions in 3, 6, 153
  missionary 125, 159
  modern 43–44, 142–43, 151–53, 156, 165, 173
  primary 145, 168–69, 172–75, 191, 194–96, 198, 200, 202
  public 117, 124
  secular 42, 44, 142, 152
  subaltern 160, 173

system of 124, 126, 138, 168, 179, 192
Western 28, 32, 153, 172, 174
educational
institutions 6, 115, 125, 128, 160
opportunities 129, 148, 161
educational policy 125, 130, 135, 141, 151, 155, 165, 169
Education Commission 1, 12, 124, 129, 145, 159, 161, 168, 172, 175, 191, 202
emotion 48, 58
employment 28, 35, 142, 145, 172, 175, 202
empowerment 29, 54
England 127, 131, 134–36, 140, 145, 147
English Protestant missions 146
enslavement 48, 116, 132, 163–64
entertainment 16, 18, 26–27, 29–30, 32, 34, 37, 52, 54–55
forms of 26, 29, 54
equality 46, 72–73, 142, 150, 154, 164, 178
Europe 46, 156, 163, 180
evangelical
campaign 133
thought 132, 148
exclusion 112, 158, 177
exploitation 8, 42–44, 49, 54, 57, 108–09, 114–15, 117, 167, 170
expression 14, 24, 28, 68, 109

faith 11, 18–19, 45, 56, 66, 69, 116, 164, 169
farces 18, 32–34, 100
First War of Indian Independence 16
folk drama 55, 57
folk theatre 54, 57
Free Church of Scotland 2, 148

Gandhi, Mahatma 126–27, 175
Nai Taleem 126, 175
work on education 127
gender 9, 46, 51, 63, 65–66, 69, 71–72, 154, 157
General Committee of Public Instruction 137, 140–41, 152
policy of 140, 152
girls 4–5, 26, 41, 44, 69, 109, 173, 191
Gondhal 113
gondhals 25
Government of India 124, 142, 179
Grant, Charles 134, 140
Observations of the State of Society among the Asiatic Subjects of Great Britain 135, 140
Grant Road Theatre, Bombay 17, 31
Gulamgiri 6, 10–12, 40, 66, 72, 124, 159, 161, 163–66, 168–70, 172, 179

Harishchandra, Bharatendu 18
Vaidiki Himsa Himsa na Bhavati 18
hegemony 3, 6, 9–12, 23–24, 36, 44, 51, 54, 65, 67–68, 70, 73–74, 114, 128, 151, 160, 163, 170
Brahminical 54, 67, 70, 151
cultural 12, 36, 128
Gramsci's notion of 163
upper-caste 10, 160
heroism 22, 25, 113
Hinduism 3, 6, 11, 41–42, 45, 69, 133–34, 147, 174
Brahminical 3, 41, 45, 69, 174
Hindu(s) 4, 16, 20, 25, 31, 38–39, 45, 72, 99–100, 128, 132–33, 136–37, 139, 146, 148–52, 156, 158–61
society 4, 45
Hindu-Turk Samvad 25
historiography 125, 129–30, 159, 162, 167
hypocrisy 10, 70, 116, 161

identity 3, 10, 28, 31, 67–68, 115, 117, 133, 161, 177
caste 67, 115
negative 68, 177
political 3, 31
ideology 6, 42, 44, 70–71, 73, 115, 159, 161–63, 176
idolatry 73, 146, 148, 158
imperialism 28, 66, 72–73, 117, 125
India 1, 8, 12, 16–20, 22–23, 34, 40, 46, 50, 68, 72, 112–15, 117, 124–32, 134–36, 138, 140–52, 154–57, 159, 162–65, 167–68, 170, 173, 177–81, 184, 187–88, 193, 200
ancient 151, 154
Eastern 18
education in 124–26, 129–30, 136, 138, 143–44, 151–52, 173
education system of 112, 138
history of education in 124, 126
North 22
post-independence 114, 125
western 1, 8, 72, 113, 129, 148–50, 155–57, 159
Indian
drama 15, 17, 29
Education Commission 124, 145, 168, 172
educational system 112, 140
modern, theatre 15, 17
nationalism 125
People's Theatre Association 20
Indologists 161, 163
inequality(ies) 177
injustice 69, 177
institutions
educational 6, 115, 125, 128, 160
modern 6, 23, 143, 154, 160
intellectuals 3, 6, 143, 148, 151
Indian 3, 143, 151
irony 55, 64

Jalsa 54

Kalidasa 15, 29, 32–33
Abhijnana Shakuntalam 15, 33
Shakuntala 15, 33, 37–38
Vikramorvshiyam 33
Kanitkar, N. B. 36
Taruni Shikshan Natika 36
Kesari 9
khel 27, 29, 46, 62
mythological 46, 62
Kirloskar, B. P. 18, 21, 33, 37–38
sangeet natak 37
kirtan 25, 30
Kirtane, V. J. 35
Thorle Madhavrao Peshwe 35–36
knowledge
forms of 67, 129
textual 69, 163–65, 170, 172
Kshatriyas 11, 139, 151, 162, 164, 181
Kunbis 2–3, 5–6, 22, 40, 42–46, 48–50, 53–54, 56–61, 63–65, 67, 71–73, 76–77, 79, 81–96, 98–106, 108–09, 119, 122, 162, 171

labour 5, 43, 86, 90, 94–95, 119, 162, 169, 171, 175–76, 182, 187, 192
Lala, Jagamohan 18
Babaji 18
language and literature 1, 3, 6–8, 14–15, 18, 21–22, 29, 32–33, 46–47, 54, 62–63, 66–69, 74, 112–13, 117, 125, 128, 131–33, 136–38, 140–44, 147, 149–50, 152, 154, 156, 161, 163, 165–66, 173, 177, 180, 184, 195
analytic and creative 112
Arabic 125, 137–39, 153

classical 32, 138, 140, 152
Dalit 14, 66–69, 117
English 4, 8, 10, 12, 15, 17, 19, 23, 31, 33, 39, 41, 45, 58, 60, 62–63, 73, 100–104, 106–08, 113, 115–17, 119, 122, 124–25, 127–29, 133, 137–38, 140–44, 146, 148, 152, 154, 156–57, 159, 161, 165–66, 168, 173, 187, 192, 195, 198
European 15, 180
Gujarati 16, 18, 156
Hindi 16, 18, 31, 62
Indian 15, 132, 137, 141, 147
Marathi 1–2, 6–8, 10, 14–16, 18, 21, 24, 26–29, 31–39, 41, 46–47, 52, 54, 58, 60, 62, 66–67, 69, 72–73, 74, 112–14, 116, 147, 149, 156–57, 158, 165–66, 168, 173, 192, 195, 199
missionary 131, 133
Persian 125, 137, 139, 143, 180
Sanskrit 7, 15–16, 29, 32, 33, 35, 37–38, 42, 47, 51–55, 58–59, 62, 125, 133, 137–39, 141–43, 150–52, 155–56, 172, 180
subaltern 68, 74
Telugu 11, 20, 27
Urdu 26, 99–100, 165
vernacular 7, 142, 144, 149–50
Western 29, 113
lavani 26–27, 29, 49, 87
learning 1, 7, 29, 33, 68–69, 85, 101–02, 112, 119–21, 125, 127, 137–39, 141, 150, 168–69, 176, 179, 187, 192, 195
higher 33, 137–39, 141
liberalism 7, 177
literary
forms 1, 9, 47, 114
genres 9, 74, 159
livelihood 31, 49, 77, 199–200
London Missionary Society 133, 146
looteche gahu ani babache shradh 64
Lord Hardinge's 1844 resolution 143
Lord William Bentinck's Resolution 140
low/lower castes 1–2, 4–6, 8–11, 14, 17, 29, 39–43, 47–49, 64–65, 68–71, 73, 112–14, 116–17, 128, 139, 147, 151, 154–61, 163, 165, 168–70, 172–77, 186

Macaulay's Minute of 1835 129, 140–41, 144
Macaulay, Thomas B. 129, 137, 140–44, 153, 155
Madras Presidency 126–27, 138–39, 146
madrassas 137, 139, 143
Mahabharata, the 24
Mahars 5–6, 70, 94, 106, 108, 122, 162, 191, 195
Manava Dharma Shastra 182
Mandal Commission 112
Mangs 5–6, 70, 94, 106, 122, 162, 191, 195
manuscripts 8, 30, 38, 41, 54
Manusmriti 105, 177
Maratha 9
Maratha history 15, 36, 113
Marathas 22, 27, 29, 35
Marathi Dnyan Prasarak Sabha 158
Marathi drama 18, 21, 24, 28, 31, 36, 38, 47, 52, 54, 66, 69, 74
modern 21, 31, 36, 38
marginalisation 165–66
marginalised groups 14, 174
marriages 11, 18, 25, 34, 36, 38, 53, 108, 158
masks and costumes 30–31
Mead, Herbert 179
Sepoy Revolt 179
Milch Cow 184

missionary(ies) 3–6, 12, 19, 42–45, 48, 50–51, 56–57, 61–62, 64–65, 67, 72–73, 76, 96–105, 108, 122, 124–25, 129–33, 135–36, 141, 144–51, 155–61, 165, 167, 191, 201
  Catholic 145–46
  initiatives 124, 144–45, 156
  lobby 135–36
  Protestant 130, 146–47, 165
  Scottish 148–50
mission female boarding school 191
Mitra, Dinabandhu 18
  Nil Darpan 18–20, 65–66
modern Indian drama 15
modernisation 125, 142
modernism 16, 18, 20
modernity 1, 20, 29, 32, 37–38, 45, 66, 117
  colonial 29, 32, 38, 66
monopoly 42, 128, 136, 163, 167, 171–72, 188, 193
  virtual 42, 172, 188, 193
moral duties 175, 197
Mughals 22, 113, 130–31, 136, 170
Muktabai 6, 70
  Mang Maharachya Dukhavisayi 6
music 25, 28, 31, 37–38, 53, 116
Muslims 2, 42, 61–62, 76, 99–100, 107, 129, 136–37, 139, 147, 156, 162, 173
myth 40, 161, 163
'Myth of Macaulay's Minute' 129
mythology 10, 17, 20, 38, 40, 72, 133, 163–65, 181
  Brahminical 10, 40, 163, 165
  Hindu 72, 133

Nagaraj, D. R. 40
  Flaming Feet: Dalit Movement in India, The 40
narratives 10, 22–23, 25, 30–31, 39, 48, 53, 55, 60, 64, 131, 162, 166
natak 18, 21, 27–28, 33, 37–38
nation 16, 20, 65–66, 72–73, 125, 163, 177
nationalism 16, 20, 33, 38, 72, 125, 132, 163
  Hindu 20, 38
national movement 23
Nibandhmala 9
non-Brahmin movement 11, 71
norms 8–9, 170, 174

occupation 2, 48–49, 77, 94, 186, 195
oppression 1, 12, 17, 23, 40, 43–44, 46, 51, 57, 67, 69, 114, 163, 166, 184
  Brahminical 12, 44, 163
  caste 17, 46, 51, 57, 67, 163
Orientalism 128–29
Orientalist 16, 32, 129, 133, 140–42, 153
  body of knowledge 128
  historiography 167
  ideas 154
orthodoxy 4, 36, 170

Paine, Thomas 3, 12, 134, 142
  Age of Reason, The 3, 12
  Rights of Man 3
pamphlets 133, 148–49
Pandurang, Dadoba 4, 158
Paramahansa Mandali 4–5, 158
Parsis 156, 174
patriarchy 9, 71, 163
peasants 6, 11, 19, 65, 68, 114, 119, 129, 148, 162
Pennington, Brian 133
  Was Hinduism Invented? 133
Peshwas 2, 7, 22–26, 29, 56, 78, 113, 155, 170
philology 115, 147, 166–67
Phule, Mahatma Jotiba 1–2, 17, 113, 124
  adult life 3

belief 70
challenge 57
characters 42, 48, 50, 63
creative use of literary forms 1
critique of Brahmins 176
critique of the existing society 11
early years 2
engagement with literary forms 9
experimentation 9
formulations of Hindu mythology 133
iconoclastic missionary 73
ideological position 163
ideological stand 56
impact on 3
indictment of Brahmanism 161
interventions 4, 6, 70, 125, 145, 160
lifelong mission 39
lifelong struggle 1, 124
literary interventions 1
manifesto for education 160
Memorial to Education Commission 145
on women's freedom and rights 153
powada on Shivaji 115
preoccupation 40, 114
prose writings 124, 159
reinvention of the *powada* 114
relationship with Savitribai 72
representation of power and authority 66
revisionist history 11
revolutionary ideas 47
schooling 12
schools 5, 70, 160
stand on imperialism 73
Vidushak 51, 54–55, 57
works 14, 48, 69, 166

plays
bookish 21, 32, 34–35, 37, 53
English 31, 33, 58
historical 34, 36
Marathi 35, 62
modern 14, 55, 66
musical 37–38
mythological 21, 25, 27, 34, 37–38
political 6, 19, 65–66
prose 32, 34, 37
Shakespearean 33, 35
short 34, 54

playwrights 6, 16, 21, 24, 28, 33, 37–38, 47, 52, 56, 58, 61, 66–67, 69
plot 19, 27, 33, 41–42, 44, 48, 52, 55, 60–61, 63, 66, 71
poem/poetry 1, 10, 25, 30–31, 40, 47, 112–13, 164
polarisation 135, 141
political
developments 21, 72, 130
history 21–22
power 28, 42, 72, 131, 136
politics 19, 28, 44, 66, 68, 112, 115, 117, 121, 166, 177
post-structural theory 47
poverty 39, 50, 169–70, 175, 192, 195
powadas 1, 10, 25, 27, 113–17, 176
Prabhakar 158
practices
discriminatory 18, 113
dramatic 15, 58, 62
exploitative 19, 45
Hindu 132, 148, 151, 158
performance 24–26, 29
performative 15–16, 21
theatre 15–16
theatrical 20, 38
Priestcraft Exposed 10, 115
print media 9
Prithvi Theatres 20
propaganda 4, 159
campaign 4, 159

proscenium stage 24, 27, 55–57, 60
prose 6, 10–12, 25–26, 30–34, 37–40, 47, 124, 147, 149, 159, 161
proselytisation 135, 146
Protestant English Missions 146
Protestant mission 146
Purogami Satyashodhak 8

race 115, 150, 161, 166–67, 180
  Aryan 115, 161, 166
  Brahmin 167, 180
radical
  interventions 3, 117
  secret society 158
Ramabai, Pandita 9, 35, 71
Ramayana, the 24, 30
rationalism 153–54
realism 34, 47, 68–69
reciprocity 46, 72
reformer(s) 1, 4, 7, 9, 11, 36, 50, 67–68, 70–71, 130–31, 143, 148, 150–54, 157–60, 162–64, 173
  Indian 9, 11, 152, 159
  social 70, 163
  upper-caste 4, 153, 164
reformism 4
reform(s) 8–9, 17–18, 36, 41, 68–69, 72, 125, 132, 134, 152–55, 157–58, 164, 175
religion 3, 6, 9, 41, 44, 63, 70, 99–100, 109, 130–33, 139, 142, 148, 150–51, 154–55, 163, 165, 185
  Brahminical 44, 154
  Hindu 132, 150
religious
  beliefs 25, 157
  conversion 46
  practices 64, 114, 140, 146, 168, 192
Revolt of 1857 145
Rgveda/Rig Veda 40, 150
  Purusha Sukta 40
rituals 11, 24, 35–36, 43, 45–46, 61–64, 69, 90, 103, 151, 158
Roy, Raja Ram Mohan 141, 152–54
  campaign against *sati* 153
  interventions in education 153
Ryot/ryot 169, 184–85, 187–88, 192–93
ryotwari system 170

saint-poets 25, 73
Sambhaji 22, 115
Sangeet natak 18, 21, 28, 33, 37–38
Sangeet Soubhadra 38
Sanglikar Hindu Natak Mandali 31
sanitation 175, 196–97
Sarvajanik Satya Dharma Pustak 11, 73
sati 35–36, 152–54
satire 10, 17, 55, 63–64, 68, 114, 116
Satyashodhak 1, 4, 8, 10–11, 53, 68, 71, 159, 174–75
Satyashodhak Samaj 1, 4, 10, 53, 68, 71, 159, 175
Savitribai 1, 4–5, 9, 46, 72, 109
  Kavya Phule 1
  school for women 5
  writings 1, 72
schooling 12, 65, 117, 122, 126–27, 130, 139, 145, 165
  indigenous system of 127, 130
school (pathasala) 1–5, 7, 10, 12, 40–41, 43–44, 46–47, 63–65, 69–70, 72, 101–03, 105–06, 109, 116–17, 119–21, 126–27, 130, 132–33, 137–39, 142–49, 152–53, 155–56, 159–60, 167, 172–74, 176, 186, 189, 191–92, 194–202
  elementary 145–47
  English 127, 156, 198
  for girls 5, 41, 44, 191

Government 10, 173, 176, 196, 201–02
indigenous 142, 144, 146, 172, 191, 198–99
mission 3, 12, 155
modern 142, 145
primary 144, 173, 176, 194–98
vernacular 139, 142, 149, 156, 197
village 119, 126–27, 143, 197
Scottish missionary 149
Scottish mission school 2–3, 12
Scottish Protestant Presbyterian missionary 148
selfishness 183, 186
Serampore Mission 146, 155
Serampore Trio 132, 147, 155
shahirs 25, 114–15
Shahuraje 27
Lakshmi-Narayan-Kalyan 27
Shakespeare 29, 33
Shantiniketan 126
Shetkaryacha Asud: The Cultivator's Whipcord 11, 40, 171
Shinde, Tarabai 70
Stri Purusha Tulana 70
Shinde, Vithal Ramji 162
Shivaji, Chhatrapati 10, 22, 25, 29, 107, 113, 115
Shudras/Sudras 2, 39–41, 44–45, 50, 99, 103, 107–09, 115–16, 120–22, 127, 166–67, 174, 180, 182–87, 189, 194
Shudratishudra 3, 10, 11, 53–54, 67, 72, 108, 116, 161–62, 164–69, 173, 177
'Sitting on the school verandah: the ideology and practice of untouchable educational protest in late 19th century western India' 159
slave 95, 119, 134, 167, 184–85
American 167, 185
trade 134
slavery 39, 116, 131–32, 134, 163, 165–66, 179, 183–84
social
developments 21, 130
hierarchy 1, 8–9, 51, 58, 142–43
issues 17–18, 46, 60
order 54, 62, 66, 73, 158, 174
structures 11, 48, 145
Society for Increasing Education amongst Mahars, Mangs and Others 5
Society for Promoting Christian Knowledge 132
Society for the Propagation of the Gospel in Foreign Parts 132
society(ies)
Brahminical 46, 199
Hindu 4, 45
Indian 71–72, 112, 130, 143, 152, 157, 162
secret 4, 158
Society of Truth Seekers 10
solidarity 14, 65, 67, 115, 163
songadya 54–55, 57
songs 25–26, 30, 37, 54, 63
spirituality 45, 158
stage
depictions 61
directions 53, 55, 58–61, 66
stories 10, 22, 24, 30, 38, 88, 164
structural theory 47
Subaltern Studies 73, 129
suicide 9, 112
Sunday schools 132–33
superiority 16, 182, 186–87, 201
superstition 41, 45, 146, 184, 186
Sutradhar 27, 30, 42, 63
system of instruction 141, 152

Tagore 126, 175
tamasha 26–27, 29–30, 54–55, 57, 59
Tarkaratna, Ramnarayan 17
Kulin-Kulasarbaswa 17

Naba Natak 17
Tarkhadkar, Dadoba 158–59
Discussion on Religion, A 159
teachers 5, 8, 10, 64, 73, 101–02, 117, 122, 127, 138–39, 157, 174, 176, 196, 198–99, 201
Brahmin 8, 10, 73, 102, 117, 174, 176
trained 196, 198
text(s) 3–4, 6–10, 12, 27, 32, 35, 40, 48, 53, 58, 62–63, 66–68, 74, 112–14, 125, 133, 137, 150–51, 153–54, 159, 161, 164–66, 170–71, 174, 177, 197
Brahminical 7, 10, 164, 177
literary 3, 48, 67, 74, 113
religious 137, 150
Sanskrit 32, 133, 150
theatre(s) 9, 15–21, 24, 27–28, 31, 33–38, 42, 51–60, 62–63, 67, 72
Bengali 16, 17
English 60, 62
folk 54, 57
Indian 15–17, 19–20, 59, 67
Marathi 15–16, 18, 21, 28, 33–35, 38, 58, 72
modern 15–17, 21, 28
mythological 60, 62
Parsi 18, 37
Sanskrit 42, 52–55, 59
Western 16, 56
the Indian Ryot 184
theory of the Aryan invasion 161
Tilak, Bal Gangadhar 9, 23
traditions 7, 10, 16, 27, 33, 37–38, 45–46, 54–55, 58, 113–15, 150, 153–55, 167, 172
dramatic 37, 46, 55
performative 54, 113
Peshwa 7, 172
translations 10, 15–16, 19, 29, 32–34, 40, 41, 74, 112–14, 117, 133, 137–38, 147, 150, 165–66, 177
English 19, 41
Tritiya Ratna 2–3, 5–6, 8–10, 14, 17–18, 21–22, 35–36, 38–41, 46, 48, 51–58, 61–66, 68–69, 71–74, 148, 150–51, 155, 169–70
an intrinsic feature of 68
as a political play 65
characters or types 47–48, 58, 63
dialogues in 64, 65
dramatic action and conflict 44
quotidian reality in 74
rejection of 9
story and plot 41
title of the play 38

United States 166
abolitionist movement in xiii, 116
movement against slavery in 166
The Good People of 166
universities 112, 144, 147–48
Untouchables 5, 147, 155, 157, 160, 162

verse 1, 10, 26, 30, 68
Vidushak 42, 44–45, 49, 51–57, 62, 64–65, 71, 76, 78–108, 150
role of 51, 62
vidyalaya 152–53
Vidyasagar, Ishwarchandra 155
vocational training 128, 146, 175

Western dramatic conventions 17, 55–56
widow 4, 8–9, 18, 35–36, 46, 70, 90, 153, 158
Brahmin 9, 70
remarriage of 4, 8, 158
widowhood 36, 71, 153
Wilson, John 149–51, 163
India Three Thousand Years Ago 150–51, 163

women 1, 4, 6, 8–9, 17–18, 26, 30, 34–36, 44, 47–49, 54, 56, 58–60, 63, 65, 69–72, 77–88, 90, 94, 104–05, 109, 129, 132, 145, 150–54, 157–59, 162, 168, 172–73
  agency of 129
  Brahmin 71
  characters 71
  dancers 26
  education of 158, 168
  injustices done to
  Kunbi 56, 58, 60, 81
  lower-caste 49, 70
  necessity of educating 145
  position of 18, 70, 158
  reform 8–9, 69, 72, 153
  social condition of 150
  treatment of 36
  upper-caste 157
  wigs for the 30
Wood's Despatch, 1854 129, 144–45, 154, 168

yakshagana 24, 27, 29